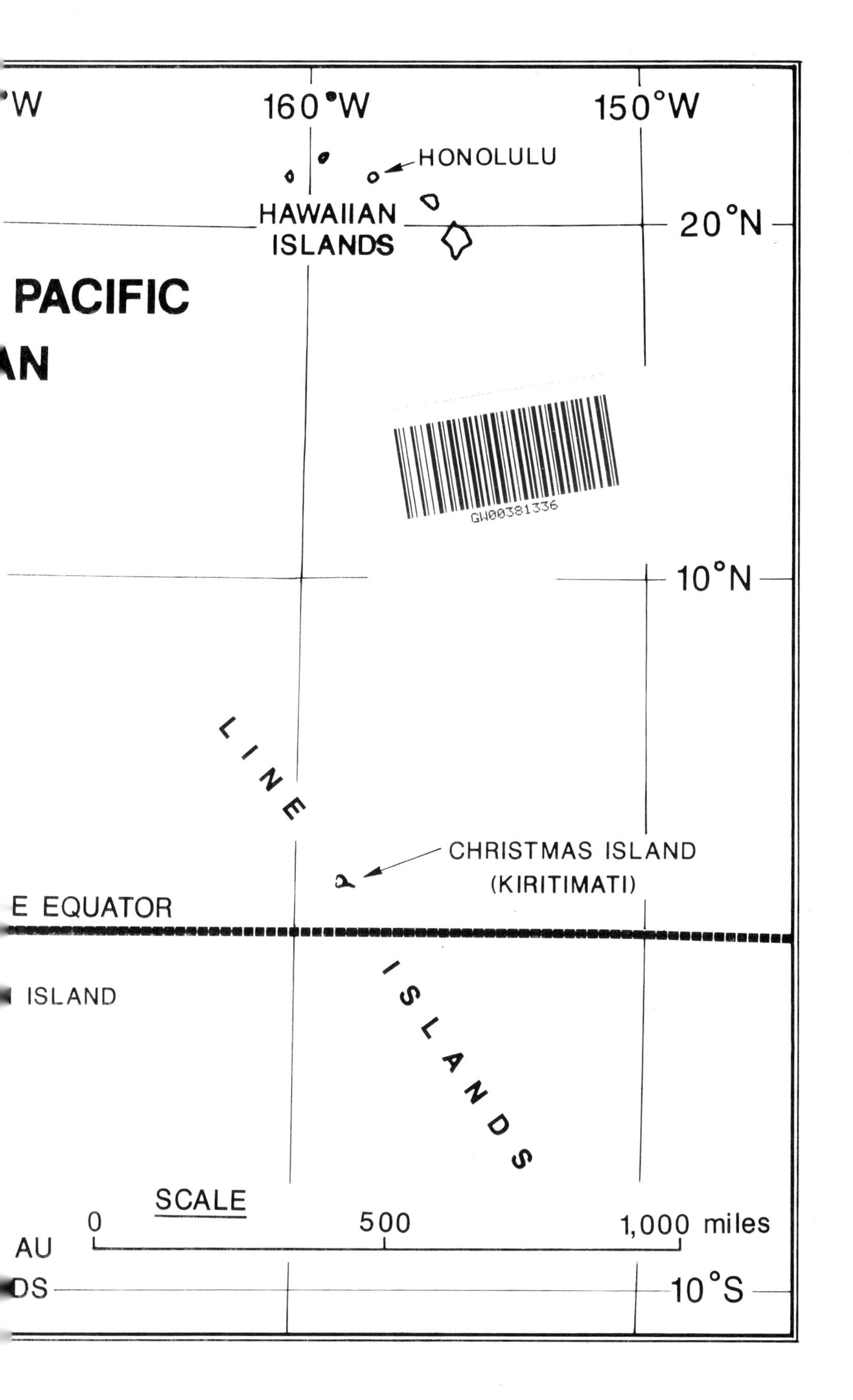
160°W
150°W
HONOLULU
HAWAIIAN ISLANDS
20°N
PACIFIC
10°N
LINE ISLANDS
CHRISTMAS ISLAND (KIRITIMATI)
EQUATOR
ISLAND
SCALE
0
500
1,000 miles
10°S

Don’t Step on a Stonefish!

By the same author

Wrong Again Dan!
Send Port and Pyjamas!

Bobbie + Diana

DON'T STEP ON A STONEFISH!

by

DAN RASCHEN

With best wishes
from Dan Raschen

Shrivenham 17th October 1997

Buckland Publications Ltd.
125 High Holborn, London WC1V 6QA

British Library Cataloguing in Publication Data

Raschen, Dan
Don't Step on a Stonefish!
I. Title
910.4

ISBN 0 7212 0848 7

Printed and bound in Great Britain by
Buckland Press Ltd., Dover, Kent.

CONTENTS

LIST OF ILLUSTRATIONS

MAPS AND DIAGRAMS

AUTHOR'S NOTE

Writing this book has brought back many happy memories and I have been helped by a multitude of people. I wish that I could include them all, but would particularly like to mention "Jack", now Major (retired) J. T. Cheeseman of Deal, my companion on our unusual trip around the islands, for his sustained enthusiasm, and for his keen attention to the accuracy of my story. I am most grateful also to Mrs Elaine Bernacchi, widow of Mr Michael Bernacchi, CMG, OBE, the Resident Commissioner of the Gilbert and Ellice Islands Colony during our visit, and to Mr P. G. Roberts, MBE, then District Commissioner of the Line Islands, both of whom are now living in New Zealand. They have provided me with much historical detail and have encouraged me enormously in my efforts.

My thanks also are due to Mr Charles Thompson, recently British High Commissioner in Kiribati, for providing updated information on the channels we planned, and to the Curator of the Department of the Hydrographer of the Navy for allowing me to pore over the charts of the Central Pacific. They confirm, better than any number of words, the vastness of the ocean, showing little other than an occasional line of soundings, all of them impressivly deep. The staff of the Library of the Royal Military College of Science, Shrivenham, have also been most helpful.

Doctor Charlton Shaw of Fairford, Rear Admiral Arthur Baxter of Fawler and Professor Cyril Wilson of Shrivenham have made very constructive comments. I doubt if the end result will please them all, but at least Judy, my wife, who has been very patient, enjoyed reading the final draft!

Those who made everything possible, including the Royal Engineers staff in London and Wing Commander Dicky Richardson, who was the Base Commander on Christmas Island, deserve special thanks. Looking back, I would not have missed the experience for the world!

FOREWORD
by
General Sir John Stibbon, KCB, OBE,
Chief Royal Engineer

I knew Dan Raschen long before we came to live in the same village, and I am delighted, both as a friend and a fellow Sapper, that he has continued to record his varied life. He has a keen sense of the incogruous, and a puckish sense of humour which is more than a match for most situations.

Dan's two previous books give many splendid examples of sapper tasks in war, but *Don't Step on a Stonefish!* is about a project, no less challenging, undertaken by the Royal Engineers in peace. I am particularly glad to be associated with it as it shows how well our Corps can cope with the unusual and the unexpected, anywhere in the world – and the need to be something of a soldier, administrator, diplomat and scrounger!

I was pleased to read how old fashioned and half forgotten engineering techniques can still be made to work when modern resources are lacking. The same return to basics lies behind Dan's very interesting thoughts on the formation of coral atolls; if you can't find out, work it out! Just what others would have worked out when anchored to a large explosive charge with its quickly burning fuze, I would be interested to hear. Dan describes the incident, in chapter 15, as "sporting".

Wrong Again Dan! took him to the age of 22, and in its foreword Sir Hugh Beach predicted the start of a saga. How right he was, as this third book still only takes Dan to the ripe old age of 35! Many of us, whether or not associated with the Royal Engineers, will look forward to more.

Chapter One

UNCERTAIN PROSPECTS

"Wouldn't it be lovely," said Marjorie in 1959, "if Dan could be sent to Christmas Island for a year. Then Judy and the little boys could come home to us."

My mother-in-law and I enjoyed finding different ways of doing the same thing and had learnt not to take each other's suggestions too seriously. I accepted her happy taunt with an equally happy smile, as she knew only too well that the last thing I wanted was to be separated for a year from my family. A few months before, the prospects of her wish coming true would have been high, but recently they had become so remote that I didn't even rise to the bait.

Many of my brother officers in the Royal Engineers had served on Christmas Island and I had expected that my turn would come to follow them. Three years earlier, the island, in the middle of the Pacific Ocean, had become the British base for testing nuclear weapons, but now a Nuclear Test Ban Treaty was promised. With no further weapon testing, there should no longer be a need for soldiers in that part of the world.

I was aged thirty-four and due to move from the Armament Establishment near Sevenoaks in Kent where, as an Army major, I had spent three happy years working alongside scientists. At home I was allowed to say nothing of my duties, other than that they were associated with nuclear weapons, so Marjorie thought I was just the man to send to a few nuclear tests. This book, however, will be about coral islands and not about nuclear weapons.

As predicted, the Test Ban Treaty was soon signed and most of my friends came home, but a few others went out to put the Christmas Island Base into mothballs. I was expecting to be sent to Germany, where I had never served, when, out of the blue, I was told that it was I who would command the only Army unit remaining on Christmas Island.

That evening I rang my mother-in-law and said, "Marjorie, you've managed it!"

"Managed what?" she asked.

"Got me posted to Christmas Island!" She sounded understandably concerned about her new found powers.

Without delay I visited the Royal Engineers postings officers at Stanmore. "Please why," I asked, "do I need to go to Christmas Island, if nothing is going to happen there?" Their answer was more polite than I expected and was roughly as follows.

"Yes, Dan, yours is an unexpected, perhaps unique, posting. We were going to send you to command a squadron in Germany for two years, but now, to our surprise, they want you back at Shrivenham the year after next to take over from a chap called Tumber."

Lieutenant-Colonel Clifford Tumber had become an institution at the Military College of Science at Shrivenham, where he taught "Ammunition". Amazed, I said, "No one could take over from Clifford and certainly not me!" It was soon made clear that the Shrivenham arrangements must stand, leaving only one year, as against the normal two, for me to command a squadron. The only squadrons which had a one year tenure of command were those in non-family stations and 73 (Christmas Island) Squadron was one of the few of those left.

"But I want to go somewhere where I can take my family with me!" I protested. That was also summarily brushed aside and I was immediately given a few details of my next posting. "We don't think there will be any more nuclear weapon tests based on Christmas Island, but we still want to keep an eye on the place. You'll be taking over from Steve Clark in June next year, 1960, and his second-in-command, Dick Sullivan, will stay on with you for a while." I knew that Steve was there, as I had served under him twelve years before in Sumatra and India, and was godfather to his son. To add to the coincidence, Dick Sullivan and I had shared a tent for some months in the Korean War.

I was then told, "You'll be the senior Army officer on the island and report to the Royal Air Force Base Commander. Your link with the Army will be through the Engineer Group Commander in Woolwich but he'll find it difficult to visit you." I was all for independence and to have my next senior officer on the far side of the world sounded unbeatable!

Before I left Stanmore I heard that the Christmas Island Base was still controlled by "Headquarters Task Force Grapple", located in the Ministry of Defence Main Building, and that the only Sapper officer remaining there wished to see me. Evidently he, Major Denys Begbie, had some unusual and additional tasks for me.

The success of my earlier Army career might have been described as patchy but now, as a married man with two small sons, I felt more responsible. To have a future in my profession, I needed to command a squadron in a manner that suggested that, some time later, I could be entrusted with a regiment: quite a thought! But, not being a natural commander, I was pretty sure that commanding 73 Squadron alone would stretch me without the prospect of "additional tasks".

I visited Denys Begbie in his office, deep underground in Whitehall. The place had an air of great secrecy and glamour but the occupants would have preferred windows with pretty girls outside. Denys was a senior and distinguished major and I was a very junior one, so was most impressed by the preparations he had made for me. He said he wasn't going to tell me about Christmas Island as Steve Clark would give me the background when I arrived, but he wanted to tell me about another aspect to my tour in the colony, by which he meant the Gilbert and Ellice Islands Colony.

"The Resident Commissioner, who is the head of the colony," said Denys, "wants some channels, or passages, blown through the coral reefs around the islands and has asked for advice. If possible, he wants us, the Royal Engineers, to do the job." I was intensely interested but my confusion must have shown. Denys then explained that "our" Christmas Island, a thousand miles south of Honolulu, was in the Line Islands, and that they were part of the colony, most of which lay two thousand miles away to the west of them.

No, that I did not realise but, with the aid of a big blue map, Denys taught me more about the Pacific Ocean in the next two minutes than I had learnt in the previous thirty-four years.

It soon became clear that I also knew precious little about coral. Pretty pink necklaces came to mind but that was definitely wrong. The islets of silver sand which I remembered off the west coast of Sumatra were also off the target, as Denys was talking of white stone slabs, and said that there would be no point in us guessing further.

Letters to and from the colony's capital, Tarawa, took around six weeks each way and all that was abundantly clear in England was that no one would know what was really wanted until some one had visited the islands. Meanwhile, government funds had been earmarked and there were rumours of a group of Australians, or even of a Japanese engineer, bidding for the job.

I assumed that "some one" to visit would turn out to be one of my officers from Christmas Island, but Denys continued, "The Engineer-in-Chief thinks that the job, whatever it may turn out to be, sounds unusually interesting and he wants you, personally, to make the reconnaissance and get it for the Corps." The E-in-C was the serving head of the Corps of Royal Engineers, a man who would say what he meant, but I had thought that command of my squadron would be my prime concern. However, my absence from Christmas Island for what would surely be several weeks had already been accepted.

"Have you read Grimble?" Denys then asked. I had to admit that I had not but remembered the name, Sir Arthur Grimble, as Denys continued, "His book *A Pattern of Islands* is a delight, all about the colony, and will give you just the background you'll need. Make sure you read it soon!" Both Grimble and the outline of the reef blasting task had obviously caught Denys' imagination, but I wasn't sure that I shared all his enthusiasm.

"Are you a sailor?" was his next question. I hesitated before I answered, as I had always been an unusually poor sailor, but my reply was "No, I am afraid I don't sail." Because bridging and watermanship were two of the prime skills of the Royal Engineers, those who sailed were highly regarded and I wished that I had been among them.

Rather embarrassed, I explained that my neck never turned very far, not since an armchair had been dropped on it in India, accidentally of course, on the night I was commissioned. If I and my neck tried to "go about" in a dinghy, we had often not reached the required posture before it became necessary to turn the other way about. "What a pity," said Denys, "as the dinghy sailing on Christmas Island is superb."

At the end of my visit, the first of several, Denys flicked in another question, "You aren't, by any chance, a diver?" Well did I remember that the specification for my job near Sevenoaks had required the incumbent to be a diver. "But I don't want to be a diver." I had said, adding, "I'm not a great swimmer and, anyway, I wear specs, so can't see in the water." Divers, I had then been told, did not need to be strong swimmers and even those with good eyesight could see nothing in the murk in which they usually worked.

Despite my wishes, a diver's medical examination had followed but, before I joined my diving course, requirements had changed, and I had never, until now, regretted that change. I should not have asked, "But how would that have helped?" to which Denys answered, "Because coral grows under water!" My relief showed when he added, "Never mind, the Navy has offered to find a couple of divers to go with you."

I was not sure that I liked all I was hearing, and Denys' parting remark disturbed me even further. "You'll probably go round the islands in a schooner and there's nothing I'd rather do."

I soon read *A Pattern of Islands* and found most of it enchanting. Life had indeed been in a different world around those coral islands before and just after the First World War. To lie near where the equator crossed the International Date Line gave an unusual setting to the scene, particularly as the IDL had been so sensibly located that absolutely no one lived near to it on either side.

My initial interest in Grimble's tales soon turned to concern and then to fright. As if the perils of ubiquitous tiger sharks were not enough, there followed hefty passages on octopuses, or octopi. They had never been my favourite creatures and Sir Arthur's descriptions of *Octopus vulgaris* "which swarms in the lagoons" and "laid out flat has a total spread of nine to ten feet" did not reassure me. That was nearly double my own spread and I readily imagined myself working in the water with those abounding and massive molluscs simply longing to grip more than my attention.

* * *

In this book I hope to tell the story of my trip around the remoter parts of the Gilbert and Ellice Islands Colony (now the independent countries of Kiribati and Tuvalu); it was based on Christmas Island (now Kiritimati), to which I am sure to refer frequently. In the next few weeks I visited various experts who would advise me on my trip to the Pacific. Almost all of them knew in detail about Christmas Island but not about the rest of the colony and none of them could explain to me how coral grew. Anything I needed would, I was assured, become available once I was on the spot.

* * *

I expected to spend a year on an assortment of desert islands, so, in preparation, I asked my friend Charles Holland, just back from Christmas

Island, what clothes I would need. "Practically none," had been his answer. When told to be serious, he suggested a pair of bathing trunks and a pair of tennis shoes, some shorts and socks, a couple of good pairs of boots and something comfortable to wear in the evenings. Christmas Island was a working island, so formal parades and occasions need not be expected. I knew, though, that conditions were changing, so added an elderly olive green bush jacket to my packing list.

Those going to Christmas Island were given a special blood test at the Army's Millbank Hospital, all to do with the hazards of nuclear radiation. With my training in that subject, I had formed the impression that the risks from well organised nuclear weapon trials were considerably less than those from a luminous wrist watch. I thus concluded that radiation would not be my greatest worry and, while I was at Millbank, took the opportunity of having my eyes tested. I would then be issued with a pair of those ghastly steel rimmed spectacles designed for wearing under a gas mask, not for fear of gas in the Pacific, but because, with their flat sides, they might fit under a snorkelling mask.

Not many days later, I was urgently summoned back to Millbank. Did I know that there were too many white corpuscles in my blood? No, I certainly did not, nor would I ever have heard of such unmentionable things, had it not been for that nuclear training. My corpuscle count apparently made me ineligible for posting to Christmas Island.

Others would have been delighted by such news but preparations for my departure were already well advanced and it would be easier to let them stand. The doctor was obviously displeased by what he had discovered as, to my surprise, he knew that I was the one person the Army most wished to send to the middle of the Pacific.

Glimmerings about corpuscles then came back to me from my Nuclear Course at Shrivenham. The lecturer had stated that not only radiation could affect a blood count. "There could be plenty of other reasons, for example, hay fever sufferers often have an excessive number of white corpuscles." That was it! "I get terrible hay fever," I said to the doctor. "Then all is explained," he replied and, with evident relief, passed me fit.

Before I left Millbank I collected my new gas mask specs, in which I looked more toad-like than ever. Judy made me promise that I would not wear them unless I absolutely had to and sent me to buy an expensive pair, with ordinary frames and green-tinted lenses, from our optician; everyone spoke of the intense glare of the sun reflected off the lagoons and of the need for care. I had always blamed my bad eyesight on undetected measles but, whatever the reason, I was now glad to have put part of my overseas planning on a proper basis.

At home I tried to study the geography of the Pacific Ocean. I knew that Honolulu, with Pearl Harbour, were in the Hawaiian Islands, way out in the middle, and that Christmas Island, as discovered by Captain Cook on Christmas Day 1777, lay just above the equator, a thousand miles to their south. I discovered that, below the equator and another twelve hundred miles south, there was Tahiti, strongly recommended by Gauguin and others. I was to learn that, in the Pacific, it was always the next island, the one just out of reach, that offered the greatest attractions.

Our family atlas had a large double sheet proudly entitled *Pacific Ocean: Communications*. On it were a few tiny dots in the vast blue area between Hawaii and Australia and very little else. The lack of communications must have eased the cartographer's task, as no shipping lanes went anywhere near Christmas Island, presumably a plus point when the place had been chosen for the explosion of hydrogen bombs.

Several dotted lines, though, converged on Honolulu, showing "San Fransisco 2098 miles", "Suva (Fiji) 2736 miles" and "Yokohama 3379 miles".

No one in London could, however, tell me how to get from Christmas Island to the islands in the colony where the reef channels were thought to be required, and which were literally off my map. Canton Island, in the Phoenix Group, also part of the colony, was known to have a good airfield, but the only airstrip in either the Gilbert or Ellice Islands was on Tarawa, nearly two thousand miles west of Christmas Island. Records showed it to be "in occasional use".

I started to wonder why my reconnaissance was to be mounted from Christmas Island to the east, rather than from Fiji or the Solomon Islands, both to the west of, nearer and more in contact with, the capital of the colony at Tarawa. However, those in London, all more experienced than I, assumed that means of transport would be forthcoming. I just hoped that they would be right.

Judy and I had had no children when we arrived in Sevenoaks, but now Bill was nearly two and half years old and Henry was ten months. With extremely mixed feelings, I left Judy and them with her parents in Cheshire. Summer 1960 had arrived and my hay fever had never been worse; that, at least, I did not mind leaving in England.

Chapter Two

ARRIVAL IN THE PACIFIC

Why was I, the only serviceman aboard, told to wear uniform to fly to and across the United States? It may have been to avoid a visa but everyone else on our scheduled flight in a turboprop Britannia wore sensible civilian clothes. It was the 5th June, 1960, Harold Macmillan was Prime Minister in England and Dwight Eisenhower was President of the United States. I was aged thirty-four and a half, rather overweight and, in my khaki battledress, overheated and obtrusive.

I sat next to an elderly lady from a Devon village who was making her maiden flight. As Devon was my own county, we had plenty to discuss: her daughter had married an American soldier during the war and lived in San Fransisco. When our delay at New York's Idlewild (now J. F. Kennedy) airport was extended, the old lady asked me if I thought she should ring her daughter, in San Francisco, to ask her to bring the car. When a further delay was announced, she asked again if I was sure that a car would not be quicker.

Our flight across the Rockies was by night, through a severe electrical storm, with the tips of the propellers forming great circles of light and massive sparks jumping off the wings. The Devon lady leant urgently across to a nearby New Zealander, whom she evidently trusted more than me, and said, "That engine's on fire!" I took immediate interest and was inclined to agree with her.

"Really!" said the Kiwi, "And what do you expect me to do about it?"

That sparky phenomenon was known as Saint Elmo's Fire but I had been more affected by the turbulence than by St Elmo, thus reminded how poor a traveller I was. By the time we reached Honolulu, after a further delay at San Fransisco, I was feeling dreadful.

Steve Clark and Dick Sullivan were there to meet me, both looking exceedingly well and tanned to a deeper walnut brown than I had ever seen. Without asking how I was, they prescribed rapid revival and, although it was only eight in the morning, I drank the first Bloody Mary of my life. It may have been the vodka, or the iced tomato juice, or just meeting old friends, but I quickly felt better.

Seeing Steve and Dick so well reminded me that, only a few weeks before, we in England had feared for the lives of everyone on Christmas Island. An underwater earthquake somewhere between South America and

Hawaii had generated an unusually severe tidal wave, which raced across the Pacific. It had reached Japan, still full of fury, and drowned hundreds of people.

That wall of water engulfed villages a hundred feet above the shore line, so our concern for those on Christmas Island, with its average height of about six feet, and lying much closer than Japan to the source of the trouble, could have been well founded. However, those on the island only noticed a couple of small fluctuations in the tide levels during the day.

This wave episode confirmed how little I knew about coral atolls and the extent to which they differed from other islands. A tidal wave, it turned out, when out in the middle of an ocean, was not my idea of a wave, one of the surf board kind, but more like a shock front. When the shock front met a shelving shore, of which Japan had many, it rolled itself up into a massive head of water. From my reading of Grimble I should have realised that coral atolls usually plunged steeply downwards from their reef edges to the depths of the Pacific Ocean. Without a shelving shore, a tidal wave could not roll up appreciably, so nothing on an atoll would be swamped, a deduction which I found reassuring.

Steve and I were allowed seven days for him to hand 73 Squadron's responsibilities over to me, so I readily agreed his suggestion that we stayed in Honolulu for the first three. Dick would return to Christmas Island but, with only two planes a week and my delayed arrival, he only just caught the first one.

I soon discovered that Honolulu and Hawaii were not the same place, also that the land area of the Hawaiian Islands, so small on the map, was about that of Wales. Yes, Honolulu was the capital of the islands but it lay on Oahu, one of the smaller islands. Hawaii was the name of the "Big Island", which boasted not only the world's largest active volcano, but also the third largest ranch in the United States. Only the year before, in 1959, had the Hawaiian Islands been admitted as the fiftieth state of the United States of America and the residents were inordinately proud of their new status. Whereas, on visiting San Francisco, they used to say that they were going "Stateside", now they took care to say that they were going "to the mainland". This was important stuff but not directly relevant to our military handover, so soon we were discussing coral.

Steve knew that the colony needed help with passages through coral reefs but assumed that I would be given details of the requirements in London, just as I had assumed that he would know what was wanted. However, the lack of liaison boiled down to communication links: the Resident Commissioner of the colony, in Tarawa, received his mail eastwards from London, via Australia, whereas we on Christmas Island received ours westwards via the United States. The gap, and gap it was, lay between Christmas Island and Tarawa, with the only direct link being by expensive telegrams. Two thousand miles of ocean plus the Date Line were, between them, a formidable barrier.

* * *

Pearl Harbour, like Honolulu, was on Oahu Island, but Steve had had little success in finding the right kind of Americans to tell us how to blast coral. The Hawaiian Islands were liberally fringed with coral and the "Defense of the Pacific" was centred on where we were, yet we could not find a soul with an interest in coral, until two US Navy Explosives Ordnance Disposal Officers offered to help.

They were Lieutenants Al Kennedy and Frank Shissler, both of them divers, who had been trying to deepen Pearl Harbour: it had a coral bottom, on which they worked in 30 feet of water, using tons of explosive at a time. Although very interesting, their work sounded different to any jobs I was expecting but, relevant or not, Al and Frank impressed us tremendously with their confidence and enthusiasm. I promised to invite them down to Christmas Island as soon as I had settled in.

On Oahu Steve and I were staying in the US Airforce Mess at Hickam, with its "BOQ" (Bachelor Officers' Quarters) above a couple of lounges and a bar. To eat, we walked a few paces to a single storey canteen building, superbly located beside the entrance to Pearl Harbour. I had previously had no notion that the only entrance to this sea-like anchorage was through a narrow funnel not much wider than a football field. Vessels could not be dispersed from Pearl Harbour quickly, which was why 7th December 1941 had come to be called the "Day of Ignomony" by the local Americans.

A detachment of the Royal Air Force was based at Hickam, to provide the lifeline for the Christmas Island Base, and Steve confirmed just how dependent the island was upon it. Its Squadron Leader promised that he would try to provide whatever I and my soldiers wanted, female company excluded, and he proved to be as good as his word.

From having been over three thousand strong a year before, the Christmas Island garrision was now down to one tenth of its previous size, which everyone hoped would prove both sufficient to maintain our considerable investment and to confirm British sovereignty. There had been some doubts on the latter point when the Americans occupied the British-claimed island during the war.

Apart from one ship a year to top up the fuel supply, all the island's needs now came by air through Hickam, using the RAF's well proven, four engined, Hastings transport planes. Two were based on Christmas Island, one for supplies from Honolulu and one in reserve, particularly for emergency medical evacuation.

A Hastings' normal range was about three thousand miles, not enough for crossing the Atlantic with confidence, so the planes were routed from Britain to Christmas Island eastwards via Singapore, Australia and Fiji, before spending two or three months on shuttle duties between Hickam and Christmas Island.

Only essential services were now based on the island, the maxim being "if in doubt, use Honolulu", a policy with which the Americans fully co-operated. Rather than, say, stationing a dental team on Christmas Island, it was considered more economical to fly patients up to American dentists in Honolulu. Later, I myself was to find this an admirable arrangement.

The local population of Oahu was of all colours, the generations of blending having achieved many original tones. I had expected to see golden-brown Polynesians, but pure bred Hawaiians were a rarity and, sadly, the beautiful girls the cinema had led me to expect were also rare. Anyway, the residents seemed happily unconcerned about either their colour or their origin.

I was told to remember the views from the hills, as there were none on atolls. Those from Diamond Head, overlooking the seaside city of Honolulu, were certainly magnificent, but I was sadly disillusioned when we saw the sands of Waikiki Beach being topped up by lorry.

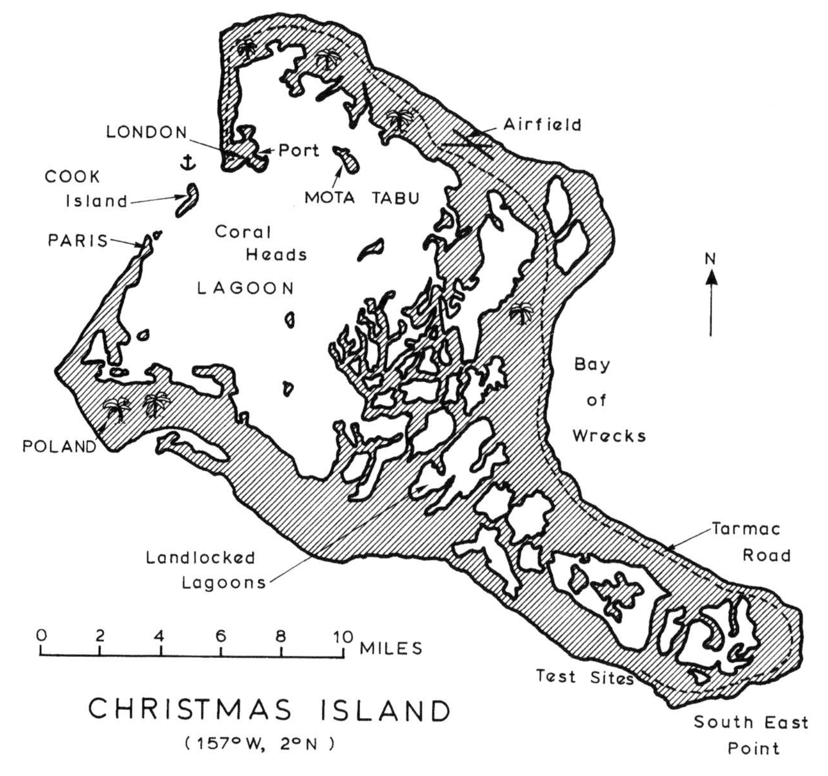

CHRISTMAS ISLAND
(157° W, 2° N)

A few other service reinforcements had arrived at Hickam during the three days before we boarded the Christmas Island Hastings. The five hours in the air over endless ocean had only one distinctive feature, great banks of cumulus cloud that lay on an east-west line, almost as if to mark the half way point. The crew, on their second tour in those parts, always expected the cloud banks, almost to the extent of using them as a navigation aid. I knew Christmas Island to be shaped like a large open-ended spanner, with a length of over thirty miles, but we came in over the sea, so there was no aerial view for us passengers.

Although forewarned of the glare of the Christmas Island sun, its sheer intensity, reflecting off the concrete runway and its surrounding white coral, still came as a surprise. I was very glad to be wearing my new glasses with their tinted lenses. The Base Commander, Wing Commander Dicky Richardson, came to meet us, and Steve and I travelled in his staff car the fourteen miles to the Port, where the small garrison now lived. We motored on the beautifully smooth, but narrow, tarmac of the newly built road.

During the remaining few days of our handover Steve explained the military requirements of my new job, but whenever I asked questions about the colony, or about Christmas Island itself, he would reply, "You'll have plenty of time to ask Percy that." Mr Percy Roberts was the District Commissioner for the Line Islands and lived on Christmas Island.

Percy was normally a modest and reticent man but the more I heard, the more I realised how considerable and unusual was his experience. He was aged fifty-three when I first met him in 1960, a New Zealander from the Canterbury area, who had been trained as a solicitor and had become a member of the New Zealand Civil Service. He must have been an outstanding athlete, rugby being his main love, but he still played a good

Percy Roberts, District Commisioner of the Line Islands.

game of cricket or tennis and was a very powerful swimmer.

In the war Percy had become an officer in the Royal New Zealand Artillery but was soon seconded to the Western Pacific High Commission and came to the colony soon after the Americans recaptured Tarawa in November 1943. In the sixteen years since then he had visited every inhabited island in the colony, some thirty of them.

Colonel Fox-Strangways was the first post-war Resident Commissioner of the colony and Percy was the Secretary to the Government of his re-formed administration, before becoming the District Officer of Ocean Island, where phosphate was quarried.

Ocean Island had had a bad war. It was severely bombed by both sides and the six remaining expatriate staff all died during the Japanese occupation. The two hundred Gilbertese whom the Japanese kept on as workers were all massacred just as the war ended; all, that is, except one, who managed to drop down a cliff before he was to be shot. It was his testimony at the War Crimes Trial that sent the Japanese garrison commander and his quartermaster to the gallows. All told, the decision to move the capital away from Ocean Island after the war had been a good one.

Percy Roberts, as a War Compensation Officer, had later visited each of the Gilbert Islands that the Japanese had occupied and then, probably because of his legal training, was made a Lands Commissioner: the ownership of land was of utmost importance to the islanders.

Percy had come to Christmas Island in January 1954 where, as District Commissioner, he was also responsible for the two other inhabited Line Islands, atolls known as Fanning and Washington. Both these had commercial coconut plantations and on Fanning there was the important cable station, operated by a few European staff accompanied by their families.

On Christmas Island, Percy managed the extensive plantations, on behalf of the colony, and supervised its imported Gilbertese labour force. When he arrived, he had been the lone expatriate on the island but, later the same year, just when South Pacific Airlines had established a seaplane base on the lagoon, the British had decided that they wanted to turn Christmas Island over to nuclear testing. Percy had witnessed every one of those tests – and looked very well on it!

His co-operation with the hordes of visitors to the island, and to his home, had become legendary. However, he realised that the servicemen could one day depart as quickly as they had arrived, so was keen to maintain his self reliance. He was an honorary member of the base's officers' mess but, as the Queen's representative locally, felt it right to keep his distance and seldom went there unless specially invited.

* * *

The strength of the Christmas Island garrison had been so greatly reduced that it was easy for Steve to introduce me to all the officers in the mess on my first evening. Excluding the crews of the two Hastings, there were about a dozen RAF officers, including Wing Commander Richardson and two squadron leaders, five Army officers, and a lieutenant commander and a lieutenant of the Royal Navy.

From those who had pioneered the base three years earlier, I had heard many tales of rugged and unpleasant living conditions. Large land crabs had proved highly unwelcome bedfellows in the tented accommodation of those days but I now found everything to be different: special pre-fabricated huts with corrugated aluminium roofs had been acquired, all with running hot and cold water and limitless electricity. I was to live in comfort in one of these new huts, a few yards from the edge of the main lagoon, which stretched away so far into the distance that only its lightest-of-green colour distinguished it from the darker and deeper ocean. The pleasant but brisk breeze could whisk snow-like rolls of salt froth off the lagoon's surface, all very pretty, but a maintenance engineer's nightmare.

I was to be, not a, but the, maintenance engineer of the base, with umpteen million pounds worth of government investment in my care but, with a can of cold beer in my hand and more available, I felt undaunted. All my companions looked reassuringly cheerful and, with further nuclear weapon tests thought unlikely, the need for prolonged maintenance was open to doubt. The Base Commander put high priority on keeping the members of the island's small garrison happy and out of trouble. "How very sensible," I thought, as anyone who became discontented in such a remote place would become a major liability.

Compared to other Royal Engineers' squadrons, mine was very small. Most of its eighty members were soldiers employed in their specialist trades and they all had definite roles on the island. A first rate job had been done in selecting "only men of good character", so I was relieved to think that my man-management responsibilities should not prove too taxing. Clearly, Dick Sullivan could run the squadron for me, if I could find some means of going on my trip around the colony.

The composition of my reconnaisance party had now been specified. It was to total four, comprising Major Raschen, as leader, a Field Engineer (Class 1), and two divers. There was precisely one Class 1 Field Engineer, as were there just two divers on Christmas Island, so my team had been selected for me.

That Field Engineer was my one and only Squadron Sergeant-Major, Jack Cheeseman. It seemed highly unusual to leave an independent squadron without both its officer commanding and its sergeant-major, but that had been accepted by our seniors in England. I was reminded of the Indian Army company which garrisoned a particularly unattractive island in the Red Sea in the 1930s. It normally had two British officers, but the officer commanding stopped a passing ship and left his second-in-command in charge while he went on leave to England. Six weeks later they were surprised to meet each other in Piccadilly.

My relationship with SSM Cheeseman throughout our working acquaintance was, by custom, formal, with me calling him "Sergeant-Major", and him calling me "Sir". However, in this book I will mainly refer to him as "Jack". Later in his career he became Major Cheeseman.

The strength of the Royal Navy on the island was only about thirty, so I was surprised when Lieutenant Commander Bill Mitford, who commanded the detachment, said to me that first evening, "I am very much looking forward to coming round the colony with you." He explained that he was one of the two divers, the other being an able seaman named Williams: however, both he and Williams had other duties, quite different from diving, to occupy most of their time. The Royal Navy was, of course, the senior service and I knew that a major and a lieutenant commander were of equivalent rank, so Bill might well have been senior to me in terms of service. However, he made it clear that he wished to join my party purely as a working diver.

An excellent opportunity to see the District Commissioner in his ceremonial role came just before Steve left Christmas Island: the Queen's birthday was to be celebrated on 11th June, 1960. The coconut plantations on the island employed nearly a hundred Gilbertese men, many of whom were married, with an indeterminate number of children, and all would take part in the celebrations.

Percy Roberts' house in the Gilbertese village had been built, with liberal use of thatch from coconut and pandanus palms, at the so-called Port of London. Later, the camp for the maintenance garrison of servicemen had been built nearby. A few additional Gilbertese men were employed by the

Tina, the author's Gilbertese batman, at Port Quarters, Christmas Island.

garrison and one of these, Tina, had appointed himself, accompanied by his two small children, as Steve's unofficial batman. I gladly took him over in that role.

The British flag had been brought to the Gilbert Islands less than seventy years before by HMS *Royalist*, in 1892. The message must have gone from island to island that, under the British, age-old habits had to change: whereas inter-island raids had previously brightened up atoll routine, other forms of diversion would in future need to be found. Slowly, very slowly, the news spread, but the authority of Queen Victoria, and of her successors, had been happily established, and now Queen Elizabeth II, in the eighth year of her reign, included the inhabitants of the Gilbert and Ellice Islands Colony among her most loyal subjects.

The heads of the services were invited to the birthday ceremonies and Steve suggested that I should attend the parade with him. So much for my not needing any smart clothes for my duties in the Pacific! Tina did his best with my shirt and shorts but, from his wry smile, I gathered that there must be a Gilbertese equivalent of our "silk purse from a sow's ear" proverb.

The District Commissioner, Mr Percy Grange Roberts, MBE, asked the Base Commander, Wing Commander K. R. Richardson, DFC, to stand beside him on the dais of planks that had been built near the flagpole. Behind them stood a line of senior Gilbertese staff, bare headed and bare footed but all with good white shirts and neatly pinned ties above their white, kilt-like, lava lavas. Bill Mitford, representing the Royal Navy, Steve Clark and I representing the Army, and Squadron Leader Bob Henderson, representing the Royal Air Force, stood in a line facing the dais and the flagpole.

The entire Gilbertese population had turned out in their Sunday best white clothes and were lined up in a most orderly manner.

A bugle was blown, the Union Jack was broken at the mast head, we saluted, and the District Commissioner read a loyal message. It was a very effective little ceremony. Less formal celebrations then began and we attended a Gilbertese concert, or batere, in the evening. It was easy to see why our soldiers did not pursue the local ladies. They were fine, big and strong, and so were their husbands.

* * *

Christmas Island is the world's largest coral atoll and Steve and I tried to view it from the top of a large oil tank at the Port. Its lagoon is the world's second largest, with Kwajelin's, of early hydrogen bomb renown, taking precedence; we could only just see the palm trees skirting our far shore. With the sun shining on it, the shallow salt water over the white coral sand of the lagoon's bottom glittered in a distinctive shade of emerald green. However, as the clouds came across, many dark and forbidding patches appeared to pock mark the previously inviting expanse of water. These were coral heads, great pillar-like growths of rock that just broke the surface at low tide.

The breeze blew almost constantly and accounted for the island's

Queen's Birthday Parade, Christmas Island, Lieutenant Commander Mitford, Majors Clark and Raschen, Squadron Leader Henderson.

Gilbertese concert.

attractive climate, seldom above 85° Fahrenheit by day, and comfortable in bed at night with a sheet and no blankets. The sea stayed at about 80°F, also very pleasant, but it was that same breeze that made the fierce strength of the equatorial sun so deceptive.

What had been achieved in turning a deserted island into a lavishly equipped test base during the three years before I arrived was well known, and I had heard the details from many Royal Engineers' officers who had been involved. Still, I had underestimated the extent of the construction tasks that had been successfully completed. With a view to quick results, a "no expense spared" policy had been adopted, which had proved refreshingly effective and probably no more expensive than the penny pinching methods used at home.

My first impressions of Christmas Island atoll, not to be confused with the phosphate island of the same name in the Indian Ocean, were very favourable, but Steve assured me that a year there was more than enough for most people. Plans to put the base on a maintenance basis had initially included the possibility of a families station, but wives and children, with all their medical and educational needs, would have defeated the whole object of feeding a minimum number of mouths.

Parts of the island were so remote that no man might have trodden there before, but an empty beer can was always found! Only Percy Roberts, who deplored the litter more than any of us, was said to know the whole island. There were certainly areas where stranded men could have died of thirst and Steve was at pains to explain that my greatest single responsibility would be to maintain the fresh water supplies. I must certainly not fall into the trap of believing that the large "fresh water lagoons", shown so proudly on the map, contained fresh water.

The unreliability of the rainfall was why Christmas Island had never been the world's most desirable piece of real estate. When it rained, as it did most years, you couldn't want a better place to plant coconuts, to eat or to sell. Every so often, however, there was a year when it didn't rain and another rainless year might follow. After Captain Cook landed on "Cook Island" at the entrance to the main lagoon in 1777, no one, so far as was known, intentionally went to Christmas Island for the next one hundred years; nor was it known what had become of any survivors from the Bay of Wrecks on the east coast.

Late in the nineteenth century, word of this large, potentially rich and uninhabited island had reached some of the none-too-scrupulous traders with which the Pacific was said to abound. One or two of them tried their luck, only to be beaten by the failure of the rains. Then, soon after 1900, came the trading companies, with large resources at their disposal. Sixty thousand acres of fertile land, free for the taking, seemed too good to miss and it wasn't long before Lever Brothers had put in a manager and a workforce. Excellent coconut plantations were established and commercial oyster farming was started in some of the smaller lagoons, not because oysters were required as a local delicacy, but because buttons were made from oyster shells.

However, the inevitable year without rain came, the small lagoons became excessively saline and all the oysters and coconut seedlings died. So did many of the established trees when further years of poor rainfall followed. Lever Brothers cut their losses and left but, over thirty years later, I was seeing what remained of their plantations, about a couple of hundred thousand mature coconut palms. Percy was to show me, in the more remote lagoons, plenty of oyster shells.

Around 1937, Father Rouget, reputedly a defrocked French priest, made Christmas Island his home, bringing with him a selection of ladies of various nationalities. Each had her house at a well separated point on the island, which included London, Paris, and Poland. There must have been a small work force in addition to the European ladies, but presumably everyone stored rainwater prudently, so survived. Meanwhile, Father Rouget arranged that sufficient coconuts were harvested and their meat dried to be sold as copra to visiting boats, thus keeping him in a manner to which he previously should not have been accustomed. Great Britain still laid claim to Christmas Island but, apart from a pink mark in the atlases, no evidence of British authority remained.

After Pearl Harbour, the Japanese started to occupy Pacific islands at remarkable speed and the Gilbert Islands were among them, but the Americans reached Christmas Island first and kept a considerable garrison there for the rest of the war. Around 1950, the re-constituted government of the Gilbert and Ellice Islands Colony, looking for possible sources of income and for occupation for an increasing population, bought the Island from Father Rouget's estate for £50,000. Since then there had been no really bad droughts and the workforce had managed to conserve sufficient fresh water for their needs.

During the Japanese War the Americans imported fresh water to Christmas Island by tanker and so had the British when they came to build the base. However, as the number of servicemen increased, efforts to find a local water supply were intensified and the answer, as explained to me by Steve, was remarkably simple. A long shallow trough was dug with a bulldozer to about a foot below the water table, which was very close to the surface. Providing that the trough was dug at a sensible place, the water was beautifully fresh as, when rain fell on the island, the fresh water formed a lens-shaped layer on top of the more dense salt water in the sponge-like coral below.

The success of the system depended on there being large expanses of land well away from the ocean shore and from the lagoons, otherwise the fresh water lens would be too thin. It also depended on the fresh water being pumped off very slowly, so that the lens was not disturbed, and on keeping the trough well away from coconut palms, whose roots behaved like churns. The system worked well on Christmas Island due to the large areas of coral and to some of them being free of palm trees. However, I was sorry to hear that it would probably not be applicable to smaller atolls, such as I hoped to visit; rain water there could only be collected off tin roofs and led into cisterns.

Every soldier to whom Steve introduced me had special responsibilities but the exception was the one and only bricklayer, Lance-Corporal White, for whom there were no pressing tasks. White had asked if he could build a church at the Port, where we now all lived, and the chaplain had jumped at the idea. There were large coral slabs everywhere, just what White said he needed, also tons of spare cement that would not keep much longer. The Lord had hinted well!

As only the foundations had been laid, Steve thought it proper to seek my agreement for this not officially essential task to continue. My first decision in the Pacific was thus an easy one. "Yes, please, Corporal White, carry on with your church and finish it as quickly as possible."

⋆ ⋆ ⋆

Royal Air Force "Welfare" had provided a lavish supply of sports equipment, including the dinghies of which I had heard in England. On his last afternoon on the island, Steve took me in one of them to Mota Tabu, a beautiful islet in the main lagoon; Dick Sullivan and Jack Cheeseman came in another. They were all accomplished sailors and I hoped that the difficulties I remembered with my neck when sailing would prove to be exaggerated. Sadly, it was as stiff as ever but the sailing, on a lovely day, provided my first acquaintance with coral in a lagoon.

With the tide just past low water, the tops of the plentiful coral heads showed up clearly, as great green or orange, cauliflower-shaped monuments. They were more difficult to see when the sun went in, and then I, the passenger, had to warn Steve where they lay. As I was to discover later, it was easy enough to hit one, in which case the dinghy would turn on its side and lie with its sails on the water. Steve assured me that it wasn't too difficult to right a dinghy if it went over, and also that the Royal Navy would be watching through a telescope, to pick us up if necessary. "Just stay with the boat and you'll be all right!" was his message. Everything sounded highly organised but I had no wish to test the system.

My imagination became more active when a shoal of fish the size of enormous salmon went past us. "Sand sharks," said Steve, "quite harmless." They looked exactly like sharks and I had been brought up in India to be wary of sharks. My reading of *A Pattern of Islands* had increased that wariness and, although some sharks were said to be harmless, I still wondered.

A little later, as we were tacking against the wind, a line of four black patches, each of them wider than the dinghy, broke the surface not twenty yards from us. "Manta rays," said Steve as, one behind the other, they wallowed along with a gently undulating motion, before sinking out of sight. "Also absolutely harmless," but, as potential companions in the water, manta rays struck me as being utterly repulsive. My confidence in my old friend's nonchalance diminished when Steve continued, "Mark you, sting rays are quite different, much smaller, and brown. You don't want to get within striking range of them."

⋆ ⋆ ⋆

The whole of Christmas Island was renowned for its bird life, but the widest and least disturbed selection of them was to be found on Mota Tabu, where we went with the District Commissioner's permission. It was a narrow coral sandbank about a mile long, covered in a form of scraggy grass and dotted with clumps of rhododendron-sized bushes, known as mau.

Before I left England, I had been contacted by a keen ornithologist couple named Ashmole, who asked me to support their request to visit Christmas Island. I doubt if my efforts helped, but they did manage to make their visit a year later and I could now understand why they were so keen to reach this inaccessible place. The variety of birds was wonderful, both in quantity and in beauty, but their noise was deafening. In terms of sheer numbers, the terns won, with the little white snowy ones being particularly attractive but, for size, the boobies and frigate birds were more impressive. The male frigates proudly sprouted balloon-like red sacks under their beaks, doubtless very fetching to their girl friends, but aerodynamically unwieldy.

The tropic birds, about the size of fantail pigeons but with vivid red beaks, would have won a prize for prettiness, but my lasting impression was of the sheer tameness of all the birds. Bishop Heber could have been thinking of Mota Tabu as the spot "where only man is vile" when he wrote his hymn *From Greenland's icy mountains.* As if to confirm our vileness, we lit a fire to make tea, caught a few baby sharks in the shallows and drank our cans of beer. Even when only a foot long, the sharks had enormous jaws.

* * *

For our return trip to the Port we had a "soldier's wind" directly behind us and, with the tide sufficient for us to clear the coral heads, we just sat back and let the dinghies take us home.

There was time for me to quiz Steve on topical subjects, such as sharks. Was it because of them that there were such strict rules against bathing over the reef edge, with swimming only permitted in the lagoon? "Not directly," was the answer.

I knew that several servicemen had been drowned when bathing in the ocean. Apparently, on every occasion the poor man had been sucked off the reef edge by a wave, then rolled on to it again by the surf. The sharp coral grazed and cut him, so he panicked, was drowned and then lost out to sea. Remarkably, all the bodies had been recovered along the shore, and "No, none of them had been touched by sharks."

I wished that I had never started the conversation, but Steve's answer was not what I would have expected from my reading of Grimble's books. I was then told that, if I were so silly as to fall off a reef edge, three things were required:–

1. Keep calm. 2. Swim out to sea. 3. Await rescue.

I wanted to establish why the Christmas Island sharks were more amiable than those Grimble had known elsewhere in the colony but it was not kind to bother Steve with further questions so late in his tour. He left for home on the Hastings flight to Honolulu the next morning.

Chapter Three

MOUNTING AN EXPEDITION

Upon Steve's departure I proudly assumed my self-designated role as Commander of the British Army in the Pacific Ocean. 73 (Christmas Island) Squadron was obviously in excellent shape and I knew how lucky I was to have my old friend Captain Dick Sullivan as my second-in-command. In the Korean War when we were of similar seniority, he had proved himself able and popular, and was awarded the Military Cross for gallantry. Unfortunately, he had been late in sitting the Army's peacetime exam for promotion to major. His lack of the necessary qualification was to be my gain, as I could happily leave him in charge of my responsibilities if I were away.

I still knew very little about coral and less about blasting the stuff, so I invited my two United States Navy diving officer friends from Pearl Harbour to come to Christmas Island as soon as possible. They accepted immediately and arrived with their shallow diving gear on the next Hastings flight. When we first met, Lieutenants Al Kennedy and Frank Shissler had said that they doubted whether they would be able to help me as their experience had mainly been with explosives on harbour bottoms. However, they were delighted to be the guests of the British and we could not have wanted two more appreciative and competent visitors.

It was very much a case of the blind leading the blind, as I still could not visualise my tasks in the colony. However, Al and Frank, with our two Royal Navy divers, Lieutenant Commander Bill Mitford and AB Williams, spent a couple of happy days working in Christmas Island lagoon from Bill's motor cutter. The divers gave tantalising reports of the beauty of the coral heads and of the multi-coloured fish which teemed around them, while Jack Cheeseman and I sat and watched. The water was only eight to ten feet deep, so the divers were often visible from above and we could hear the bubbles from their air bottles breaking the surface.

To show willing, I donned my gas mask spectacles and a snorkel face mask, but nearly knocked them off again as I jumped over the gunwale of the cutter, a good couple of feet above the water. I was delighted to find that, for the first time in my life, I could see under water and what the coral revealed was astounding. Climbing back into the cutter was more difficult than jumping off it and, when I was hoisted aboard none too gently, I remembered my very sensitive shins.

Even if we were not able to ask Al and Frank precise questions about coral blasting, they did provide us with many useful tips about working in coral waters. Some that were new to me were:

1. Don't go into the water soon after an explosion. Sharks are attracted by dead fish. In the same way, don't go in if you have open cuts and, if you cut yourself when in the water, come out. Sharks love blood.

2. Don't empty your bladder into the sea. Urine means men and sharks are interested in men.

3. Don't be attracted by the unbelievably vivid blue of an open clamshell and never put your finger or foot into one. To do so would be painful, and fatal if you were out of your depth.

4. Don't step on a stonefish!

The rules about sharks and clams seemed obvious, when you thought about them, but "What is a stonefish?" I had to ask. Neither Al nor Frank had ever seen one but Frank answered, "Luckily they are quite rare but there are thought to be some of them on most reefs. They are like a flatfish with spikes and look just like their surroundings. They say you die in agony within a few hours of treading on one." For that I thanked him and took particular note of his advice to wear shoes at all times in the water.

The two Americans departed on the next shuttle plane back to Honolulu, saying to be sure to contact them when I was next there, which was certainly my intention.

* * *

How do you make a reconnaissance of ten or twenty small islands lying in two million square miles of ocean when you have no means of transport? In England, everyone had assumed that, if I used a little initiative, I would find a way of moving round the colony. Now that I was confronted with the problem in earnest, no practical suggestions were on offer.

Despite some qualms about the inhabitants of the seas, I very much wanted to make the trip but my personal disappointment would be as nothing compared to that of my seniors in the Corps of Royal Engineers. In a nightmare I reported to them, "You remember that reef blasting job you wanted? So sorry, I never managed to make the reconnaisance."

I hoped that if I could reach Tarawa, the capital, I could then find ways of moving between the islands of the colony. As Steve Clark had advised, I consulted Percy Roberts, who said he was sure the colony would help if possible but stressed that he had not made such trips himself recently. When he had travelled in the Gilberts soon after the war, there had still been Americans with whom to hitch lifts.

Transport remained my main problem. A bird would fly 1,800 miles from Christmas Island to Tarawa, rather further than from London to Moscow. Ships in the area were a rarity and, if a plane could be diverted, there would be hardly anywhere for it to land and most of the lagoons were said to be unsuitable for seaplanes.

Time and money also reared their ugly heads. Nobody had put a definite limit on my time of absence from the Army on Christmas Island, nor on

Bill Mitford's from commanding the Royal Navy there, but Bill and I thought that about a month would be acceptable. The prevailing winds would change in September, after which the atoll approaches became hazardous and Dick Sullivan would be due for relief about then too. Every week of delay decreased the chance of my trip ever starting.

However keen the Army might be to work for the Colonial Office, officialdom would demand a transfer of funds. I knew that the colony had been allocated about £70,000, at 1959 prices, for the whole task, including my reconnaissance, and the more that cost, the less there would be for the main work on the channels. As expected, exact costings proved difficult to obtain but I was quoted the price for using a Hastings aircraft at three miles for £1, meaning over £1,200 to Tarawa and back. Colony vessels would work out at about £100 a day and the pay and allowances of the four of us in my recce party, totalling about £15 a day, would all have to be charged. I just hoped that my estimate of £4,000 for the reconnaissance would prove to be in the right parish.

Bill Mitford was also very keen that the expedition should be mounted soon. He wanted to practise his skills as a diver and would welcome some diversion from his rather limited role on Christmas Island. "With all the resources of the Royal Navy behind you, Bill, what shipping can you arrange for our reconnaissance?" I asked. He admitted that the only ship available was a motor fishing vessel (MFV) of forty tons that had been left at Christmas Island because it could not get itself home; in fact its range was only two hundred miles.

I had already heard of the MFV's lack of capability. She had once made a daring round circuit of Christmas Island, about 150 miles in all, but that was when larger vessels were around to offer a tow in emergency. Recently the MFV might have run an errand to Fanning, another of the Line Islands, as it happened that the European staff, who tended the ends of the undersea cables that surfaced there, had families that were already as large as they wished. The gist of the message received on Christmas Island was, "Run out of contraceptives. Please supply."

Christmas Island had always been a non-families station but those on Fanning had rightly surmised that the necessary articles would be available for servicemen going on leave to Honolulu; stocks in the sports store were found to be mountainous. However, the short trip to Fanning and back would have been too much for the MFV and, with great regret, the trip could not be authorised. Apart from one ship, a Royal Fleet Auxiliary, that would bring fuel to Christmas Island in many months time, Bill knew of no other RN ships in the Pacific east of Japan.

A Bank Line vessel came twice a year to collect the copra from the Christmas Island plantations, but it then headed eastwards towards England, via the Panama Canal. The more I thought about shipping, the more remote the chances of mounting my reconnaissance by sea appeared to be.

How could I "show my initiative"? Nothing came to mind so, as my office was next to that of the Base Commander, I chatted my problems over with him again. Wing Commander Richardson enthusiastically supported the idea of the reconnaissance and would be happy to ask the Commander-in-Chief of Transport Command for his personal assistance, but practicalities had to be faced. The only airstrip in the Gilbert Islands was at Tarawa, just where I wanted to go, but its condition was uncertain. However, a Hastings was known to have used it, without mishap, quite recently. Hope at last!

I suggested that one of the Hastings now on Christmas Island should, on its way home to England via Australia, make a diversion to Tarawa before going on to Fiji. A relief plane a month later could make the trip the other way round and pick us up. This sounded simple, until some annoying details were mentioned. There were no ground staff at Tarawa and, more importantly, usually no fuel; it had to brought in by ship in drums, which meant infrequently and at long notice. There were also technical implications, among them limits on flying hours. The financial factor was always in the background, too, as many Hastings miles could be added to my estimates and would exceed the available funds.

I had arrived on Christmas Island on 9th June and now, a month later, had made no progress in arranging my reconnaissance. My report to London only confirmed my sense of frustration. "Stuck for transport," I signalled, which was, of course, already well known.

* * *

Even without the promise of my reconnaissance, my Christmas Island command was one that many of my contemporaries envied, so I did my best to learn about the island and its possible engineering needs. "Know the ground" was a useful maxim, so I went out most days in my Land Rover: I was particularly attracted to the south-east end of the island which, being as far as possible from the Port, had become the actual test site for the nuclear weapons.

The Americans had had a little trouble in estimating the power of their early thermo-nuclear weapons, and Eniwetok and Bikini atolls had been knocked about rather more than they intended. Consequently the British showed due caution with their first home-made H-bomb on 19th June 1957 and, although the aircraft that carried it took off from Christmas Island, the bomb was exploded as an airburst near a deserted atoll, Malden Island, a few hundred miles away. Apparently the result had been very much as predicted, causing only the expected level of damage, and the only known inhabitant, a pig that was living wild, was said to be none the worse for its unique experience.

It was then considered safe to explode subsequent British weapons over the sea off the south east point of Christmas Island itself. This meant that all the instruments and cameras could be positioned along the coastline and installed and serviced much more simply than on Malden.

Before the end of the British trials on Christmas Island in 1959, sufficient confidence had been built up for some of the nuclear devices to be suspended below tethered balloons and exploded at a height of a few thousand feet over the end of the island. A year later, I found the ground directly under the bursts still clear of scrub and grass, but no other effects of the large bangs were obvious. I found the concrete blocks, with steel shackles to which the balloon wires had been attached, as good as new.

On my visits to south east point I learnt that fine big crayfish, lobsters with large tails but no claws, abounded on the reefs nearby. They had survived the nuclear explosions overhead and on a moonlit night with a low tide could be picked off the wide expanse of flat coral between the shore and the reef edge. However, it was remarkable how seldom the timing of moon and tide was convenient but, when they were, a hundred large crayfish were a fair catch. I assumed that if crayfish were available on Christmas Island, so they would be elsewhere, but sadly discovered that the more populated atolls were almost fished out.

* * *

I had almost given up hope of setting off on my trip around the colony, when the District Commissioner paid an unexpected visit to my office. Previously Percy Roberts had asked to borrow a bulldozer so that the coconut plantations could be extended but this time was obviously different. "Dan," said Percy, "His Honour the Resident Commissioner makes periodic visits around the colony. This year he thought he would have to miss us out but I've just learned that he can include us. He'll be here in a week, staying just one day." My heart leapt as Percy continued, "Would you like me to ask if he could take you and your party back to Tarawa? He'll be calling at the Phoenix Islands on the way."

Before Percy had had a chance to add provisos, I had said, "Yes!" Those provisos turned out to be considerable, but I was too relieved with a sense of new hope to take them as seriously as they deserved.

The first point to note was that colony vessels were very small and had next to no space for passengers. His Honour (H.H.) had his wife on board with him and, although they were on *Moana Raoi*, the biggest and probably best of the ships, she was still small. There could well not be room for four more passengers. "That wouldn't matter," said I, "as we could sleep on deck." All Percy replied was, "Things on colony vessels, Dan, aren't quite like that."

The second snag was, "You would have to find your own way back and the colony would probably need assurance that you could do so." The only way to get back would be for the RAF to pick us up from Tarawa, so Percy came next door to the Base Commander with me to explain the proposal, ending with, "If H.H. says he can take the party, can you say that you will get them back?" I added that fuel for a single Hastings trip had now been positioned at Tarawa airstrip and that I was sure that the reconnaissance funds could run to one return flight from Christmas Island.

I knew that Wing Commander Dicky Richardson's decision would be difficult, but he took the broad view and recommended the one return Hastings trip to Transport Command. While we awaited their approval, there was no harm in Percy asking whether H.H. would be prepared to have me and my party on board.

I sent a telegram to my Army superiors in England saying, "Unless instructed otherwise, hope to depart Christmas Island on 17 July for reef blasting recce, returning in about a month." I gave the transmission of that message low priority, because I knew that the less time there was for decision, the more difficult it was to say no! I had spent 1946 in Sumatra, and later had reached the Korean War, both against the odds, by using the same approach.

H.H. the Resident Commissioner replied quickly from *Moana Raoi*, to say that I and my party would be most welcome, but very cramped. Transport Command took longer, asking for further assurances from the Base Commander, which he willingly gave. They were awkward assurances; I imagined that very little thanks would come his way if all went well and knew that, otherwise, he could land in trouble. Meanwhile, as I had hoped, I received no reply to my own signal.

Percy obtained an outline itinerary for the reconnaissance from the Superintendent of Marine in Tarawa and I attached a copy of it to the short directive (to myself) which Wing Commander Richardson asked me to draft. He signed it on 13th July 1960 and gave it back to me with his best wishes. We copied that directive, for information, to the many authorities associated with the reef channels project; a map of the proposed route, much of which proved to be largely fictitious, was attached.

I had not allowed myself to believe too seriously that our trip would materialise, all to avoid excessive disappointment if it did not. Now there was a mad rush to complete arrangements which really should have been made earlier. I had not previously appreciated the weight and bulk of the diving kit and, for Jack and me, it was more like trying to pack for a holiday at an unknown destination when we did not know how we would be spending our time there.

All we knew with certainty was that we would be working on coral or in the sea. There were endless tools and gadgets that we thought we should take with us, perhaps for measuring levels, perhaps for testing the purity of the drinking water. Eventually the essentials boiled down to a compass, a crowbar for chipping samples of coral, a cord knotted at intervals for measuring distances over the reef, and a six foot long wooden rod with which we could measure the depth of the water. Jack kept thinking of a large number of smaller items that might be useful, such as hammers and large nails for marking out centre lines, and these were accumulated into several sandbags.

From the tentative itinerary, I could see that our visits to individual islands were likely to be hurried, sometimes lasting only a few hours, so everything we wished to see and question would need to be recorded quickly. Army life had taught us how to fill in forms and, if there were no suitable form for a certain need, we should devise a pro-forma of our own. Not knowing our precise task, the framing of the pro-forma questions proved difficult! However, the list we did produce proved to be much better than had we left matters to chance.

One question that I was sure we must ask the locals was phrased, *Hazards (fish, currents, etc) to working parties?* Based on what I had read and heard, we expected some interesting answers to that one. Our one and only Army clerk typed up a suitable two sided form and ran off fifty copies for us to take with us.

The visit by His Honour the Resident Commissioner was a great occasion for the District Commissioner and his Gilbertese work force, but one in which we servicemen would have no official part. We were, in effect, H.H.'s guests on one of "his" islands, for which the Base Commander hoped we could show our appreciation by staging a dinner in our mess. After some doubts about the suitability of the tides for sailing, H.H., Mr Michael Bernacchi, and his wife accepted our invitation to a Guest Night on the Sunday evening of their visit.

The MV *Moana Raoi* arrived late on Saturday and we saw her moored to a buoy outside the Port the next morning. It was reassuring to hear that she drew too much water to come into the lagoon but, nevertheless, at only 490 tons, she looked extremely small and much smaller than any other ship in which I had previously traversed the oceans.

H.H. and Percy, who was naturally also invited to dinner, spent the day together and we arranged with *Moana Raoi's* master that Jack and AB Williams should go aboard before dusk, taking Bill's and my kit along with theirs.

The Bernacchis and Percy arrived at the mess at 7.30 p.m. for what became a very happy evening. None of us knew much of diplomatic life and had been slightly awed at the prospect of entertaining a Resident Commissioner. Mr Bernacchi turned out to be a well built man aged nearly fifty, clean shaven, suave and with greying hair; there was no mistaking his air of authority. He had a ready and dry sense of humour and was an excellent mixer. Mrs Bernacchi looked ten years younger than her husband and, from the moment she entered the room, we knew that she enjoyed meeting people. With dark hair and a sparkling personality, she took enormous interest in everything and was exceedingly welcome in our all-male mess.

It turned out that H.H. had been in the Royal Navy, joining through Dartmouth and Cambridge University, but later transferred to the Colonial Service, only to be recalled to the Navy for the war. He knew the form that Guest Nights took and obviously enjoyed them as much as any of us. When it came to mess games, both he and Mrs Bernacchi showed themselves to be exceedingly nimble and the time for us to catch the launch out to *Moana Raoi* was marked by H.H. standing on his head in a manner that none of the rest of us could equal.

Chapter Four

A SHAKY FIRST LEG

We boarded *Moana Raoi* at midnight and sailed for Canton in the Phoenix Islands. Immediately Bill Mitford and I were shown to our tiny two berth cabin and I was thankful to find that Jack had booked me the lower bunk by putting my kit on it. It was several years since I had been in a ship but I could already sense that the rolling and pitching still would not suit my queasy tummy. Knowing the demands for tidiness of the Royal Navy at sea and in deference to Bill, I stowed my clothes, but was thankful to lie down with the minimum of delay.

The deck being washed down outside our cabin window signalled the end of a none-too-restful night and a cup of tea presented by the ship's steward, a charming Solomon Islander, started the day officially at seven o'clock. Our cabin had much in common with a room in a doll's house and it was a wonder that everything fitted in. A very narrow passage led from the outside to the even narrower door, which opened inwards, thus preventing access to the drawers under my bunk; the open door also prevented the occupants of the bunks from seeing who was entering. There was an undersize hanging cupboard, a settee that would have been suitable for children and a tiny desk at which I would later write my visit reports and tour diary.

Bill had a beard of distinctive goatee shape but I needed to shave, so he used the miniature wash basin with cold water only, before I got up. On subsequent mornings the kindly steward brought me a jug of hot shaving water.

Moana Raoi proceeded westwards at about eight knots with a gentle corkscrewing motion, for which it was difficult to account, as the air on deck was nearly still. A glance over the rail, though, made the constant churning swell of the Pacific Ocean, to which the ship was reacting, all too apparent.

Our cabin was just behind the quarter deck. Forward of the bridge was the ship's hold and, on top of it, *Moana Raoi's* motor launch, with two large surf, or copra, boats, one on either side. Forward of the hold was the forecastle, carrying a sturdy mast with a couple of derricks and their winches; anchor cable and more winches occupied further space, but the whole of the forward part of the ship was submerged under Gilbertese passengers. I now understood why Percy Roberts had said we would not be able to sleep on deck.

We visited the bridge and the ship's master, Captain Vic Ward, showed us around the ship, a tour taking about one minute; he suggested that the best place for us to sit was the tiny triangle of deck over the stern, well clear, please, of the two miniature lifeboats.

Vic took Bill and me with him into the little dining saloon for breakfast. The Bernacchis were already there with Jack and AB Williams, together with another large man, "Bud" Flanagan. He was the ship's engineer and, apart from Vic, the only member of the crew not of local origin.

The saloon was said to seat eight at a pinch and, as eight we were, it was very pinched indeed. There could be no question of anyone sitting aloof, though I had been worried as to how Williams would mix in. I guessed that he had not met many Resident Commissioners, let alone their wives, but shyness proved not to be Williams' problem; he was soon making the running of the conversation.

Everyone was, I thought, being unnecessarily hearty and I felt severely tested even before Bud apologised for the greasiness of the fried egg he passed to me; that finished me. I went to that triangle of deck, found myself a seat and tried to sip a cup of coffee. Later, I was joined by the remainder of my reconnaissance party, who all expressed their condolences, but their confidence in me cannot have been increased by my miserable appearance. I made a brave attempt to accompany the others to lunch but, as we were filing into the saloon, Bud just mentioned that the pork chops were a little on the fat side.

The saloon seated seven much more comfortably than eight, so I didn't take it too personally when it was suggested that I might continue to take my meals on deck. I accepted without argument and, for the next four days, Mrs Bernacchi took great trouble to organise dainty trays for me. However tempting those trays looked, my sustenance became five cups of Marmite-flavoured hot water each day. Bud just mentioned that the Major's waist line could stand a few more days on that diet.

News of happenings elsewhere on the ship reached me rapidly. Jack and Williams were sharing a cabin somewhere below and seemed to be coping well, but Jack and I were shaken when Williams announced that he had brought two bottles of brandy and a bottle of whisky aboard with him. On Christmas Island he was an accomplished beer drinker but, as the rules stood, he should not have been able to obtain spirits; he told us he had been sold them by a member of the sergeants' mess. With mixed feelings, I mentioned AB Williams' bottles to Bill, who confiscated them without delay. I was then worried that, in such a small team, goodwill might become at risk, particularly as Williams himself had brought his assets to our attention.

I need not have worried; Williams was proud of having obtained the spirits and highly interested in seeing what we would do when faced with the predicament he had engineered. Bill had acted just as Williams thought correct, to the extent that he, Williams, became better company than ever. As a fellow passenger, he drank evens or better of whatever was on offer, which was often H.H.'s personal whisky: after all, he, Williams, would have been only too glad to contribute to the liquor pool!

There is a well known temptation to analyse one's companions on a sea voyage and Williams would probably have won a competition for the most interesting character aboard. For much of the time he led us to believe that he was really thick, with very little life above his waistline, yet his light reading was algebra books. When not so occupied, he would demonstrate an astonishing ability to play patience on an open deck in a gusting breeze, without losing any of the cards. In the evenings, he shamed us all with his beautifully pressed trousers and brothel creeper shoes of exclusive pattern.

The doings of the well known Mitford family were seldom dull and Bill certainly fitted that pattern. He was intense by nature, precise in his beautiful manners, and confident in his beliefs, to the extent that he inspired confidence. As my companion in such a small cabin he had the great advantage of being slight of stature; keen on physical fitness, he was strong and wiry.

Jack Cheeseman was just the man to be the sergeant-major of an independent squadron of Royal Engineers, meaning that he was full of character and resource. Although he had the traditional qualities of a warrant officer, including a very deep and, if necessary, loud voice, his military appearance was softened with a ready smile and a need to wear spectacles. He was aged thirty-three, a year younger than me, and his presence was quickly felt. He settled into life around the colony with the greatest of ease and, as we wore civilian clothes for most of the trip, was often taken to be the major in charge. Never was I taken to be the sergeant-major!

Some anticipate the next meal at sea with keen interest but, not being inclined to eat, I found my first few days in *Moana Raoi* increasingly boring. The more seasick I felt, the more I wished that I could have met the person who named the ocean "Pacific". Out in its middle, with nothing in sight, day after day, certainly it was uneventful, but never pacific. I read a couple of Evelyn Waugh books which did me good, then started another, but the hero went mad on a sea cruise.

Bud, as chief engineer, kept an eye on the wireless operator and brought us up to date with world news by typing out a news sheet which became daily more depressing. The Belgians were having real trouble in the Congo and the Soviets were behaving in a most unfriendly manner. If a nuclear war were to start, *Moana Raoi* was probably at the safest place in the world; even that thought did not encourage me greatly, but one incident in the daily routine did interest me increasingly.

Mrs Bernacchi, realising that she and her husband would be aboard *Moana Raoi* for several weeks, had made extensive preparations for the voyage, one being to bring with her a window box of chives to add spice to the galley's products. This box was positioned on the deck where I sat and was watered religiously twice a day. The ship's cat, a friendly fellow, took great interest in the chives, but it wasn't long before I realised that he was not so much attracted by the herbs, as by the excellent cat litter under them. Daily he did his duty in the chives box and on most days chives adorned the cooking as served in the saloon. I kept quiet on this subject until I again felt up to eating proper meals myself.

Vic Ward, the master, was the first person who was able to explain the type of work on which my advice was likely to be sought and it was a great relief to discover what was in mind. Above sea level, a coral atoll was only a pile of coral rubble, surrounded by a flat fringing reef of coral stone. Some fringing reefs were very wide, nearly half a mile, as we had seen outside the Port at Christmas Island, but some were only a few yards across. All reef flats were covered by a few feet of water at high tide but dried out completely at low tide; "that means that we can only work our work boats, the ones beside the launch on top of the hold, to the shore for a very limited time each tide."

Vic explained that, often, ships could not find an anchorage near the islands, so had to chug up and down at a safe distance from the shore while the tide level prevented the surf boats from working. Each surf boat could carry about three tons and, when loaded, drew about three feet of water, which was as deep as all but the highest tides ever covered the reef flats. Tides were obviously going to play an important part in my life and the truth started to dawn when Vic said, "What we need is some form of channel, deep enough to take a loaded surf boat over the reef edge and to the shore at any stage of the tide." He added, "You'll see what I mean when we visit Hull and Gardner Islands at the end of the week."

As outlined by Vic, the loading of copra sounded a very tedious business, especially when many return trips to the shore were involved. The surf boats were about ten feet wide, so the minimum requirement would be for a channel wider than that, with three feet of water in it at lowish tide. Thankfully, I could say that such a task sounded manageable, but I hoped the reef flats would not be too wide at the channel sites.

Bill Mitford had also been listening to Vic and was understandably disturbed by what he had heard. To work at low tide there would be no need for divers, nor would there with only two or three feet of water over the reef flat, so he was wondering why Christmas Island had been stripped of its divers for the project. Vic reassured him, by saying that at the reef edge, where the coral dropped away steeply to the depths of the ocean, lay the worst problems. Even on a still day, waves broke on the reef edge once the tide was covering the reef flat, and that was why the copra boats were also known as surf boats. Between each wave the surging water exposed the jagged edge of the reef and the skill of manoeuvring the boats over it lay in choosing the right wave on which to surf from the deep and turbulent water to the calm shallows over the reef flat.

This form of surfing, with unwieldy boats, sounded highly hazardous and it was easy to understand that going out over the reef edge, when fully laden, could be even more testing than coming in with less aboard. "I imagine that making a suitable entrance, or funnel, through the reef edge will turn out to be the most difficult part of each job," said Vic, "and I can't see how that can be done without divers." Copra boats were too valuable to lose through accidental bashing on the reef edge.

Vic foresaw a further need for divers on the barrier reefs; the strip of water connecting a navigable lagoon to the ocean was often full of coral heads and for a copra boat to hit one of these in a tide race could be fatal. Vic mentioned the island of Aranuka as an example and added, "You certainly won't be able to work on coral heads without divers." Bill and Williams at once looked much happier.

Although the islanders were natural seamen, both the master and chief engineer were kept busy. *Moana Raoi* was Vic Ward's third command in the colony and, as the largest vessel in the fleet, he was very proud of her. "What does *Moana Raoi* mean?" I had to ask.

Vic looked embarrassed. "Calm sea!" was his reply.

Few ship's masters can have known the central Pacific like Vic Ward, and it was fascinating to listen to him. What most struck me was just how deserted that part of the ocean was. In his ten years around the colony, he had only twice seen another ship that was not on colony business, and even they were rare. Exceptions were a couple of missionary vessels, which were almost part of the colony, and the ships which visited Christmas Island during the weapon tests. The chances of collision at sea sounded remote but so did the chances of rescue, if ever the need arose.

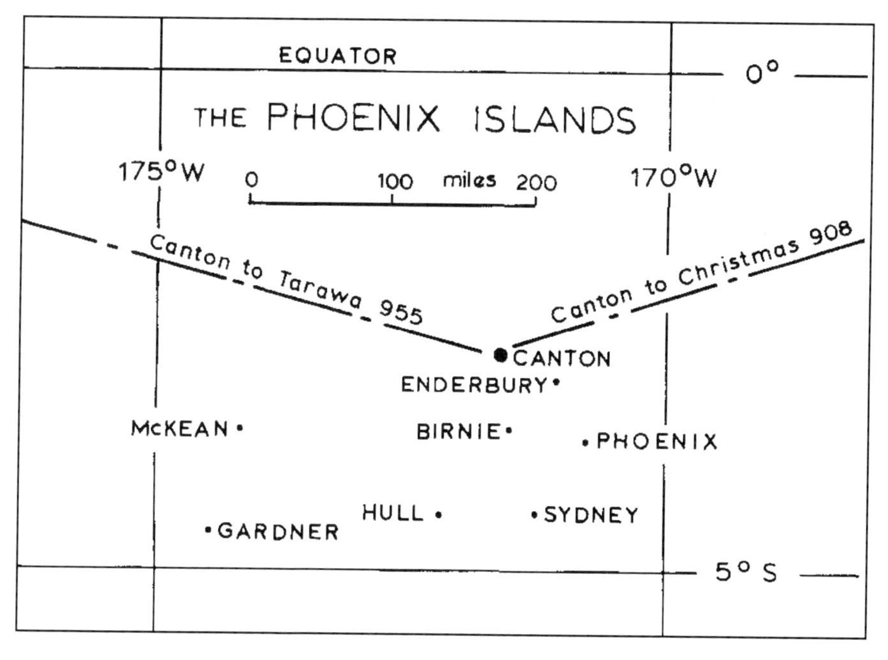

We were due at Canton, the main island of the Phoenix Group, on Friday evening, almost five days out from Christmas Island and were told that Canton differed greatly from the other islands we would visit. True, it was an atoll with a lagoon but the Americans had developed it in the Pacific War as a supply base and, more recently, as a staging post for aircraft. The engineering might of the United States had considerably widened and deepened the lagoon entrance and a small harbour had been built with a quay at which *Moana Raoi* could tie up. However, the entrance to the lagoon was still a beast to navigate, except at a slack tide and it was to catch the tide at Canton that we had needed to sail from Christmas Island at midnight on Sunday.

Many of *Moana Raoi's* crew of nearly thirty worked the copra boats, but that did not explain those hundred, or so, Gilbertese passengers who covered the forward part of the ship. We were told that some were being taken home after contracts on Christmas Island, and others were reliefs for the plantations on Hull and Gardner Islands. Just how that quantity of people managed to live was better not asked but there were piles of coconuts everywhere, so perhaps they were for both food and drink.

Before we left Christmas Island I had requested permission to bring some explosives with us, to experiment with the blasting of coral, but had been answered, "Sorry, no!" Most of the islanders smoked, which would have been dangerous enough, but the cooking fire that one Gilbertese family lit on deck beside the hold confirmed the sense in Vic's answer.

We had crossed the equator from north to south on Tuesday, 19th July, seen a few flying fish skimming the ocean, and caught a couple of small tuna on the troll lines over the stern; the lures looked like gigantic and gaudy salmon flies. By Thursday, our fourth day, I was starting to get my sea legs and began to write my tour diary, which, thirty years later, provides some basis for this book.

* * *

That same Thursday evening, Bill Mitford became ill. I had ventured into the saloon for supper but fairly soon afterwards retired to Bill's and my cabin, where I found him writhing in agony on my bed, the lower bunk. I had no idea what was wrong with him, so went to the Bernacchis for help and they called in Vic Ward.

We could get no sense out of Bill but he was obviously extremely ill, the most likely assumption being that this was a recurrence of previous stomach trouble. I understood that, some months before, Bill's previous operation for appendicitis had given trouble and that he had been flown from Christmas Island to Honolulu for further surgery. All was said to have been well since then but that was obviously no longer the case.

With no doctor aboard and with no one medically qualified, Vic, as master, knew that responsibility rested with him and acted calmly and decisively. He had a good, simple, medical book and a fairly sophisticated first aid kit, but before consulting the book, we all agreed that the first need was to try to alleviate the pain. So Vic injected a large dose of morphine into Bill's arm and, after ten minutes, it had some effect.

Vic stayed with Bill, while Mr Bernacchi, putting his Royal Navy experience to good effect, and I drafted signals asking for a plane to be sent to Canton to take Mitford to hospital. Life or death depended on those messages getting through but transmitting them proved full of problems. *Moana Raoi's* wireless was small and, even had it transmitted strongly enough over many hundreds of miles through the inevitable atmospherics at night, it was unlikely that anyone, anywhere, would be listening for a message. Mainly to conserve batteries, but also to make the life of the lone operator on each island tolerable, wirelesses only opened up "on sked" (schedule, in English!) for a very few minutes at a time. Even then, there was an element of luck in catching the sked, due to the changing time zones across the ocean. Burt Lancaster and the ship's wireless operator kept trying to make contact throughout the night, but without success.

The tranquilising effects of Bill's first dose of morphine wore off quicker than we expected and never was a medical book studied more avidly. Whatever Bill's previous history, we diagnosed peritonitis, meaning a burst appendix. In that case, the book's only answer was immediate surgery, impossible on *Moana Raoi.* The book added that, if surgery were not possible, death could be expected within twenty-four hours. We were due at Canton in twenty hours but some delay would then be inevitable before any surgery was possible. However, the book advised that penicillin might help, so Vic added an outsize injection of it to Bill's previous morphine.

I stayed with Bill until one in the morning and then Jack came until 3 a.m., when Williams took over until five, then I resumed duty. Vic had been up most of the night and given Bill two more large injections of morphine, the second of which really numbed him. Meanwhile, despite incessant tapping, our messages had not been passed on the wireless.

Presumably because I had become so absorbed in Bill's health, my own seasickness had completely disappeared and, while I was eating my first large breakfast of the voyage, Burt arrived with the marvellous news that a message had, at last, been passed. During the night he had also managed to get an extra knot out of *Moana Raoi's* engines and we were now due at Canton two hours earlier than planned.

Bill remained desperately ill throughout the morning but our hopes rose when, firstly, we were able to confirm that Canton Island had its own doctor and then, at 2 p.m., with the island in sight, we received a message that a Hastings would be leaving Christmas Island shortly and should land on Canton at 7 p.m. It could take Bill direct to Honolulu.

I had to face up to the effect of Bill's impending departure from our party. I knew that one diver should never work unless help were available from another and AB Williams showed me his Royal Navy Diving Manual, which ruled that "No diver must dive, except in emergency, without a trained attendant being present", so Williams must not dive alone. He accepted the implications as inevitable and prepared to leave us at the same time as his fellow diver, Bill Mitford.

Without the divers, only Jack and I would be left for the reconnaissance but we now felt that many of our tasks could be tackled from above water. If all went well, the two of us could still prove useful. H.H. had come to the same conclusion and Jack and I were reassured to hear that he was in favour of us continuing on our own.

By arriving at Canton early, Vic had set himself a severe test of seamanship. Instead of entering the lagoon at high tide, with slack water in the entrance, the flood tide was rushing in, so that *Moana Raoi* was thrown forward as if through a plug hole. This was exactly what Vic had planned to avoid but he successfully made the sharp turn that was immediately required to avoid grounding just inside the lagoon entrance and we were soon alongside the Canton quay. Bill Mitford had been lucky to be in Vic Ward's hands.

The first aboard were Mr George Bristow, the British District Commissioner for the Phoenix Islands, and Dr Dick Zandee, a Netherlander who was the resident medical officer for Canton Island. Dr Zandee saw Bill in our cabin and quickly diagnosed a strangulated hernia. He was concerned at just how ill Bill was and wanted him moved to the dispensary at the airfield, two miles away, as quickly as possible. The doctor had a United States Navy "Corps man" (sick berth attendant) with him, but the passage to our cabin set a problem, as it was too narrow for the "litter" (stretcher).

Bill, fortunately, was conscious and understood our predicament. Other than drag him along the floor, there seemed no way of moving him to the deck, but Bill managed to stagger the few paces himself and was lifted on the litter over the ship's rail and on to the quay.

The Bernacchis, George Bristow and I were at the Canton airfield at 7 p.m., when the Hastings landed just after dark. We were delighted to find that one of the two Royal Air Force doctors from Christmas Island, the surgeon, was on board, and he and Dr Zandee examined Bill in the dispensary. Meanwhile, the Hastings crew prepared for the seven hour flight to Honolulu. Both doctors, however, decided that Bill was too ill to risk the flight and that they must operate as soon as possible in the Canton dispensary.

We were enormously relieved to hear, the next morning, that all had gone well, in spite of the difficulties involved in performing the operation. The medical team consisted of the British surgeon, the Dutch doctor, the US Navy Corps man, a visiting American lady, who had once been a nurse, and a Gilbertese medical student. They could not give a general anaesthetic, so had had to use a spinal one, which left Bill capable of taking considerable interest throughout the operation. It was now planned to let him make his initial recovery without being moved from Canton and then to fly him to Honolulu later.

To our surprise and delight, there was private mail waiting for Jack and me at Canton, deposited by a homeward bound Hastings from Christmas Island. It was that aircraft that had picked up *Moana Raoi's* signals for help and, by sheer luck, Wing Commander Dicky Richardson, the CI Base Commander, had been on it, making a brief leave visit to Fiji. With only one Hastings left on Christmas Island, only Richardson could authorise its emergency flight to us with the surgeon. The amazing speed with which such effective action had been achieved was to the great credit of the Royal Air Force.

Knowing that Bill Mitford was in good hands, George Bristow had taken the Bernacchis and me back home for dinner. We had to cross the large lagoon by launch and were very late but Mrs Bristow produced a magnificent meal. I had not expected the invitation but was even more pleased to be there when George discovered that we had both soldiered in Sumatra in 1946.

The Hastings took the RAF surgeon back to Christmas Island the next morning, together with AB Williams, the diving gear and my letter to Bill Mitford's father reporting good progress. The problem of Williams' bottles of spirits had earlier been settled, by Jack and me buying them off him.

The Bristows again asked the Bernacchis, with Jack and me, to their house for lunch. One of our fellow guests was the American lady who had assisted at Bill's operation, who was full of praise for the spontaneous teamwork of the Dutch doctor and the British surgeon. Earlier that morning Mrs Bernacchi had shown me the ruins of the Pan Am Hotel near Canton airfield; although it had been built only ten years before, the new generation of planes could overfly Canton, and the pointsettias growing wild around the hotel were sad reminders of recent glory.

The rest of Canton was devoid of vegetation, just white coral sand and rubble with no palm trees, but we were assured that other atolls would be different. In the absence of other information, I tried to theorise about coral atoll formation and am including some of what resulted in the Annexe at the end of this book. My ideas were certainly oversimplified and are still probably wrong, but they may give newcomers to atolls a few opening gambits.

Mrs Bernacchi had also taken me to Canton's two post offices, one British, one American (the island was a condominium), and I bought a set of the beautiful Gilbert and Ellice Islands stamps. There had been a competition in the colony for their design, with a prize of £40 for each that was selected. Very few stamps were actually used there on letters but useful revenue came from philatelists.

A little out of phase, I will now say that we heard, some weeks later, that Bill Mitford's recovery had gone completely to plan. Surgery was completed in Honolulu and, not long afterwards, he left the Royal Navy to become a Church of England parson.

Chapter Five

SOME PHOENIX ISLANDS

Vic Ward had taken *Moana Raoi* out of Canton lagoon while the tide was right, so when we rejoined her after lunch she was lying out to sea. The launch trip took us close to the wreck of the American liner *President Taylor,* which must have been a fine ship of about 20,000 tons. During the war, when she was a troopship, there had been a disagreement between her master and the senior officer aboard as to whether so large a ship could enter Canton lagoon.

Initially, the master had refused to take the risk but, shortly afterwards, Japanese submarines were reported nearby. The *President Taylor* then tried to enter the lagoon, but the entrance proved to be too shallow. After the war, two American couples moored a yacht nearby and spent their time removing what they could from their prize, and selling the spoils. Fortune again failed to shine on the ship as, first, husbands swapped wives, and then their yacht burnt out.

I took the precaution of taking some Avomine seasickness pills well before we sailed and was thankful that, this time, they worked. George Bristow accompanied us and the Bernacchis were surprised that I felt fit enough to join Jack and them to play Scrabble after dinner.

Most of the Phoenix Islands had been uninhabited until 1939 but, because of their fairly reliable rainfall, three were thought to be potential coconut plantations, so land was offered to anyone in the colony who cared to take it. We were due to visit Hull and Gardner, inappropriate modern names that had replaced the former Orona and Nikumororo. Some of those who moved had brought their problems with them and, unfortunately, remained of poor reputation; we were advised not to judge all the colony's inhabitants by them.

Moana Raoi was the one ship due to visit Hull in the year 1960. She would deliver supplies, collect copra, with which future supplies could be bought, and make some voluntary exchanges of families between islands, all very welcome. There proved, however, to be one snag: it was Sunday. With its population of about one thousand, Hull boasted both a Roman Catholic priest and a Methodist pastor, and the allegiance of the inhabitants was split between them. The only thing on which all were agreed was that work was not allowed on Sundays and neither side would bend its religious rules.

There were good reasons why *Moana Raoi* could not wait another day and George became involved in some tricky negotiations with the local authorities. It was a long while before the implications of "no ship for another year" really sank in, but George eventually managed to save face for everyone, by the judicious use of the International Date Line. Yes, it was Sunday here in Hull but in Tarawa, the capital of the colony, it was Monday and no commandment said that work could not be done on Tarawa's Monday. After this was agreed, H.H. the Resident Commissioner went ashore and was politely greeted.

Because the tide was high, the surf boat carrying Jack and me rode easily over the reef edge, whereupon most of the other occupants jumped into the shallow water covering the reef flat, and walked the boat to the shore. The water around Hull was the clearest I had ever imagined; it was a revelation to peer from the boat into the black depths of the ocean and then see the beautiful and steeply sloped side of the reef coming up towards us as we approached its edge.

The chart of Hull had been made during the war in 1943 and was of much better quality than some we were to meet later. There was no anchorage marked, so *Moana Raoi* stood off about a quarter of a mile while her launch towed the two surf boats from ship to shore and back. Later, Vic found that he could anchor in 12 fathoms (72 feet) about 150 yards out from the reef edge near the west tip of the island, where the reef shelved more gently than elsewhere. I asked how he found the place, to be

The reconnaissance party in working dress: the author with measuring rod, and Jack Cheeseman with crowbar.

answered, "If I can see the bottom, I know I can anchor but, for safety's sake, the wind needs to be blowing off the shore." The main village had its copra shed near the same west tip, so Vic's anchorage was worth recording.

Very luckily, for our first task, the type of surf boat channel required on Hull was easy to understand. There was already the start of a natural channel, or chute into the reef edge on the line that the boats were working. How could this be extended right across the reef flat up to the shore of the island? The total distance was under one hundred yards, the sea was delightfully calm and, given time and explosives, Jack and I were sure that the job could be done.

He and I had gone ashore in our working kit, consisting of bathing trunks and tennis shoes. He was armed with the crowbar and measuring line: I carried the wooden measuring rod, a copy of our questionnaire pro-forma, and my notebook, but we had not foreseen how quickly our records would become sodden with sea water.

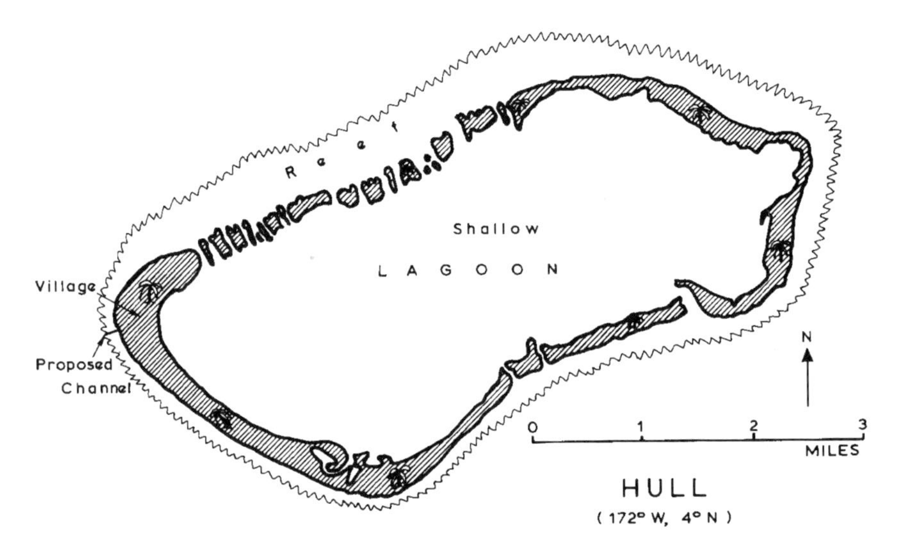

White men were a rarity on Hull and two, up to their waists in the water on the reef and performing strange antics, were too good for the village children to miss. The only available policeman was escorting H.H. on his rounds, so we had to fend for ourselves; the children were highly excited and, as they spoke no English and we spoke no Gilbertese, we couldn't keep them quiet. Each time Jack and I shouted distances and depths to each other, our message was drowned by the delighted din of childish chatter. We took our time and only hoped that what was recorded in the soggy notebook would proved legible and accurate. A very special aspect of our reconnaissance work now came home to us: if we forgot to take any measurements, or to ask any relevant questions, there would be absolutely no means, not for years, of anyone filling in the gaps.

Vic Ward wished to sail again as soon as possible and hoped that Jack and I could obtain all the information we needed during the four hours the tide allowed his surf boats to work. Work, the boats indeed did, and ton after ton of copra was offloaded from the island into the boats, and then into the ship's hold, all at a great pace. It was now easy to understand why such a large cargo handling crew was required, all working frantically, as the tide was a hard task master.

Jack and I had come a long way to see that reef and we particularly wanted to inspect it with the tide out, which we later did as, fortunately, H.H.'s business on the island detained him. While the tide was dropping we sought answers to the questions on our pro-forma, but almost everyone in authority was accompanying the Resident Commissioner. Eventually, we tracked down the island's wireless operator, who spoke English and answered with confidence.

The boat channel would lead to the edge of the village and we knew that large explosions and villages made poor partners. We tried to explain the dangers of blast and flying stones to the wireless operator, to whom, of course, such things were unknown, then asked, "Please, is there not some other place, away from the village, suitable for the channel?" His reply was a polite, but firm, "No!" We British visitors could not be expected to realise that the west tip of the island was protected from the prevailing easterly winds, so was the most sensible place to cross the reef, thus the village had been built there.

The wireless operator's attitude at first surprised us but, when we had a better look at the village, we realised that there was not much that explosives would damage. All the huts had wooden frames, with palm leaf roofs and sides, which would be easy to repair; otherwise, there were only rainwater tanks and they were strong. We were assured that the village

Hull atoll from MV Moana Raoi *showing her launch and deck passengers' daily rations.*

could quickly be evacuated but, having seen the children, we wondered. The only things that would be worth moving, said our informant, were some medicine bottles in the dispensary, lying only 20 yards from our proposed channel. By now the wireless operator had been joined by several friends, who said they also wanted "his" channel, and would be pleased to help dig it.

The time came to ask about the safety of workers on the reef. My questions about dangerous fish were greeted with amazement and incredulity. Perhaps I had misunderstood my reading of Grimble but, contrary to expectations, I recorded against the *Hazards to working parties?* question, "Apparently none".

The lack of vegetation on Canton Island, only 120 miles away, compared with Hull's overall covering of palm trees, was striking. All a matter of rainfall, we were told, but please can someone explain why two coral atolls, so close together and separated by the same ocean, winds and currents, should be so different?

When he had asked for the channel at the western tip of the atoll, the wireless operator had added, "But, when the westerly winds blow for a few months from September, we won't be able to use it so, could another on the other side of the island be made as well?" The far side of the island was six miles away and we had no hope of getting there and back in the time available. However, a glance at the chart showed that the fringing reef there was very wide. We said we were very sorry, but there would be no suitable channel site there, an answer that was accepted. Anyway, if only one ship

Surf (or copra) boats on tow.

Ship's visitors return to Hull.

visited Hull each year, its arrival should be scheduled to coincide with favourable winds!

When the tide had dropped and the reef flat dried out, Jack and I had the chance to check the measurements we had taken when wading in the water. The children had lost interest in us and gone home, so we were working under much more controlled conditions. We also had a chance to check the nature of that reef flat, or slab of coral rock, on which we were walking. It seemed as hard, and nearly as flat, as a concrete airfield, and the crowbar bounced back quite dangerously when we tried to chip off samples. There were very few cracks, or fissures, and no obvious lines of weakness in the rock; our first impression was that, for blasting purposes, we could use the same methods as for hard chalk or solid limestone. Later we realised that this could be wrong, as the consistency of the coral varied greatly once the hard crust of the reef flat had been broken.

* * *

Life on Hull seemed even less exciting than we had expected; there was little evidence of sea fishing and prospects in the shallow lagoon looked poor. There were no sports pitches and no electricity, so many of the diversions of the modern world were lacking; even the batteries of the wireless station were charged by wind power. However, the inhabitants looked well fed, strong and fit, but not everyone seemed devoted to Hull and many more of them accompanied the copra boats out to *Moana Raoi* than returned to the shore. Vic Ward had spent the earlier part of the morning swimming off the ship but now needed to exercise his authority to reduce the chance of stowaways.

We sailed soon after midday while I started to draft my official reconnaissance report and made a note in my personal diary:–

"We could certainly improve the channel at Hull considerably with explosives, if it weren't for the probability of knocking down the village. Remembering our experience with the girls' school in Sumatra, I feel sure that this would not be popular, so it looks more like a job for one man and one boy for one month, rather than for ten men for two or three days."

* * *

Gardner Island, at the western end of the Phoenix Group, was our next objective and turned out to be a charming little place, about half the size of Hull, but more varied in character. A couple of large sharks were cruising on the surface between the ship and the reef, so Vic Ward did not go bathing. At high tide the shore consisted solely of a bank of coral sand about six feet high and the whole island from the seaward side appeared to be covered in coconut palms.

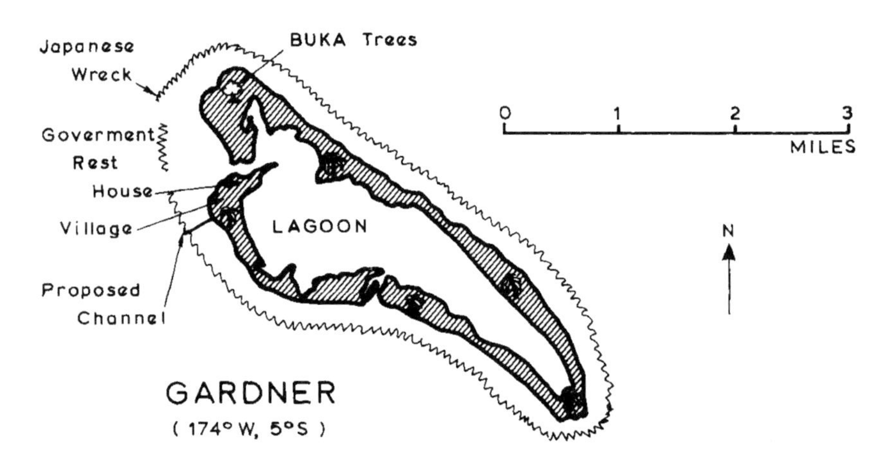

The chart showed the average depth of the Pacific Ocean between Hull and Gardner to be 3,000 fathoms, or over three miles, and the reef edge at Gardner sloped even more steeply than that at Hull. There was no question of *Moana Raoi* anchoring, so she had to chug along the coastline while the copra boats worked to her. The steersman of the boat which took Jack and me ashore misjudged the wave on which to surf his boat, hitting the reef edge, and he was toppled into the water. The speed with which he managed to clamber back into the boat was impressive, showing that he had some regard for the local sharks.

The spot at which we were asked to plan a boat channel had everything in its favour; in particular, it had no village at the end of it. No village meant no children and Jack and I were able to work with speed and confidence. As at Hull, the reef flat was not very wide, so we knew that, given enough explosive, a reef channel could be blasted. Our early observations proved perhaps too encouraging, as we were to discover later when we met more difficult tasks.

⋆ ⋆ ⋆

George Bristow had gone ashore with the Resident Commissioner, so I was gratified to be offered the help of Gardner's Chief of Kaubure, or chief headman of the island, who normally would accompany H.E. The local policeman was with him to interpret our questions.

That Chief of Kaubure must have had hidden depths, or he would not have been in his important position, but we never plumbed them. The policeman's English was adequate but the CoK was a difficult man to interrogate. We went through our questions very slowly but to each one the CoK would first answer "Yes", only for the policeman soon to say, "Sorry, he meant 'No'." Sometimes, though, the CoK started by saying "No" quickly followed by "Yes". After our fifth question the policeman had to tell us, most apologetically, "He says he really cannot say." We then took to asking the policeman what he personally thought and the CoK was not affronted by being omitted from our question and answer session. We just hoped for the best.

For the *Hazards to working parties?* question on Gardner I recorded my own answer:

"Sharks seen just off reef, opposite proposed channel. They sometimes come over the reef flat at high tide but no one has been harmed. On account of them, as well as for other reasons, work around low water would pay but a rifle proves a good deterrent."

Vic Ward carried a .22 inch rifle on the ship and the sharks had disappeared after he had taken a few shots at them.

Jack and I walked along the beach to see if there were any alternative sites for channels but found none. However, we were very interested to see bukas, bushy-topped trees from which dug-out canoes were built. Before sawn timber was imported, there must have been a severe problem on the islands that had no buka trees. We found the Government Rest House on the edge of the beautiful lagoon, where George Bristow was going to stay a few days before a specially arranged vessel took him back home to Canton. The Bernacchis were with him and from them we learned some recent history of the island.

When the Phoenix Group was resettled in 1939, the British District Officer, Mr Gallagher, had a good rest house built for him to live in. Unfortunately he died in 1941 of something like appendicitis, so the islanders had erected a fine tomb for him, beside which we now stood. Appendicitis was still high in our minds, following Bill Mitford's stomach trouble so, by mutual consent, we agreed not to re-open a medical discussion.

⋆ ⋆ ⋆

We then visited the village trade store which, hardly surprisingly after a year without resupply, was almost out of stock. Jack and I had formed a first impression of the delightfully basic economy of an island, which proved to be essentially correct. A local went to his trade store to see if there were anything he wanted to buy: if so, he harvested some coconuts from his trees, dried the meat and sold the copra to the Wholesale Society representative. The local then bought what he wanted from the trade store, also run by the Wholesale Society, which then ordered new stock. So, no sales from the store meant no money for replacement goods and no need to produce copra. Another good reason for not producing copra was that the locals might need to eat all the coconuts.

Whatever the reason, the inhabitants of Gardner had not produced as much copra as had been expected, so *Moana Raoi* was ready to sail a little early for Tarawa. Gardner to Tarawa was 844 nautical miles, or nearly 1,000 land miles, meaning four days at sea.

Without George Bristow, Mr and Mrs Bernacchi, Jack and I were the only remaining "first class" passengers. As it would be the Resident Commissioner, Mr Bernacchi himself, who would decide whether our reconnaissance proposals should be recommended to London, we could not have asked for a better opportunity to hear his views. He, in turn, was keen to hear our reactions to the first tasks we had seen. The idea of reef channels had been his, so the topic was dear to his heart.

Earlier, Jack and I had talked over the many questions to which we had no answers. Our experience with explosives had been gained as military engineers, training mainly for the demolition of bridges and roads, usually in a hurry and perhaps in the face of the enemy. We knew the wartime methods and how to calculate the quantities of explosives required, and would normally err on the generous side. That done, in military life, we asked for what we wanted, and expected others to provide everything we requested. Here, in the colony, things would be different! There were no resources available, except plenty of willing labour and anything that was required had to be ordered by mail, bought and imported.

The explosive techniques to blast the coral reef flats would involve a form of quarrying but, unlike the faces of most quarries, our coral rock would be lying flat. We knew that it would be best broken up by boring holes into it, filling the bottoms of them with explosive, and lifting off the coral rock layer by layer: to drill boreholes one needed a large air compressor with its pneumatic drills. I asked Mr Bernacchi if there were any such equipment we could borrow in the colony, but he knew of none, so I suggested the purchase of a set. That would be very expensive, and the weight of about three tons would set as big a problem as the cost: a compressor would fully load a copra boat and would almost certainly capsize it, so we started talking of lashing two boats together to form a raft.

Vic Ward entered our conversation at that stage. Not all colony vessels carried two similar copra boats and, even if a raft were constructed, how did we see it, with a compressor on board, being surfed over a reef edge? Just to confound us, he added that, of all the vessels, only *Moana Raoi* had derricks strong enough to lift three tons.

A military alternative for drilling boreholes consisted of specially shaped explosive charges, which focused their effect to blast a deep narrow hole into rock. Because of their conical shape, they were known as "beehives", but beehives were expensive, made a terrible bang and, without complicated modifications, did not work under water.

Jack and I knew of self-contained, man-portable drills, much like a small outboard motor, but with a drill on the end rather than a propeller, but even on dry land, their reliability was suspect, so they would be unlikely to work when drenched with salt water. Our quarrying problems seemed insoluble and we wished that we had done some experimental work before we left Christmas Island but, then, we had not been aware of the nature of our tasks.

H.H. understood our concern but was in no way dismayed. Not all the tasks would be the same and he was sure that suitable methods would come to our minds as we toured the colony. While I was engaged in these weighty discussions with her husband, Mrs Bernacchi was having a field day, washing most of Jack's and my clothes. We were enormously grateful, particularly as August Bank Holiday weekend in Tarawa was wont to be highly social, and we should arrive just in time for it.

It was a pleasure to hear of the affairs of the colony from the Bernacchis' own lips for they were obviously absorbed in them; we readily caught their enthusiasm and it was a great relief to be thinking of things other than coral for a while. Mr Michael Bernacchi had been appointed Resident Commissioner eight years earlier, in 1952, the same year that *A Pattern of Islands* was first published, but Sir Arthur Grimble's experiences, as recorded in it, dated from around the 1914-18 War.

In the Second Great War, the Japanese occupied the Gilbert Islands but had not taken the Ellice Islands. Very few of the pre-war Europeans, except a few Roman Catholic missionaries, had survived, so there was an inevitable lack of continuity of government. The first Resident Commissioner since then, Colonel V. Fox-Strangways, had certainly set the colony back on course, but none of Mr Bernacchi's predecessors had stayed very long in post. However modestly they talked, it was apparent to us that the influence of both him and his wife on the progress of, and life in, the post-war colony must have been immense.

Anything H.H. and his government could do was restricted by finance and he gave us some details of the colony's income, which came mainly from copra and phosphate. The whole of the annual copra output of 7,000 tons was taken by Lever Brothers, having been collected and marketed by the colony's Wholesale Society, with the price varying greatly from time to time. The colony took 25% in tax, the rest went to the producers.

The phosphate from Ocean Island, which was solid guano deposited by birds millions of years before, was all taken by the British Phosphate Commission. The colony received twenty-one shillings a ton totalling £250,000 a year from it, about equalling the income for the copra, so the colony's total income in 1960 would amount to about £500,000.

Looking into the future, the phosphate on Ocean Island would be worked out in less than twenty-five years and the price of copra was expected to drop, as other producers were entering the market. Also, the population of the colony was rising, so that meant less coconuts to spare for copra. Even if the long term economic prospects of the colony sounded none too rosy, we were fascinated by the current arrangements. Because any money under Colonial Office control had to be spent as Parliament in London directed, the Wholesale Society was in being to provide funds that could be spent as the colony itself wished.

The Resident Commissioner was, on behalf of the Colonial Office and the Queen, head of the colony, but he was also the managing director of the Wholesale Society. Wearing one hat he levied taxes on himself wearing another. The system worked, but not for nothing was the colony sometimes know as the Gilbert and Sullivan Islands.

I wondered who were Gilbert and Ellice, after whom the colony was named. It turned out that Ellice had had nothing to do with Gilbert. Captain Gilbert of the ship *Charlotte* reported some islands in 1788 and they had later become known as the Gilbert Islands. Captain De Peyster of the ship *Rebecca* found other islands south of the Gilberts in 1819, which he named after his ship's owner, Mr Ellice. I only hope that Ellice appreciated the honour he had been paid, otherwise they should have become the Gilbert and De Peyster Islands.

* * *

It was a great pleasure to be in a colony that was not only off most maps, but felt "out of this world" as well. Among the islanders, commerce had hardly raised its filthy head: the better educated men admitted that they worked, but stressed that they did not wish to become rich. There was no such thing as a rich Gilbert, or Ellice, islander. Time honoured customs allowed any member of a family to sponge on any other, so the moment anyone started to become successful, he discovered flocks of previously unknown relatives. Even though most of the islands were out of sight of each other, word of an apparently rich relation spread inexplicably, and further impecunious kinsmen soon arrived on the rich man's island. With no need to work, and with no wish to be rich, there was no need for a trade union.

My over-simplified explanation of the colony's economics might suggest that the islanders were idle and completely devoid of ambition, but that impression would be wrong. Generations of sheer survival on their tiny islands, enlivened by the need to fight fierce neighbours, had bred two extremely strong and cheerful races, gifted with abundant initiative and intelligence, either of which could be mobilised as and when the spirit moved.

The most highly educated islanders were the assistant medical officers, one at least of whom was stationed on every island, and on whom the inhabitants depended entirely for their medical care "until the next ship". The AMOs were trained for four years at Suva in Fiji and returned to the colony with a much broader view of the world than most of their contemporaries. The Bernacchis were delighted to have heard recently that the first ever Gilbertese had been accepted at Cambridge, not for a full tripos, but for a year. H.H.'s college had been Magdalene, so doubtless his influence had helped. Mrs Bernacchi was knitting the clever young man a heavy and a splendid grey woollen pullover.

It was more normal to talk of the Gilbertese, rather than of the Ellice, islanders, because of the 40,000 of the former and only 5,000 of the latter. For the convenience of British colonial government, the two sets of islands had been paired off, probably because they were adjacent strings of coral atolls in a remote part of the Pacific. In fact, they were very different, with the Gilbertese being of Micronesian origin, and the Ellice of Polynesian, and their languages had nothing in common, also. In a determined effort to integrate the two races, the Ellice islanders had been given a full part in the running of the colony and probably had slightly more than their fair share of the government jobs.

Wednesday, 27th July 1960 was, for us, not a day, as we crossed the International Date Line from Tuesday to Thursday. The zero degree of latitude line lay through Greenwich in busy England, but here, on the other side of the world and astride the 180 degree line, there was nowhere and no one. The Pacific Ocean, with its rolling swell, looked just the same, but now had a natural current helping to push *Moana Raoi* towards Tarawa. Vic called it "the set", saying that it could vary unpredictably in its strength and, in the Ellice Islands, was sometimes as strong as two knots. I rather missed the significance of the set at the time, but later appreciated its importance.

* * *

Mrs Bernacchi had been telling us of what to expect in Tarawa and much of it sounded very pleasant. However, one remark left us disquietened. "There is sure to be a lot of people waiting to quiz you about coral blasting." Neither Jack nor I had ever blasted an ounce of coral and, for all we knew, we might soon meet men who had blasted the stuff in bulk as a pastime. I had admitted my ignorance on the subject to her husband but Mrs Bernacchi had been too polite to believe me. I just hoped we would not be asked too much about coral blasting before we had learned something about it, but meanwhile I felt a complete fraud. My worries did, however, reinforce my wish to note any information I could obtain about coral and coral atolls.

Most of Mrs Bernacchi's comments on life in the islands were much more light hearted. In particular, her tales of the visit of H.R.H. Prince Philip, Duke of Edinburgh, to the colony in April 1959 deserved special note and, among her memories, the visit to Gardner, the atoll we had just left, had a special place.

The Bernacchis had been with the Duke in *Britannia* as they sailed from Tarawa towards the Phoenix Islands. Canton Island was to have been the first stop but, as there was a little time in hand, the Duke said that he'd like to go ashore for a picnic. With no other land nearby, Gardner was therefore selected for the impromptu visit. Since no one aboard, apart from the Bernacchis, had ever been there, Mr Bernacchi had been asked to go on the bridge and navigate *Britannia* to Gardner. Mercifully, H.H. had found the island, no easy task, and then found the right place to approach, by looking for, and then homing on, the white flagpole.

The inhabitants of Gardner noted the approach of the unknown vessel with interest and, to his great credit, the magistrate was, with the help of a picture postcard, able to identify *Britannia.* To show due deference, he then put on his uniform. After a good start, things went less well. The first outrigger canoe sent out to greet *Britannia* crossed the reef with insufficient caution, owing to the excitement of the occupants, who included the magistrate. They all got drenched, so in no way looked the part for a right royal welcome to "the husband of the woman king" (no word for queen existed in the Gilbertese language).

Gardner Island's one resident surf boat was then launched, to be rowed to *Britannia,* but it had not been in the water lately, so leaked, and slowly started to sink. However, after some delays, Prince Philip's party reached shore safely with "about a ton" of picnic kit. He and the visitors had said all the right things about Gardner and the inhabitants felt doubly proud to have been added unexpectedly to his programme.

It was surprising to hear how many of the important parts of H.R.H.'s visit planning had been undertaken by islanders who normally had little official standing. Neli Lifuka, the splendid Ellice islander and highly effective supervisor of *Moana Raoi's* cargo handling teams, was also the hereditary High Chief of Vaitupu, said to be the most beautiful place in the colony. When it was agreed that Vaitupu should be included in the Royal Tour, Neli was left in sole charge of the island's arrangements, and had put on a wonderful show.

With thirty-six hours to go before we were due at Tarawa, Vic Ward was confronted by two more small crises, which he brushed off as matters of routine. First, the ship's Gilbertese cadet officer ran a temperature of 105° Fahrenheit, as high as a human being should go. I expected to hear that Vic had given him a good dose of penicillin but, instead, he had chosen sulphur pills from his medicine cupboard, and the cadet's temperature had dropped dramatically.

No sooner was that young man on the way to recovery, than one of the women Gilbertese passengers on the forward deck threw a fit and tried to kill her husband with a coconut knife. She also tried to throw their baby overboard and, when that too had been prevented, attempted to jump off the ship herself; all rather pathetic in retrospect, but stirring at the time. Once the lady had quietened down, Vic had been the family comforter and very good he proved to be in that role.

Chapter Six

TARAWA, CAPITAL OF THE COLONY

Tarawa was the only place in the Gilbert and Ellice Islands of which I had heard before I knew that I was going to the colony. It had been one of the first islands the Americans had freed from the Japanese in the Pacific War, which the news bulletins in Britain had mentioned frequently in 1943. Their pronunciation was *Tar-* (as on roads) *ah-wah*, but I found the locals said *Tara-* (as in taragon) *wer*. What made Tarawa special, compared to most atolls, was that it had a large and mainly navigable lagoon.

It was eight o'clock on the morning of Saturday, 30th July 1960, when the south side of Tarawa came into view from *Moana Raoi's* bridge, and Vic Ward invited me to come and look. Mrs Bernacchi had bet me that he would do this but I kept my straightest face. "Do you see the land ahead of us, Dan?"

"Yes, Vic," said I, dutifully.

"And near the left hand end of it, do you see a black cloud?" asked he, to which I, quite truthfully, answered "No, Vic."

"Oh, Dan," he continued, "your eyesight must be even worse than I thought. I can assure you that there is a heavy black cloud. It lies over that part of Tarawa called Bairiki."

I then asked the desired question, "Why does a black cloud lie over Bairiki?"

Vic's delighted reply was, "Because Bairiki is the centre of government of this benighted colony!" Some years later Vic changed jobs to become a most loyal member of that same government.

It took us another three hours to round the south-west point of Tarawa, before entering the lagoon through the barrier reef which bounded the west side of the almost triangular atoll. The lagoon was full of shoals and coral heads, all well charted, but we anchored a long way from its shore. Jack and I had been assembling our belongings, which, in addition to the crowbar and our other reconnaissance kit, now included a couple of sandbags full of increasingly smelly coral chippings.

Tarawa, from the south, looked like an island about twenty miles long, with a solid bank of coconut palms along its whole length. Now, from the lagoon, we saw the other side of that long strip of palms and, as the tide dropped, the strip split up into a string of islets. *Moana Raoi's* launch transferred the Bernacchis, Jack and me towards an end, Bairiki itself.

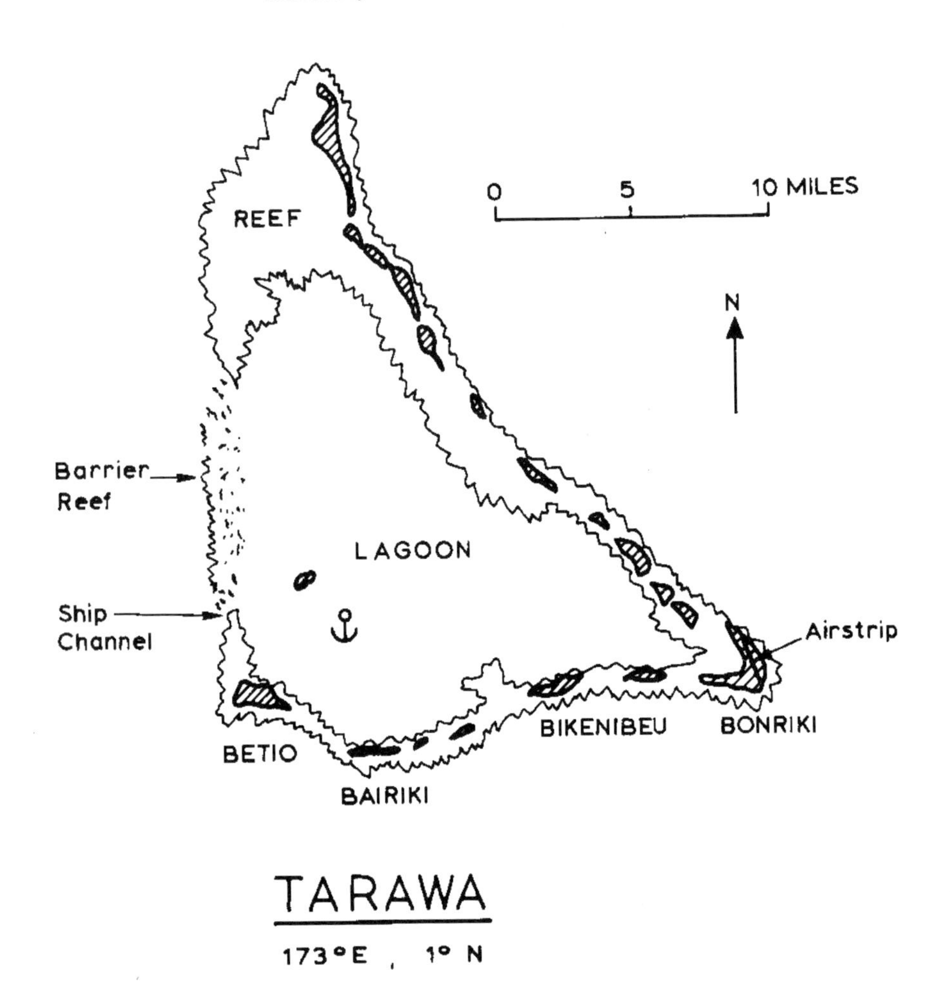

I had certainly not expected the show of pomp which awaited us. Bank Holiday weekend or not, all the members of the headquarters European staff of the colony, plus their wives, were at the landing stage to welcome the return of His Honour the Resident Commissioner and his wife to the capital. The men wore white shirts and shorts with white stockings and the ladies had pretty summer dresses, hats and white gloves, all with appropriate shoes.

As on Christmas Island for the Queen's Birthday celebrations, there was a flagpole with a bugler beside it, with local officials in attendance. Most of them were in khaki but their coloured belts brightened up the proceedings. Jack and I felt that our dress was highly inappropriate for such an occasion, though our slacks and vividly coloured "aloha" shirts from Honolulu were an improvement on what had been acceptable afloat. We hung back discreetly but were quickly called forward to be introduced.

There had been talk of a visitors' hostel on Bairiki, so I expected that

Jack and I would be put up there. Instead, the invitation for us to stay with the Bernacchis at the Residency for a few days came as a very happy surprise. It was not until later that we realised just how great was their kindness, particularly after being away from home so long themselves. Jack and I clambered into the Resident Commissioner's long wheelbase Land Rover behind the Bernacchis and their Gilbertese chauffeur, and we made the trip of a few hundred yards to the Residency. Bairiki was a very small island but the vehicle justified its representational status, silver painted and with a brass crown screwed on the bumper because, when the tide was low, it could reach most of Tarawa across the sandbars between the islets.

H.H. had warned us earlier of delay before continuing our reconnaissance, because we had arrived at a time when most of the colony vessels would be collecting island magistrates and headmen for a conference, so very little transport would be spare. However, he was sure that the Superintendent of Marine, Captain Douglas, would have revised plans ready for us; signals had put these in hand before our arrival.

No sooner had Jack and I been shown our splendid rooms in the Residency, than we were collected by Mr Roy Davies, the Secretary to the Government and Number Two to H.H. He took us home to join his charming Australian wife and their two small girls for a magnificent lunch, all very different to the "no families" year we had expected on Christmas Island.

Captain Gerry Douglas, the Marine Superintendent, collected us from lunch and took us to his office. He was a large, fresh faced, man aged about thirty-five, younger than I would have expected in view of the seniority of some of the ships' masters under his control. He carried his authority easily and was very keen that our reef channels proposals should succeed. He produced a revised itinerary for us, which meant we would be away another four weeks, but would have to change ships in the middle. He had also rearranged his own programme to allow him to accompany us all the way round.

We were to sail in the colony vessel, MV *Ninikoria,* after the holiday, on Tuesday, 2nd August, and Gerry added that he would be bringing Anna, his wife, with him. Mrs Bernacchi had mentioned Anna Douglas, charming and good looking, so the prospects were pleasing.

* * *

The islet of Bairiki was even smaller than we had realised and Gerry had no trouble in directing us back to the Residency for tea. Mr and Mrs Bernacchi had been given a fairly free hand to build the kind of home they wanted on Bairiki and the result was a very pleasing single storeyed building, much in the shape of a 'T' lying on the ground, except that its trunk sloped to the right. As we approached, the gravel drive was being raked by a large and happy Gilbertese man; seldom can there have been more orderly gravel, as he had been raking it at lunchtime also.

As we faced the front door of the Residency, the kitchen area was behind trees on the far right and, adjoining the kitchen, was a large dining room with, on the left, the guest wing which Jack and I were to occupy. The drawing room was about thirty feet square and faced south on to a veranda, beyond which was the wide reef flat and the Pacific Ocean. The guest wing led off one side of the drawing room and the Bernacchis' private wing off the other, with a huge curtain dividing the drawing and dining rooms, so that the two rooms could be thrown together. Outside the guest wing there was a tennis court, and the servants' quarters and laundry were in separate buildings behind the kitchens. The walls were of wood and the roofs of top quality pandanus thatch, all most effective and eye catching.

In the guest wing, Jack had a huge bedroom, and I the "bridal suite", with vast beds and its own writing room attached. The female touch was evident in the furnishings, all very different to our utilitarian accommodation on Christmas Island. All we needed to complete this perfect romantic setting was our wives, but need we must! Mrs Bernacchi apologised that there was only one bathroom in the guest wing but Jack and I just goggled in reply. With masses of running hot and cold water, our laundry removed and returned beautifully ironed by the staff, all was quite beyond our belief.

⋆ ⋆ ⋆

In the evening H.H. took Jack and me for a stroll round Bairiki. At high tide, the islet was shaped like a wedge just over half a mile long, with the Residency near the pointed end, but now, with the tide having dropped four feet, the sandbars and reef flat had surfaced, and the whole place looked much bigger. The colony's main jail lay only a few hundred yards from the Residency and H.H. proudly showed us round. The atmosphere was most friendly, with everyone glad to greet him: the wire fence was not so much to keep the inmates in, as to keep outsiders out. There was accommodation for twenty-one male and seven female prisoners.

As we were introduced to the smiling prisoners, I recognised Tanako, the large Gilbertese who had been cheerily raking the Residency gravel. H.H. explained that they were all in for long sentences, mainly for murder and manslaughter, but hastened to add, "We tend only to have pleasant murders, like knifings in a fit of temper, or something stupid when they get drunk, which they simply mustn't." The strictest law in the colony was that alcohol, for the locals, was forbidden.

If the fence around the jail was flimsy, that dividing the male and female parts of the establishment can only have been intended as a gesture towards propriety. We couldn't help noticing that one of the lady prisoners, of whom there were four, was pregnant. We gained the impression that such things happened occasionally, no one quite knew how.

Near the prison was the communal piggery tended, of course, by the prisoners. The Bernacchis owned two pigs, one of which had reached his allotted span. Tanako, their prisoner-gardener, had been asked to kill the pig but, for once, he had looked sad and abashed. He had asked if he might be excused the duty "as he was extremely squeamish, and could not stand the sight of blood." His request had been granted and a friend had done the deed.

Mrs Elaine Bernacchi, Jack Cheeseman, Mr Michael Bernacchi (H.H. The Resident Commisioner) at Tarawa.

We asked why such a kindly fellow as Tanako was in prison, and received the reply, "Yes, such a pity, but he killed his mother-in-law by stabbing her with his toddy knife, so has to stay here for a while."

Our sightseeing tour included the Girl Guides' hut and the Bairiki cafe, which was selling hot drinks and doughnuts; most of the local Gilbertese had money, because they worked in the government offices, which were also on our walk. As we approached the Residency again, we passed a delightful little Gilbertese cemetery, with the gravel-covered plots picked out with upturned beer bottles, presumably mourning gifts from those who were allowed to purchase beer.

Mrs Bernacchi told us that Tanako had knifed his mother-in-law because she had accused him of sleeping with the wife of his brother during the latter's absence on another island. Soon after Tanako had arrived in jail, one of the Bernacchis' house girls became pregnant; her husband had died a couple of years before, so it had taken tactful questioning to elicit that Tanako was the father-to-be. Far from causing embarrassment, he had proved his worth by spending much of his day looking after the baby, rather than raking the gravel to excess, thus allowing the house girl to get on with her work.

Those of us in the Residency had been invited to a party in Betio that evening. H.H. had declined but Mrs Bernacchi undertook to take Jack and me with her. Betio was the islet and port at the south west end of Tarawa and the hub of the colony's commercial life. At low tide Betio and Bairiki were connected by land but, with changing tides, it was easier to make the trip both ways in the Residency launch. The four mile journey down the lagoon took forty-five minutes, lovely at dusk, and even more beautiful returning by moonlight.

Our hosts at the buffet supper party were the manager of the Colony Wholesale Society, an Australian named Bruce Dean, and his wife, whose generous hospitality was typical of the great kindness we met throughout our stay. There were about ten couples already there, all of them British or Australian, with their lives much more comfortable than I expected in such a remote place.

Almost as soon as we arrived at the party, we were shown the latest Colony News Sheet, which had been published that very evening. Sadly, I have lost my own copy of it but I well remember that the headline read: *Reef blasting experts arrive.*

The gist of the article's opening sentence was, from Jack's and my point of view, as ominous as the headline:

"When H.H. the Resident Commissioner and Mrs Bernacchi arrived back at Tarawa today, after their tour of the colony in MV *Moana Raoi*, they were accompanied by Major Dan Raschen and Sergeant-Major Jack Cheeseman, who had joined the ship at Christmas Island. Both are Royal Engineers and are experts in all forms of work with explosives. They have come to advise the Government on the blasting of reef channels on many of the islands."

Jack and I expected to be bombarded with embarrassing questions but, mercifully, those questions never came. By expressing, frequently, our genuine appreciation of the beer and of the white wine, both Australian, we managed to keep off any deep conversations on blasting coral.

Our fellow guests included three masters of colony vessels and their wives, with Vic Ward among them. We were really enjoying the party when the electricity generator on Betio closed down at midnight but, before we left, another of the couples there, the Turpins, had invited us back for lunch with them.

The next day the Bernacchis stayed at home but arranged for their launch to take Jack and me down to Betio again for the Turpin's lunch party. Its helmsman was getting to know us and we only wished we could ask him about the lagoon and its coral heads, but he spoke very little English and we spoke no Gilbertese. In this we were not alone; Mrs Bernacchi had a useful working knowledge of the language but very few of the other expatriates, with many of them on short tours in the colony, spoke the language.

Dick and Peggy Turpin's guests included most of the people we had met the previous evening, plus nearly as many again. Jack and I basked in our novelty value, but it was as nothing compared to that of the nursing sister, newly arrived from England. Apart from some nuns, she was the only white spinster in the colony. I thought that Jack and I were the first members of the British Army to visit Tarawa in recent years, but apparently a Major

Harry McIntyre had been there only two years before. Harry had a great reputation in the Royal Engineers and everyone certainly remembered him most happily in Betio.

* * *

Those who lived on Betio were proud to tell us that the Battle of Tarawa, when the island had been retaken from the Japanese, had been fought mainly on their islet. After lunch, Dick Turpin spared himself from his own party to drive me round what he knew of the battlefield. Even though Tarawa had no proper port, it was the stategic centre in that part of the Pacific, and Betio was the place that most attracted military interest. It was a low lying strip of coral, two miles long and never wider than six hundred yards, with an area at high tide of around a hundred acres; at low tide, wide reef flats surfaced all around it.

Percy Roberts had told me something of his own experience when he had arrived in Tarawa directly after the American victory and I was able to check the details later. Japanese marines landed on Tarawa three days after the attack on Pearl Harbour on 7th December 1941, and had smashed the radio station and any boats they could find before departing. The Japanese Army had arrived to occupy the Gilbert Islands a few months later but, in the meanwhile, Major Holland, of the colony's Education Department, had made plans for most of the Europeans to escape in a small launch. Using a wireless that had been hidden from the Japanese, his party contacted Suva in Fiji and arranged for a rescue ship to rendezvous with them, which it did. Almost miraculously, they and some shipwrecked Americans, whom they had picked up on the way, reached Suva safely.

Japanese (ex Singapore) gun on Betio, Tarawa.

That had left five Europeans and seventeen New Zealand servicemen to be captured and interned by the Japanese. However, after the first U.S. air attack on the islands on 15th October 1942, all twenty-two prisoners had been paraded and murdered, which accounted for the lack of continuity in the government of the colony from before the war.

Earlier that year, on 15th February, Singapore had fallen and, soon after, the Japanese, realising the importance of Tarawa, decided to turn Betio into a fortress, no easy task on an island at most eight feet above sea level. However, good concrete emplacements were constructed and digging, so far as the high water table allowed, was put to good effect. Some of the British eight inch guns from Singapore were shipped to Betio and, somehow, re-emplaced. Ironically, as at Singapore, they were pointed in the wrong direction. In the middle of 1943, a Japanese Rear Admiral, Keijo Shibaski, whose career prospects I would *not* have envied, reported after his inspection, "Tarawa could not be taken by one million men in one hundred years."

The Americans occupied Funafuti in the Ellice Islands early in 1943 and Admiral Nimitz selected Tarawa for "the first long stride" of his drive back across the Pacific. In mid November that year the bombardment of Betio by the battleships and aircraft of a large United States fleet, under Admiral Spruance, began. It was expected that most of the Japanese defenders would be killed before the assault by the 2nd US Marine Division, which started on 21st November.

The American Task Force Commander was accompanied by the Australian skipper of a Burns Philp Company vessel who knew the colony, but his advice, to attack on a rising tide, with the tide half up, cannot have been understood. The timing of the assault went wrong; some blame was placed on the Americans' tide tables, originating from a reference point on the coast of Chile, but the six hour error was beyond excuse. The *half* tide advice had been noted but the proviso that it should have been *rising* had been missed.

The attack went in at dawn on a falling tide. The pathfinder vessel missed the entrance to Tarawa Lagoon through its barrier reef and many of the assault craft grounded much earlier than had been expected, to be left high and dry as the tide fell further. The heavily laden Marines then had to wade ashore in daylight under intense machine gun fire, only to find deep depressions in the lagoon reef in which some drowned.

However, with indomitable courage, by nightfall a toehold had been gained ashore.

The Japanese resistance had been utterly underestimated. Even the landing of six light tanks on the next suitable tide had not deterred the defenders, who had quickly knocked them out and later occupied them by night. Two of the tanks, with their machine guns still working, were manned as Japanese pillboxes out on the reef flat. I took a couple of snaps of one of those tanks, rusty and lying on its side, but still with a rubber track on the sprockets.

The battle of Tarawa ended on its sixth day of land fighting. The original Japanese garrison was said to have numbered 4,836, of whom 2,619 were combatants and the remainder mainly Korean labourers. A total of 17 Japanese and 129 Koreans were found alive at the end of the battle. The Americans had lost 1,019 dead and thousands more were wounded. Tarawa had been a costly way of learning hard lessons.

Soon after, the Americans turned almost the whole islet into an airfield, like a huge, unsinkable aircraft carrier. Not until they left in 1947 could the Gilbertese replant the place with coconut palms, so that, apart from the larger pieces of rusting ironware and a few piles of ammunition, Betio now again looked like any other small coral atoll. Its life bustled and the expatriate community seemed little affected by the haunting history of their homes.

During my tour of the Betio battlefield, Jack Cheeseman had remained at the Turpin's lunch party, which was still going strongly when we left at tea time. The launch had us back on Bairiki at six o'clock, "just in time for drinks" as the Bernacchis said. At a very congenial dinner for the four of us, Mrs Bernacchi asked Jack and me to call her Elaine and we all swapped, or checked, ages. She was rising 38, but when she had arrived in the colony as the Resident Commissioner's wife had still been only 29, when she found that her official title in Gilbertese meant "the old woman". I already knew that Mr Michael Bernacchi CMG, OBE (we continued to call him "Sir" or "Your Honour") was 49. His father had been a scientist and antarctic explorer, which perhaps accounted for Michael being a member of that exclusive London club, the Athenaeum.

* * *

August Bank Holiday Monday started badly for Jack, as he trod on his spectacles when getting out of the bath. He had no spare pair, but managed adequately to repair the cracked ones. His favourite pipe, which was almost his wand of office, was also not suiting him that morning, but we were still both delighted to lunch with Gerry and Anna Douglas, who was just as attractive as we had been led to expect. Our fellow guests already seemed like old friends and we were swamped with further invitations, most of which, sadly, we could not accept.

We excused ourselves early, as Elaine Bernacchi had promised to take us along the whole south side of Tarawa, while the tide was low. At the far end lay the Bonriki airstrip, from which we were due to be collected at the end of our reconnaissance and I wanted to confirm that it could still take a Hastings.

H.H.'s police corporal drove us in the Land Rover the fourteen miles from Bairiki to Bonriki, hopping from islet to islet over the sandbars that joined them. The airstrip was still there and we checked its length against the vehicle's mileometer. No trouble on that score but its width was questionable, as new rows of coconuts had been planted along the sides.

We stopped many times on our way back and there could have been no better guide than Elaine. On Bikenibeu we saw the King George V Boys' School (which included representatives of almost all the inhabited islands among its 120 boarders), the Elaine Bernacchi Girls' School and the colony hospital. The locals, including the schoolchildren, came flocking out to meet their old friend Elaine. George Pitkeathly, the Colony Chief Education Officer, was among them and we found time for beer. Visitors, whoever they were, were of great interest.

We were shown round the hospital by the delightful Irish matron, Margaret White who, despite our hurry, was determined to show and tell us everything about her "wonderful job". Few hospitals can have had happier patients and the problem was to tell who they were as, if one member of a family were admitted to hospital, the rest went too to look after non-medical needs.

We just beat the tide back to Bairiki and, while we were preparing for our start the next morning, discovered that our precious crowbar was missing. Perhaps it had been considered an inappropriate article to deliver to the Residency but H.H. made it his Bank Holiday task, not an easy one, to borrow another for us.

We missed our diver companions on many scores, but without doubt, administratively, two of us fitted more easily into colony life than four. That weekend of wonderful hospitality ended on Tuesday with an early breakfast, so that we could visit the Bairiki Trade Store. Elaine said we would need presents to give in return for some the islanders would probably give to us. I spent about half a day's pay, mainly on sticks of tobacco and large quantities of sweets. Later I was to wish I had spent more.

Chapter Seven

MARAKEI AND MAGISTRATES

The colony went to work again on Tuesday, 2nd August, and the MV *Ninikoria* came across Tarawa lagoon to lie off Bairiki. A launch picked up Gerry and Anna Douglas, Jack and me.

Ninikoria's master was Warrington Strong, who had recently been a lieutenant-commander in the Royal Navy and was attracted to *Ninikoria* when he saw her being built in Hong Kong. Her first master, Alex MacAdie, had moved on quite quickly and "Warry" left the Navy to take her over. Both he and his ship were, therefore, fairly new to the colony.

At 270 tons, *Ninikoria* was only just over half the deadweight of *Moana Raoi,* small by most standards but the right size for performing colony duties economically. Her sister ship had had a little trouble with her metacentric height, meaning the way she balanced on the water: unfortunately, she, and everyone aboard, had disappeared without trace. She was presumed capsized, so, on the insistence of MacAdie, *Ninikoria* was built a few feet longer than her ill-fated sister and everyone believed that all stability problems had been overcome. Very interesting, but I wished I had heard all this later!

Apart from Warry, who was aged about forty and very lively, the only other ex-patriate member of the crew was the elderly New Zealand chief engineer. Gerry and Anna occupied the cabin suite on the deck aft of the bridge which, presumably, was intended for the Resident Commissioner when he was on tour. Jack and I each had good little cabins facing forward over the well deck which was smothered with Gilbertese passengers. How the itineraries of the ships were publicised, how the passengers knew when and where to turn up and how a ship's crew knew who, or who not, to take with them, we never knew.

We left Tarawa lagoon through the gap in the barrier reef, then sailed northwards up the coast before turning towards our first destination, the island of Marakei. Another island, Abaiang, was in view on our port beam most of the way but, as had been the case when we approached Tarawa, all we could see was a long line of palm trees. We had already learnt that, from a distance, most coral atolls looked like that.

The most notable event in our half day's journey to Marakei was that we passed another vessel. She was the ketch *Morning Star,* a missionary ship from the Marshall Islands, and had been expected in Tarawa for many

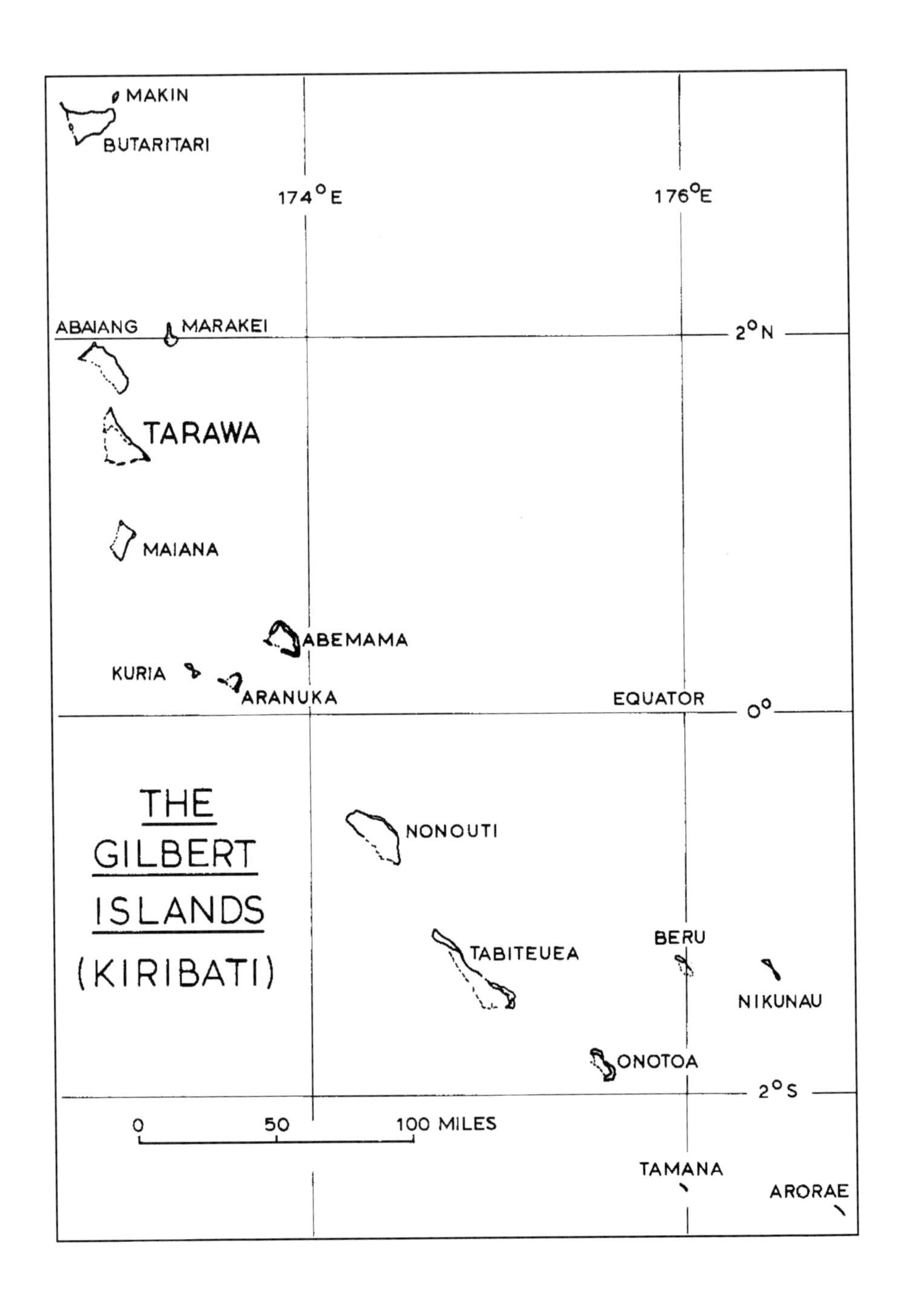
MAKIN
BUTARITARI
174° E
176°E
ABAIANG
MARAKEI
2° N
TARAWA
MAIANA
ABEMAMA
KURIA
ARANUKA
EQUATOR
0°
THE GILBERT ISLANDS (KIRIBATI)
NONOUTI
TABITEUEA
BERU
NIKUNAU
ONOTOA
2° S
0
50
100 MILES
TAMANA
ARORAE

days, where the one and only customs officer was eagerly awaiting the chance to board her. Unless he proposed to impound the missionary, we much wondered what he really hoped to achieve. *Morning Star's* engine had broken down, thus the delay, but she looked lovely under sail, just the kind of boat I imagined Denys Begbie meant when he briefed me in London about probably travelling in a schooner. I was exceedingly thankful that I was not; even my few hours in *Ninikoria* were turning my tummy, and a ketch would surely be worse.

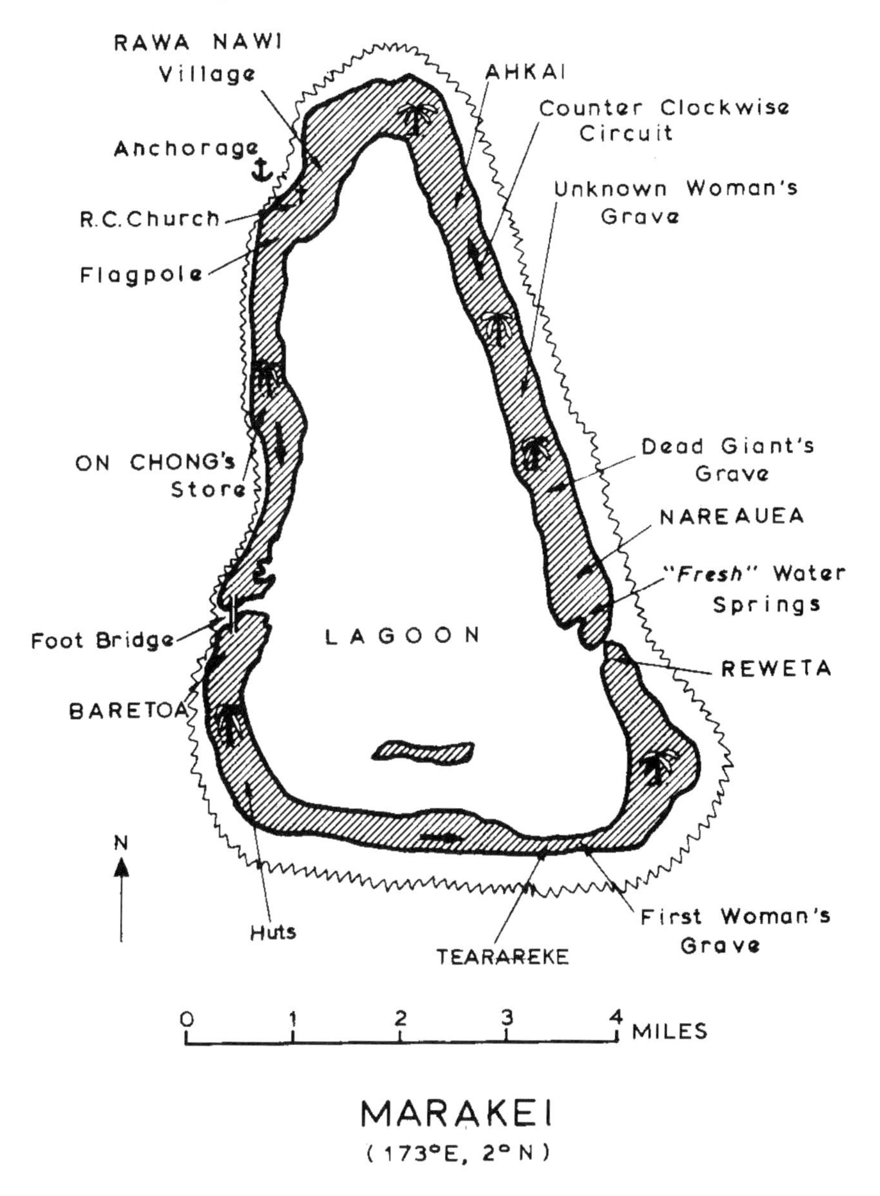

MARAKEI
(173°E, 2°N)

The war had missed Marakei and the island remained so much off the beaten track that its chart, as provided by the Admiralty Hydrographer in England, was based on "a sketch by Captain Wilkes of a United States expedition in 1841". "Surely it means nineteen forty one?" Eighteen was correct and, to keep visiting mariners on their toes, the Admiralty had added "Marakei Island is reported to lie five miles westward of the position quoted." However, to spoil their lordships' fun, we were approaching Marakei in daylight and *Ninikoria* had radar.

Gerry Douglas was uncertain what types of reef passages the inhabitants of Marakei wanted but, for a start, in his capacity as Superintendent of Marine, he decided to make his own map of the pear-shaped island, which he sketched with the help of the ship's radar scanning the shoreline. The result, much as shown on page 75, was considerably more accurate and less misleading than Captain Wilkes' earlier effort; copies of Gerry's map were issued to all colony vessels after our return to Tarawa.

We approached the white flagpole at the Government Station, near the stalk end of the pear. Rawa Nawi, the village in front of us was the largest of six, with the island's population of about two thousand high for its size. The copra shed had been built there and a passage from sea to shore had been requested. Warry anchored *Ninikoria* in ten fathoms of water about a couple of hundred yards from the shore. Captain Wilkes, of blessed memory, had, quite rightly, marked this anchorage as "precarious", meaning that there was no swinging room on the anchor cable if the wind changed, but the breeze from the north east allowed us to remain at anchor overnight.

* * *

There were two hours of daylight left, so there was time for us to start work. Jack, in his favourite blue shorts and blue shirt with his gym shoes, was carrying the crowbar, the compass and a notebook. I wore my green bathing trunks and tennis shoes and was responsible for the measuring rod and the coil of line knotted at ten yard intervals. Our manner of dress was practical, but must have looked truly awful.

The launch taking us ashore passed some formidable coral heads at the entrance to the proposed channel, great yellow and orange pillars coming to the surface from twenty feet below, but we grounded safely on the sandy shore. Almost directly in front of us lay a wooden building with glass windows, and to the side of it was a much larger church, also of wood and with masses of glass windows. Sure enough, the locals wanted the new reef channel to join the shore just where we landed, nearly opposite the Roman Catholic priest's house, and only fifty yards from the church. Our previous worries of, at worst, breaking some bottles of medicine with our proposed blasting, did not compare with the prospect of breaking church windows or, possibly more heinous, those of the priest's own house.

As we waded ashore we realised that the shoreline was not like the solid fringing reefs on Hull and Gardner. Here at Rawa Nawi, a shelving sand beach, liberally dotted with rocks of coral rubble, sloped up to a very narrow reef flat, which then merged with a six foot high bank of silver sand. At the top of the bank were the palm trees and the village and, behind them and out of sight, lay the almost wholly enclosed lagoon.

The hordes of children studying our every movement were our immediate problem but, as soon as we walked up that sand beach, we foresaw problems with the channel too. You don't blast sand under water: you dredge it, and you keep dredging it, and if you haven't got a dredger, and Marakei had not, you're stuck! The tide range in the Northern Gilberts was seven feet, greater than elsewhere in the colony, so there was no doubt that any channel dug in sand would quickly silt up. There would be time later to consider how the engineering might be done, but our first need was to make a sketch map of the channel site.

In the absence of any good maps for reference, we needed to pinpoint the proposed channel, so that anyone following us could find the exact spot. This was easier said than done as permanent land marks on the shore line were hard to find. My report for Rawa Nawi read:–

"A line of nine coconut trees along the shore runs north to south. The required channel, at compass bearing 283 degrees, ends opposite the fourth tree from the south end, which has a red painted mark ten feet above the ground."

I just hoped that those trees stayed there! Next, we needed to plot the depth of the sloping shore at known distances from the reef flat and, now that it was apparent that the mad visitors were going to perform for them, the jabbering and giggling of the children increased dramatically. The village policeman had sensibly stayed at home, so we were, as at Hull, left unprotected.

I tied the end of my knotted measuring line to a small coral rock on the shore and Jack recorded that, at distance zero yards (from the rock), the water depth was zero feet. Simple stuff for simple folk! The tide was low and I started to back out to sea, pulling the line taut behind me and stopping every ten yards when I reached a knot.

My antics were altogether too much for the children, some of whom splashed around me in the water, but many more stood on the shore, howling with laughter. Jack and I could, of course, not understand a word they said, but did not need an interpreter to comprehend "now we have seen everything!". Severely tested, but undeterred, I continued to sing out the distances and depths: 10 yards, 1 foot; 20 yards, 1 foot 6 inches; 30 yards, 1 foot 9 inches, and so on. Unfortunately some of the children were learning to count in English, mimicking me and making it no easier for Jack to record the correct figures.

As the water became deeper, all the children left me and, now that I was alone, I realised that I had not yet enquired about sharks, but I could not be seen to falter in my duties now. When forty yards out, I was standing in three feet of water, well up on my bathing trunks, but 80° Fahrenheit is a pleasant temperature and I was enjoying my backwards wading on a beautiful evening. I had to continue to the full depth of a loaded surf boat, three feet six inches, but the bottom, of coral sand, remained surprisingly level for the next twenty yards.

In the hope of seeing when the water would deepen, I clambered on to a convenient clump of coral, but made the mistake of expecting it to take my weight. Dead coral can be as hard as rock, but live coral justifies names like "branch", or "stag horn", and can be soft. One of my feet give way under me, down went my shoe, and up scrunched some branch coral, grazing my shin as it did so. After a few seconds it hardly hurt and, more important, it didn't bleed. I had no wish to test the validity of the "sharks love blood" theory.

I continued backing out to sea, more slowly as the water deepened slightly but my distance from the shore continued to measure seventy yards. "It can't be," shouted Jack. I pulled to tighten the line and found that it was completely loose, just like losing a good fish. There was nothing for it, but to wade ashore again, only to find that the knot which tied the line to the rock had become undone. I had always rather prided myself on my knots and lashings, so was not used to them just coming undone. I thought I detected a child among the spectators with a satisfied smirk, but there was no point in venting my wrath. I tied a doubly sure knot, and backed out to sea again.

Jack had, I thought, found my exertions in the water unnecessarily funny, so I took him with me when we went to call on the RC priest, knowing that our visit was unlikely to go well. He was a Belgian and was reputed to be capable of withdrawing his support on matters of British Government

Gilbertese children.

policy. The priest was not too pleased to see us, so I was at my most tactful, explaining to him that his parishioners had requested a channel to the shore close to his house and church, but that the explosions would probably break the windows of both. I ended, rather lamely, with, "We wonder if that would matter?"

The holy father mustered a remarkable command of the English language with great rapidity and force. We were left in no doubt that to break even a few panes of glass would certainly matter, in fact, even one pane would be out of the question. However, after he paused to draw breath, we were sure we heard him say, "Unless . . . "

"Unless what?" was our swift and hopeful reply. The words "good compensation" came through quite clearly to Jack and me.

Perhaps it was our lack of clothing, or perhaps we had disturbed his supper, but our meeting with the pastor had gone even worse than I had feared. He was still glowering as we departed, with me promising to keep damage to a minimum. Between ourselves, Jack and I shared his dislike for that channel and hoped that he might dissuade his flock from demanding one at that spot. It would be such a pity if, after the windows had been broken, the channel silted up again.

* * *

It was dark when we boarded *Ninikoria* again, and we were glad to dry off before our evening meal. Gerry had arranged an early start for us in the morning, as the ship's schedule demanded we sailed in the afternoon. He fully appreciated our reservations about the Rawa Nawi channel and said he would help us look for alternatives but, even more important, whatever we did, we must comply with a local requirement: all new arrivals had to traverse the whole coastline of Marakei in an anti-clockwise direction.

Legend had it that the original inhabitants of the island had been two giants. On landing, they had set off to walk around the island in opposite directions, but the giant who walked clockwise died and the giant who went anti-clockwise lived. Ever since, everyone new to the island had to go the whole way round, anti-clockwise and without retracing their steps, or they too would die.

This was, of course, complete nonsense, except that, and it might be worth noting, the current Resident Commissioner, Mr Bernacchi himself, had not had time to go round the island when he first visited in 1956. He had, unaccountably and immediately, become severely ill and had to be evacuated first to Tarawa and then to New Zealand for treatment. Who knew what would have happened in the same circumstances in olden times? Just to be sure, Gerry had arranged that bicycles should be borrowed for us all. "It is only about five miles," he had assured us. Had I glanced at the map he had just made, I would have known the distance must be fifteen miles but I would not have slept so soundly. Anna Douglas must have realised the truth, as she had decided not to go ashore at Marakei.

Next morning I put on some lightweight socks, in the hope of protecting my shins from further coral scratches. Although I was no great swimmer, Jack preferred that I worked in the water, while he kept the records in our notebook dry; however, we all got wet going ashore at 6.30 the next morning. Gerry brought Willie, the ship's bosun, as interpreter, and we were met by the village carpenter, who was to be our guide. The bicycles were of better quality than expected but none of them was fitted with brakes, a feature which Jack was the first to notice. Gerry explained that, because coral atolls were flat, brakes were considered an unnecessary luxury and it was worth saving their cost.

We lashed the tools of our trade to the bicycles and set off in the prescribed anti-clockwise direction. Those pestilential children were still at home, the track near the shore proved to be more of a road than a footpath and, in the still of the early morning, Marakei was a very lovely place. Its rainfall was higher than Tarawa's and the ground was highly fertile, so everything was growing splendidly. All the flat ground had been covered with coconut and pandanus palms and there were many pits full of prolific babai plants. Babai roots looked like logs of wood but, if boiled carefully as a vegetable, were considered a delicacy. They then tasted like logs of wood.

The just-past-dawn chorus of birds was more noisy than beautiful. There were masses of white, dove-like terns, similar to those on Christmas Island, but the small grey herons and a form of crow that sounded as if it had been crossed with a cuckoo were new to me.

As well as satisfying the needs of the old legend, we had to remember our quest for an alternative channel site. After we had cycled only a couple of miles down the west coast, I saw on my right a gently shelving shore leading into calm, sunlit, water, with no sign of a reef edge; all that was there was an old hut which, our guide told us, had once been On Chong's Store. Gerry agreed that the place had possibilities.

Conditions for bathing were perfect and I, already wearing my swimming trunks, was into the water before the others had parted from their bicycles. The sea was as clear as in the Phoenix Islands and my gas mask specs under a face mask proved surprisingly effective. I floated gently seawards, looking down on large lumps of coral lying on the firm bottom below. A channel could easily be cleared with a little explosive and, with no houses for miles, there was nothing to damage. An additional advantage of the site was that the water deepened to four feet at less than forty yards from the shore, so that only a short channel would be needed.

Gerry soon caught my enthusiasm for the place and was already talking of moving the copra store there from Rawa Nawi. That such an apparently perfect place had not been used previously, except perhaps by On Chong, seemed unbelievable and we guessed that the lack of an anchorage nearby must be the snag.

Ninikoria had two launches and the smaller one was fitted with an echo sounder; Gerry volunteered to fetch it and be back within the hour. As he fully intended to complete the circuit of the island that same day, he hoped that he could temporarily retrace his steps with impunity. Meanwhile, Jack and I stayed to make a site plan. The centre line of our proposed channel would lie along a series of interconnecting pools, each about six feet deep.

They lay between small crags of growing and overhanging coral, around which innumerable little striped fishes popped in and out with no regard for the one large green parrot fish, who dawdled among them. I was still peering down into the water when the launch with its helmsman, bringing Gerry and his bicycle, chugged in from the sea.

The echo sounder, although small, proved to be highly effective; we enjoyed guessing the depth of the water and checking the true figure off the sounder. We could see the bottom at a depth of fully eighty feet and wondered if that was the world clear water record. The echo sounder unfortunately confirmed our fears about the lack of an anchorage; even if there were no precise reef edge, the side of the island went down to the depths of the Pacific Ocean very steeply indeed, which was perhaps why the store had not proved successful. Nevertheless, On Chong (in fact not an individual, but a company of traders) had chosen an excellent lee shore for the seaside shack.

Penny toll bridge on Marakei.

We were much heartened when Gerry deemed it would be a better proposition to work copra boats from a ship coasting off On Chong's Store, than from one anchored, but with its boats limited by the tides, at Rawa Nawi. With time short, we remounted our bikes and the helmsman took his launch back to *Ninikoria.* Our guide, the carpenter, whom we named Thomas Cook, warmed to his task, and Willie interpreted his utterances in good faith, though even he, another good Gilbertese, became a little incredulous as the stories unfolded.

My backside, clad only in a pair of wet swimming trunks, was finding the almost non-existent saddle of my bicycle most disagreeable but, mercifully, we were soon forced to dismount. A very rickety footbridge crossed a shallow creek that connected the sea with the lagoon. T. Cook, as he had become, had forgotten that there was a one penny toll on it; none of us was carrying money, so the chances of our completing the round tour of Marakei looked ever slimmer; luckily, however, the toll keeper was absent.

Further on and nearer the south-east corner of the island, the locals had requested an additional reef channel at a place called Teararekè; Gerry had not been able to understand why a channel was needed there, as copra was not stored nearby. We found that the distance between the lagoon and the sea was short at high tide but long at low tide, due to the wide expanse of dry reef flat. If the fishermen took their canoes out from the lagoon, where they kept them, to the sea at high tide, they found themselves confronted by a wide stretch of land when they returned at low tide, and canoes were heavy to carry.

I sympathised with their request but Gerry said the money was for copra boat channels and not for luxuries. Soon, though, he relented slightly and allocated low priority to the task; so our kit had to be unlashed from our bicycles and Jack and I went on to the reef to make our plans. It didn't take us long to confirm that the reef was excessively wide, so we regretted that the fishermen would have to keep humping their canoes.

T. Cook wished to press on, as he was itching to show us the grave of the

Coconut break on Marakei with Gerry Douglas, Willie, Jack Cheeseman, the gravekeeper and "T. Cook".

First Woman of Marakei, which was a little further on. This was the first we had heard of the lady, who presumably had been imported to the island by the surviving giant. One of T. Cook's friends tended the grave and must have known that we were coming, as he had put on an official looking waist belt and an air of importance.

Elaine Bernacchi had told us that, although visitors to Marakei were so rare, some elementary tricks had already been learnt, and there would be no harm in leaving a small present if we were shown anything supposedly special. From our small stores bag Jack produced twenty-five cigarettes and a couple of packets of sweets and laid them, with appropriate deference, upon the not-very-impressive tomb. The quality of our gifts must have been above the norm, as the grave tender asked our names and muttered them in a pious manner, as if wishing us well.

T. Cook, honest fellow that he was, admitted that the gifts would not be used by the late and long departed lady but by his friend, the grave tender. He was a little surprised when we said, through Willie, "Yes, we did expect that!" In gratitude for our generous and correct behaviour, T. Cook nipped up a convenient palm tree and threw down a good coconut for each of us. They were opened for us with a slash of his knife and, while we were drinking the "milk", the three Gilbertese started to discuss the uses to which coconuts and coconut palms, could be put. Some were:

Food

1. The meat is good food, and the milk is full of vitamins.
2. If the meat is grated and squeezed through a cloth, a form of coconut cream results, good on puddings.
3. The processed cream makes coconut oil and that makes margarine or soap. Alternatively, the meat can be dried to form copra, from which all manner of good things, including ice cream, can be produced.
4. If the new coconut leaf shoots are bound and cut, the sap can be collected, in a coconut shell, to produce toddy. This can be drunk raw or, (broad smiles) illegally, fermented. Either way, it is full of health giving properties.
5. The toddy can be boiled to give a sweet caramelly sauce, again good for puddings and loved by children.
6. The green husk of a raw coconut makes good chewing, and cleans your teeth at the same time.

Clothes

Grass skirts are not made of grass but from boiled coconut leaves. Admittedly, party skirts come from the boiled leaves of the pandanus palm, but palm leaves are good enough for every day use.

String

The fibres of coconut husks make string. The women plait it by rolling the fibres up and down their thighs, an excellent, if painful, way of removing the hair.

Timber
Coconut wood is used for the larger parts of buildings but pandanus is better for the smaller.

Thatch
Again, pandanus leaves are better but coconut leaves make useful thatch.

Fuel
What better fuel could one want than dried coconut husks? To light the fire, rub the dried fronds of two coconut leaves together.

Matting
Coconut husks make coir matting, too.

⋆ ⋆ ⋆

Gerry kept pressing Willie to make a move, but, egged on by his companions, Willie asked us if we knew that there were fourteen distinct stages in the formation of a mature coconut, with a separate Gilbertese name for each of them? We admitted we did not, but no doubt whatever was left in our minds that, in the islands, coconuts were important.

As we cycled up the east, and more windy, side of Marakei, T. Cook added more and more impromptu halts to our tour. In spite of Gerry's exhortations to keep going because the ship must sail on time, he showed us:

(i) a "fresh" water spring a few inches from the edge of the salt water lagoon. It tasted of sulphur, absolutely foul;

(ii) another spring, with slightly fresher water, where we had to bend down before cupping our hands to drink. The local villagers crowded round us in support of their friend, but then laughed in an embarrassing manner at our inelegant drinking postures;

(iii) the tomb of the giant who died going the wrong way round the island. It was untended, but had potential as a tourist attraction; and

(iv) the tomb of a woman completely unknown to us. It had an attendant but, due to the lack of warning, we had no presents left. Gerry, luckily, still had a stick of tobacco.

It had taken us over four hours to complete our anti-clockwise circuit of the island. T. Cook really had shown outstanding aptitude as a guide which, considering the lack of visitors to Marakei, was amazing. We thanked him as best we could and sent some tobacco from the ship for him.

I was tired and sore, but the island magistrate was not due aboard *Ninikoria* for a couple of hours, so Gerry took me in the launch down the west coast, looking again for anchorages. The echo sounder brought home to us just how steeply the side of the atoll shelved down into the depths. Less than a hundred yards from the shore the reading soared clean off its scale so, sadly, we found no new anchorages.

We were sorry to leave Marakei but did so feeling encouraged. The channel at On Chong's Store was worth pursuing and the coral heads at Rawa Nawi could be removed without breaking the Belgian priest's windows and would make an interesting job for divers.

Against the "Hazards" question on my reconnaissance report I wrote:–

"Apparently none. Plenty of jellyfish, but the locals eat them raw. Many of the other fish are said to be poisonous, so ask! Flies are bad, as are the hordes of inquisitive children: if work were to proceed, the village constable, with big stick, would be needed."

* * *

Our next call was Abemama, Robert Louis Stevenson's island, which lay about 150 miles south east of Marakei. For reasons not explained, we were due to pick up the magistrate there at four o'clock the next morning. Mercifully, my seasickness pills were working, so I could write my Marakei report in *Ninikoria's* saloon as she rolled and pitched along, but poor Anna Douglas succumbed to the sea and remained in her cabin, no longer envious of her husband's cruises around the colony. To decypher our notes and record them in a way that someone in England might understand, was testing me: one thing was certain, I had no wish to leave my family for another year, so would not be volunteering to return and see the project through.

We were trolling lines over the stern in the hopes of augmenting the larder and caught a couple of barracuda about the size of salmon grilse. They had fearsome, pike-like, heads, so their capture inevitably reopened the tales of their ferocity, but they made excellent eating. Evidently if you said "shoo" to a shark, it would swim away, but if you tried that on a barracuda, it would attack with redoubled fury. On that theme, one of my ancestors entered his small shipyard one evening thinking the guard dogs were locked up, but was attacked by them. With no means of escape, he went down on all fours and put his throat at the level of their snarling teeth; ancestor and dogs were still eyeing each other when he was rescued later. I had no wish to put any of these useful tips into practice!

Before supper that evening I was near the troll lines when obviously a good fish was hooked. I blew the whistle provided to alert the engine room and we dropped to four knots, about half speed. The chief engineer then arrived to pull in the fish, which fought in a manner I never imagined possible. After about a quarter of an hour it first surfaced, and showed itself to be a truly lovely tuna about five feet long. Eventually it was aboard and weighed 105 pounds, less than I had expected, considering the way it had shown its individuality when being dragged by a 250 ton ship for nearly half an hour. For its length it had great girth but, with its two pairs of long, crescent shaped fins and similar tail, the overall effect was of tremendous power and perfect streamlining.

* * *

Prior to coming to Christmas Island, Jack had been instructing young officers in the use of explosives, so probably had as much recent experience in the art as anyone in the Royal Engineers, but when we had first met Gerry, we had told him of our lack of practical experience in coral blasting. He had promised to beg some explosives for us from Ocean Island, where phosphate was continually being blasted. Now, we were delighted when *Ninikoria's* wireless operator reported that fifty pounds of high explosive should arrive at Tarawa in time for our later trips.

Due to "unpredictable currents" we were four hours late reaching Abemama. How we could have collected the magistrate in the dark was not clear, but he was certainly not in sight when *Ninikoria* cautiously entered the lagoon in daylight. Atolls either enclose a lagoon, in which case they are known as "lagoon atolls", or have no major lagoon, and are "reef atolls". Abemama, we were assured, was a good example of the former: its lagoon was, at its widest, about ten miles across, and surrounded by either a thin strip of land covered in palm trees, or, when the coral was submerged by high tides, by the barrier reef.

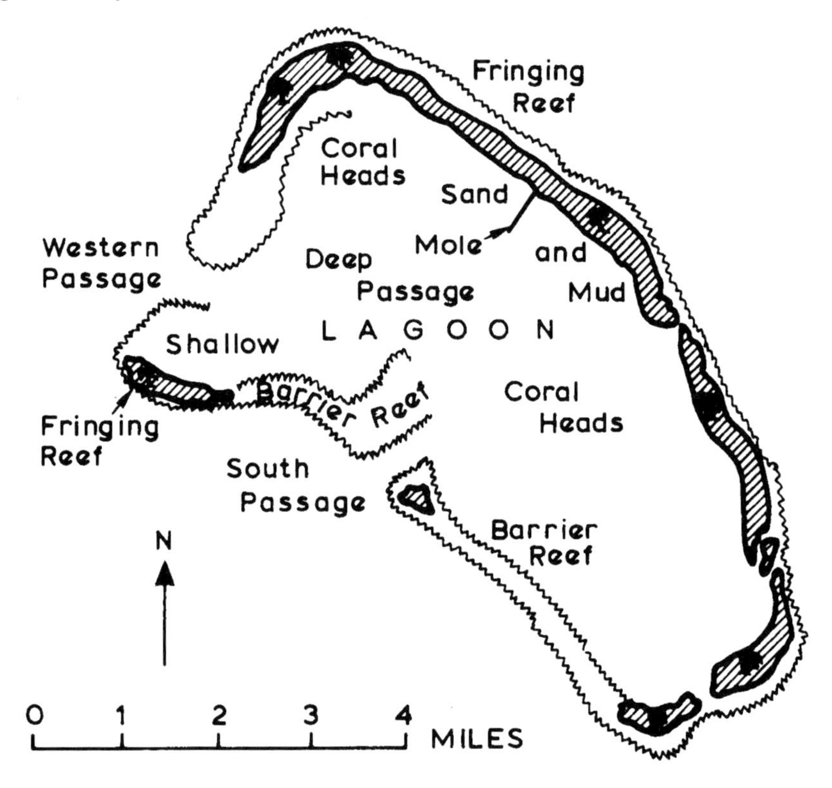

ABEMAMA

(174° E, 1° N)

Stevenson lived on Abemama in the late 1880s, soon after he had written *Treasure Island.* He had gone there to study the life style of the then King of Abemama, whose methods were those of "the bad old days" before the coming of the British Flag in the 1890s. Stevenson's interest in Abemama soon waned and he left, already a sick man, in 1889, to die in Samoa five years later.

The Japanese occupied Abemama early in 1942, but when they heard that the Americans had retaken Tarawa in November 1943, every one of the thirty-five men in the Japanese garrison committed suicide. The Americans tried to turn Abemama into a base for their advance across the Pacific and had built a mole, or loading quay, from the shore towards the deep water of the lagoon. Gerry wanted to know how this mole, which had silted up with mud and sand, could be brought back into use.

Although we had a good look at that mole and its mud, we knew that to bring it back to its former glory needed more than a few men for a few days with a few tons of explosives. Gerry was disappointed, but that was what he had expected to hear. After my positive report on Marakei, I had to write a thoroughly negative sequel on Abemama.

The magistrate was eventually located and collected, and we left in the afternoon, by when I had asked many questions about the local sharks and other aquatic hazards. Grimble had written about Abemama, so I hoped to compare his often frightening experiences with the answers now volunteered by various local dignitaries. As we had found elsewhere, the islanders were surprised that I had even asked, and answered that there was nothing about which to worry. In England, I had never doubted what I had read in Sir Arthur Grimble's books, but now I was very relieved to find that things seemed to have changed since his day, not only ashore, but on the reefs as well. That said, Jack and I were surprised how little the locals swam outside the reef edge; we also realised that Grimble knew those islands in a way that we, and most others, never would.

Chapter Eight

KILLER CLAMS AND BARRELLED OYSTERS

The last island to which *Ninikoria* would take us before our return to Tarawa was Maiana and we were roused early the next morning to find ourselves anchored off its north-west corner. Gerry Douglas had asked us to pay particular attention to Maiana, because it was an island capable of producing plenty of copra but, as Superintendent of Marine, he was having difficulty in shipping it out.

We were told two other items of local importance, firstly that we should beware of the outsize killer clams to be found on the Maina reef and, secondly, to expect the local ladies to be wearing only grass skirts. We had seen examples of the Maiana clamshells, long since dried out and bleached by the sun, in the Residency garden on Tarawa; each half was thirty inches across the jaws and weighed as much as I could lift. No one explained why Maiana in particular should be blessed with such monster shellfish but I knew that I would be paddling among them.

Until now we had not met anyone actually wearing a grass skirt, though at the far end of Marakei a few of the women had been topless, but their skirts were of cloth. Cloth was the one type of import the islanders considered essential, sufficiently essential to encourage the production of copra to be sold to the Wholesale Society.

We were visiting Maiana on a spring tide, with a rise and fall of six feet, and there were the magistrate and many loads of copra to collect. It was dark and unpleasantly chilly as we left *Ninikoria* in her larger launch, which was towing both her copra boats. We were sure to be drenched with spray, so our bathing trunks and tennis shoes were sensible garb, but did not allow for the cold: I also had on my stockings, hopefully as a protection against coral scratches.

Wet handkerchiefs were no more good for cleaning our spectacles on the equator than on a soggy Scottish grouse moor; our notebook was reverting to pulp and my shivering hand would not write, a pity, as Gerry kept making observations that deserved note. If, as we crossed the barrier reef into the lagoon, I had been asked whether I was enjoying my trip around the islands, my answer would have been a definite and miserable "No!"

Neither Gerry, nor any member of *Ninikoria's* crew, had ever visited the government station on Maiana. It lay six miles, a full hour, across the lagoon and we had difficulty in seeing its white flagpole. "If only we can find a way for colony vessels into the deep lagoon," Gerry had said, "we will have solved the problems at Maiana," but now he had to admit excessive optimism; in front of the government station at the lagoon edge lay a full quarter mile of mud and coral rubble. We had bumped the barrier reef as we crossed it on the rising tide, but the tide still had not risen sufficiently for us to avoid the long squelching plod from launch to flagpole. My stockings were a mixed blessing, as they never allowed my grazed shins to dry out and heal and were now clogged up with mud.

Although we would be spending the whole day and the next night at Maiana, Gerry made sure that we picked up the magistrate on this first trip. After making arrangements to load pandanus thatch, for which the island was renowned, we returned to *Ninikoria,* before setting off to look for a more suitable entrance to the lagoon.

Maiana, like Marakei, still only had one of Captain Wilkes' 1841 sketch maps in use as its chart. Poor fellow, he deserved marks for trying but his sketches can never have been very accurate and in 1960 were proving more of a hazard than a help. It was easy to understand why the colony had been pressing the Admiralty to spare a Royal Navy survey ship for a prolonged visit. HMS *Cook* had been past only a year before and reported how much charting needed to be done, but no one knew when the surveys would be undertaken. In the meanwhile, Gerry Douglas was trying to prevent the colony vessels under his control being misled by faulty charts.

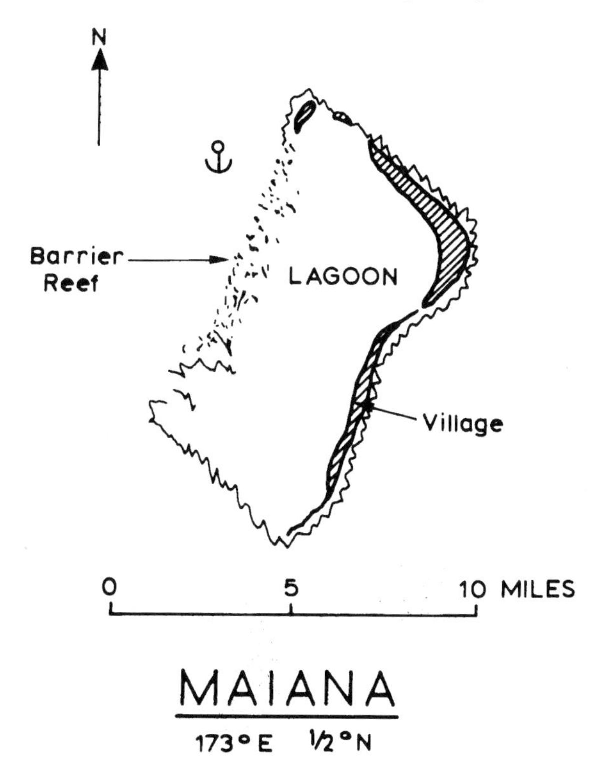

Maiana was a lagoon atoll, much like a rectangle in outline ten miles by five and *Ninikoria* took us well clear of, and along, the west facing sides. The barrier reef between the ocean and the lagoon was known to be dangerous as some parts of it never surfaced, even at low tide. We now turned and, very gently, approached that reef. It was high tide, so it was completely submerged and nothing showed up on the radar screen. Captain Warrington Strong had the old chart, but a look out on the bows proved to be more reliable and luckily he saw the reef edge, coming up from nowhere, long before the chart suggested land. Warry ordered full astern and all was well; he had no inclination to take his ship near to the reef again, and left Gerry to take Jack and me in the echo sounding launch to look for the natural channel which he so much hoped existed.

We started by traversing the barrier reef, which was about a mile wide and covered by a few feet of water, from ocean to lagoon, and then back the other way. When we paused, which was quite frequently, Jack and I flopped out of the launch, to stagger around on the uneven and submerged coral, while attempting some purposeful prods with the crowbar. I found that reef highly unattractive, up to my waist in water with my specs permanently opaque with spray, and I could only place my feet where they decided to settle. With all the crevices between the jagged coral, I imagined it was a veritable Utopia for killer clams and octopuses, let alone stonefish. My morale dropped even further when a shoal of sand sharks ("I promise, quite harmless," Jack repeated) darted past. Meanwhile, I was collecting new abrasions through my stockings, which were aggravated by my repeated clambering back into the boat.

If the depth of water were still so shallow as to allow us to wade, we knew that we could not have found Gerry's supposed channel, but he was still so keen to find a better place to enter the lagoon that we took more and more trouble to estimate levels and distances. From the first, it was obvious that to blast a channel of sufficient depth right across the wide reef would be a huge task, but it wasn't until I estimated the explosive requirements at over 1,500 tons that Gerry accepted the difficulties.

The tide was dropping, so, to my great relief, we returned to *Ninikoria.* Then, when Gerry was thanking us for our efforts, he added, "I think we may still have a couple of hours here on the high tide tomorrow morning, so I wonder if you would mind looking at one more place where there just could be a channel?"

Seldom have I been more sorely tested: I had grown to loath that Maiana barrier reef and Jack also had not enjoyed our perilous wading upon it. However, on the principle of "The path of duty is the way to glory," I answered, "Yes, by all means, Gerry."

At 4 p.m., with three hours of daylight left, Gerry took me off in the launch again to look for a new passage further up the reef. Anna had recovered from her sea sickness and had been finding the day on *Ninikoria* rather dull, so she came with us, saying, "I want to buy a pig." Again, we found neither the slightest indication of a reef passage, nor, after we managed to land on a small inhabited islet, of a pig for sale. There was, however, a cheerful girl aged about twelve. She was bare topped, developing fast, and wearing a real "grass" skirt. Although we were probably her first white people, she was in no way shy, and delighted to have her photograph taken.

Anna was a great help, particularly as she spoke Gilbertese, and soon the girl in the grass skirt was joined by two others, and then by masses of boys, all of whom wanted their photos taken. I had soon finished my scarce film but saw no harm in continuing to click my ancient Agfa box camera.

When the children eventually dispersed, an elderly and apparently European woman came up to us. She spoke no English, but Anna talked in Gilbertese with her. The old lady explained that she was the daughter of the English trader Benjamin Corrie, a character who, as I knew from Grimble, had an important place in the history of Maiana. As if to verify her credentials, she took us to her father's grave, but then, after polite farewells, shuffled off to her Gilbertese village. We felt rather sorry for her but there was nothing to suggest that she was in any way sorry for herself.

As long as the tide would permit, pandanus thatch was brought to *Ninikoria* from a loading station just inside the barrier reef. The thatch seemed a bulky and uneconomic load, but space could be found on the ship, and roofing was required in Tarawa, where we should be back within twenty-four hours. It had been a long day, but my sleep was disturbed as loading of the thatch started again in the moonlight. Next morning we

A "grass" skirt on Maiana.

Palm thatch and lagoon mud on Maiana.

heard that things had gone particularly well, with the previous record number of loads being equalled.

Then, of course, a record breaking trip had to be attempted, but the larger launch, with two surf boats in tow, grounded on the barrier reef as the tide fell. As dawn broke, Jack and I could just see the launch well aground, with its surf boats, which drew less water, still afloat beside it.

Warry ordered the smaller launch to go and help but, having behaved perfectly the previous day, its engine would now not start. The surf boats then started to ground, so their steersmen decided to use their initiative while there was still scope for action. Both boats, which had no means of propulsion, were cast off from the large launch, and started to drift with the falling tide towards *Ninikoria*. With great skill, one of the boats was steered directly to our ship, but the other steersman slightly misjudged the current and just missed. He and his boat drifted past, tantalisingly close, but none of the lashings that were frenziedly thrown from ship to boat and boat to ship quite made the distance. It was our great loss to be unable to understand the wealth of advice and entreaties that passed either way.

By 7.30 a.m., *Ninikoria* was faced by three problems. Her larger launch was heeling over ever further on the reef, her smaller launch was in the water, but would not start, and one of her two copra boats was drifting out into the Pacific Ocean. Jack and I, with no responsibilities, found all this hilarious, but had to be careful not to show our true feelings; but, when it became evident that we would have to wait another six hours before the tide could put matters right, we, too, became concerned. Our return to

Tarawa might be delayed by nearly a day, as ships did not normally venture into its lagoon by night.

At last the old Kiwi chief engineer managed to coax the small launch into starting. It was a diesel and its reluctance was overcome with the aid of a little cigarette lighter fluid, evidently an unorthodox, and possibly dangerous, solution. The drifting copra boat was then collected, greatly to its steersman's relief.

With both copra boats aboard, and with several hours to wait before the large launch would float clear, *Ninikoria* took us down the coast again, to lie off that part of the reef through which Gerry still hoped we might find a channel. We learned later that the occupants of the large launch were considerably dismayed when they saw their mother ship weighing anchor and disappearing out of sight.

Our renewed efforts to find Gerry's supposed channel proved even more dispiriting than the day before and our wading on the crumbling coral was more difficult because the tide was running. With the nearest land five miles across the deep lagoon, and *Ninikoria* well out to sea and unable to come closer to us, it was just as well that the launch kept going. More by luck than good judgement, neither Jack nor I stepped on any unfriendly creatures: dull perhaps, but we preferred it that way.

I had been up early that morning, consolidating all the Maiana measurements we had taken, which looked like leading us nowhere. Explosives would not solve the island's problems, and I asked Gerry whether the colony could obtain a small, low draught, landing craft, of which some from the war might still be available. He answered, "Yes, we probably could, but it would need to be maintained, and we are running as many vessels as we can afford already." Hovercraft, with their ability to go over sea, mud and land, would have been ideal, but they were only in their infancy.

Jack and I received a signal inviting us again to stay at the Residency on our return to Tarawa, and were, of course, delighted to accept. I realised that H.H. the Resident Commissioner would wish to hear of our progress, also that much of my report would make poor listening. Of the three islands we had visited on *Ninikoria,* only at Marakei were we fairly confident that coral blasting could help.

* * *

Knowing the journey back to Tarawa from Maiana was short, I had become over-confident that my sea sickness was behind me. How wrong I was, but at least it proved that the pills could help! *Ninikoria,* despite her rolling, was a good modern ship, so we were sorry to leave her and her master, who admitted, with a happy smile, that his life in the colony was very different to what it had been in the Royal Navy. No one, including him, spoke well of *Nareau,* the ship that would take us on the last, and longest, leg of our reconnaissance.

It was when we arrived back at the Residency that we received the excellent news from Christmas Island that Bill Mitford was recovering well in Honolulu.

We had to finish dinner that evening without delay, as we were all expected to attend the Girl Guides' Concert in the Bairiki maneaba, or meeting house. Almost all villages had their maneaba, a long and large thatched building with no doors, but open below the low eaves of the thatch. To enter, we had to duck down, to a height of about three feet and, in my case, stagger into the room. Those inside would, before the British brought peace to the islands, have been at a great advantage, as an intruder's head was presented in the perfect position for chopping off.

Elaine Bernacchi was the leading light of the colony's Girl Guides, so we were greeted most warmly: that show was a tremendous achievement but, as its language was Gilbertese, I did not fully appreciate it after a busy and uncomfortable day.

While we had been away, the Bernacchis must have discussed the potential help which Jack and I should be able to give them: by reputation, the Royal Engineers are infinitely resourceful. After breakfast the next morning we were confronted with an extensive list of little jobs which, it was suggested, we might care to undertake. They included the fitting of a chair leg, securing some guttering and unblocking a drain. Had we worked every day and night, we could not have repaid the wonderful hospitality we were receiving but, Sapper, or not, I had never been a very handy man. I was sure almost all the tasks were more in Jack's line than mine.

Jack was his co-operative self, but he did murmur that he worked so much better if a pipe were to hand. He had lost his getting the tuna aboard on *Ninikoria,* and was looking forward to getting across to Betio to replace the treasured briar. Elaine picked up the topic of the pipe and promised that Jack would have his chance to visit Betio, but tomorrow. This morning would, however, so far as she was concerned, be jobs for Jack. That suited me very well, as I knew that if I attempted any of the tasks, I would introduce permanent doubt regarding the renowned achievements of my Corps.

It was an inspiration when I asked if Corporal Teki, H.H.'s police orderly, could cut my hair on the Residency veranda. I knew that H.H. had his own hair cut by Teki, so was confident that all would be well, that was until I saw the decidedly rustic barbering implements. However, all was well and I thanked Corporal Teki as best I could. With my hair cut, everyone agreed that I ought to be completing my report on our visit to Maiana, so I was taken off the jobs rosta. My most pressing task, though, was to draft a telegram to Christmas Island to ask for a Hastings aircraft to pick up Jack and me from Tarawa on, if possible, 25th August. That was in nearly three weeks and should allow time for the necessary flying clearances to be obtained.

Thirty four people were due at the Residency for Sunday lunch, another good reason for keeping out of the way while the preparations were made. Jack and I were most happy to help pass round the drinks and the party went well from the start. Many of the guests showed considerable interest in our travels, interest that was the greater because few of those present had ever been outside Tarawa itself.

Elaine had managed to import a frozen clump of twenty five dozen New Zealand oysters: they had come via Suva, Fiji, and at three shillings a dozen were good value anywhere, providing the basis for a superb seafood cocktail. The main dish was as good as its name was unpronounceable, but consisted of chicken, pork and crayfish, all lying on a vermicelli base.

At 3.30 p.m., Wyn Jones, one of the better known guests, thinking the party was breaking up, quietly took George Pitkeathly, the Chief Education Officer, Roy Davies, the Secretary to the Government, and me to his house on the lagoon edge to play bridge. Assisted by further beer, Wyn and I won four old pence at a penny a hundred.

When we had been leaving the Residency, H.H. had been doing his celebrated standing-on-his-head-on-the-floor act, but the party was really ending when I returned at 5.30. Elaine said that the guests had not outstayed their welcome. "When I get worried," she added, "is when people come for lunch carrying torches to see themselves home." That evening H.H. said that he felt tired, but soon revived after a few taunts from Elaine and a little of his own whisky, proffered by Jack.

* * *

It rained all Sunday night and well into the next morning, when Gerry Douglas met us early to discuss the arrangements for our trip on the motor vessel *Nareau,* which we were due to board that evening. Anna Douglas had decided not to come with us, as "She is sure she would be sea sick in *Nareau.*" I fully sympathised and my dark forebodings of our next trip became darker. Gerry also told us that the promised high explosive, fifty pounds of it, plus the necessary accessories, had arrived from Ocean Island and he would bring it with him. Wonderful prompt action, but I was rather surprised, as the regulations for carrying explosives on passenger vessels sounded very tight.

After he had bought a new pipe, Jack and I spent the day checking the availability of engineer resources in the colony, thus confirming that there was next to nothing of use to a blasting team. Bob Hilton, the Public Works Superintendent, showed us round his stores, which included a few tools and a little timber, but most items were bespoken for minor local tasks. However, given money and time to order, three months at the least, almost anything could be obtained.

The only items available in abundance on Betio were empty gas cylinders. The Americans must have imported them after the Battle of Tarawa and left them behind. The Gilbertese had put many of the steel cylinders to good use, mainly as bells, including the church bell(s), the tea bell, the school bell, the fire bell and the knocking-off bell. To us, the bells all sounded exactly alike, so we asked how they knew that, say, the fire bell was being rung. With the delighted smile of one who knows the right answer, the Gilbertese foreman told us, "That is simple. It is painted red."

Most of the shipping that the colony possessed was lying in the lagoon off Betio. *Moana Raoi* was certainly the largest vessel, and then came

Ninikoria, which we also knew well. The next largest ship, at about a hundred tons gross, was *Nareau,* now the focus of our interest: she looked tiny, but *Tungaru* was even smaller and was admitted to be of an uneconomical "middling" size. Smallest of all were a pair of two-masted boats, little larger than our forty ton motor fishing vessel back on Christmas Island. These were *Kia Kia* and *Te Matapula*; both words meaning tern, the most common colony bird, in Gilbertise and Ellice respectively. They were useful for liaison purposes (children to boarding school, patients to hospital, and so on).

A ship similar to *Ninikoria* was due to be built "to replace *Nareau*", and we asked what the new vessel would be called. We already knew that Ninikoria meant "courageous" in Gilbertese, so the natural question was "Will her name mean courageous in Ellice?"

"Well, no, there could be some problems with that one," was the answer, "because the Ellice for courageous is *Faka Ma Lucy.*" Yes, there might well be problems, particularly if, at the launching ceremony, the champagne bottle failed to break.

We knew many Ellice words could raise English speaking eyebrows: Elaine Bernacchi delighted in visiting the government offices not far from the Residency, so that she could say "Good morning, Faka Ofo" to an official of that name. Nor was he alone, as there was an island in the Tokelau Group, just over the Date Line from the Ellice Islands, also called Faka Ofo; not only the British have fine family names!

Chapter Nine

ARANUKA

I swallowed a large number of sea sickness pills before Jack and I boarded *Nareau,* armed with a packet of anti-cockroach powder which Elaine Bernacchi had thoughtfully bought for us.

A deity named Nareau had been the legendary creator of the Gilbertese Universe, so the naming of the ship was understandable, but I wondered whether her intended scrapping might not prove a delicate matter. H.H. himself asked me not to pursue that question, saying, "*Nareau* must go!" He explained that she had been built in Australia at considerable cost only ten years before, but had never proved satisfactory. Her designer had forsaken shipbuilding before she was launched and moved into the hotel business, where success had again eluded him.

Nareau turned out to be better than we had been led to expect, not a difficult achievement. Gerry Douglas and I shared a two berth cabin directly over the stern. From it, glazed swing doors, rather like French windows, opened on to a tiny triangle of deck directly above the propellers, which thrashed in the sea only just below. It was fortunate that those doors

MV Nareau.

proved to be watertight when shut, as *Nareau* was only seventy feet long and quite capable of pitching up and down sufficiently to swamp the deck outside. Our cabin had its own shower, wash basin and WC, but all were designed for small people, and Gerry was large. Jack had a cabin to himself amidships and realised that he had probably drawn lucky.

Nareau carried neither radar nor echo sounder and had no freezer for food, so that meant no fresh meat or vegetables. Her cruising speed, also, left much to be desired. Gerry had relied on her maker's claimed eight knots, or more than nine land miles an hour, to plan the schedule of our trip. Now, her master told us that we should not rely on more than five knots against the wind: she had a high silhouette and the wind direction really mattered.

Bill was in his last year before retirement: already on the cautious side, he had no intention of blotting his copy book now. He was not going to strain his ship's engines and, even with the wind behind us, we never made more than six knots. Gerry's plan had been to visit those of the southern Gilbert Islands which needed our attention and then to carry on south to as many Ellice Islands as time would permit. However, after our first twelve hours in *Nareau,* we were four hours late in arriving at our first island, Aranuka. In the circumstances, Gerry decided to change his plan and Bill readily agreed.

Nareau had one great advantage, in that she was so little in demand that she was for our sole use, so there were no magistrates to collect, copra to load, or contract workers to exchange. Within the limits of fuel and food, her timetable could be as flexible as we wished.

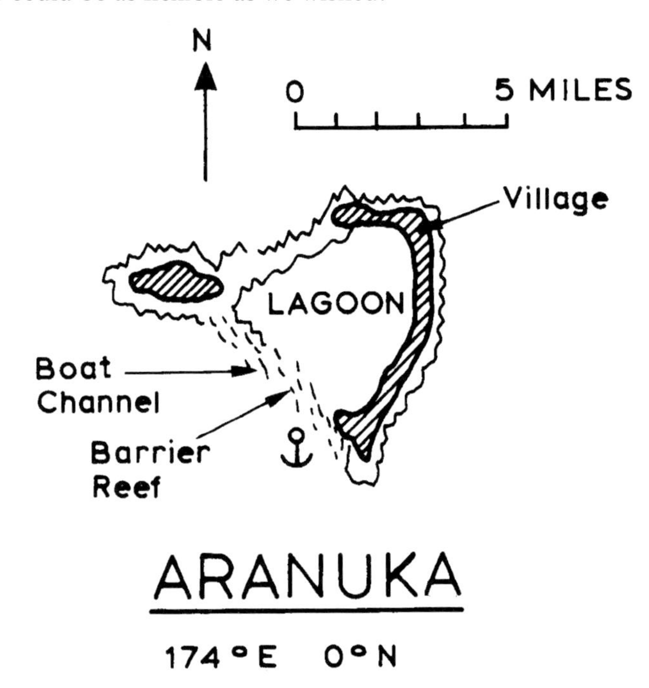

If only for the sake of tact, the Ellice Islands needed to be included in our reef reconnaissance but, unless we were careful, we might never reach them. Gerry's revised plan was that we should complete our reconnaissance of Aranuka and then go direct to Nanumea, the most northerly of the Ellice Islands. After that, there might be time to visit other islands nearby before we came back up the Gilberts. This sounded very sensible but, first, a new type of task awaited us at Aranuka.

Aranuka Island lay just north of the equator. Its chart was another of those based on the sketches made by Captain Wilkes in 1841 but had been updated at an unknown time by an unknown person. We would have had greater faith in it, had its originator not chosen to remain anonymous, but Bill assured us that members of his crew knew Aranuka well: it was a small lagoon atoll shaped rather like a wishbone, with the gap between the feet spanned by a barrier reef which enclosed the lagoon. Neither the Japanese nor the Americans occupied it during the war and it wasn't long before we understood why, particularly as Abemama, which was bigger and had better access, was only twenty miles away.

The statistics of Aranuka were quoted as 479 Gilbertese producing about 150 tons of copra a year, both small in comparison to many of the other islands, but if access could be improved, more people might live there and more copra might be produced. Access from ship to shore was by boat through a gap in the barrier reef, which the chart marked as "hazardous", and then three miles across the lagoon to the government station on its north edge. It was on the passage through the barrier reef that our advice was being sought.

We approached in *Nareau* from the north, so had to skirt the north and east shores of Aranuka. Bill gave them a very wide berth but, through binoculars, the reef flat looked very broad and, with a fifteen knot wind blowing on to it, also very rough.

Aranuka was the ninth atoll that Jack and I had visited, so we well knew that any channels constructed on the north or east faces of the islands would be unusable from March to October, when those winds really did prevail. We also realised that the local inhabitants, over the centuries, had probably discovered the best means of hopping on and off their islands, so it would be highly unlikely that we, in a visit of a few hours, would find much better places.

It took an age for *Nareau* to bring us round to the south side of Aranuka but at last Bill anchored at a good safe spot in six fathoms, though still several hundred yards off shore. The ship's launch then took us a further half mile along the coast until we were roughly opposite the reef passage. We were assured that it would be obvious, either as a gap in the reef at low tide, or by an absence of breakers at other times.

We were apparently at "other times", though Gerry had been hoping that our arrival would coincide with low tide. The tide tables were based for reference on a port called Apia in Western Samoa, well over a thousand miles away, and there could easily be an error of an hour or so; we had experienced the effects of unsuitable timing when *Moana Raoi* had been thrown by the tide into Canton's lagoon. Here at Aranuka, we were facing one of the highest tides of the year but our launch headed into it and over the reef edge with no great trouble. Fortunately, as Bill had promised, the launch's helmsman knew the way.

The gap in the outer barrier reef was substantial, about fifty yards wide and twenty feet deep, and a series of posts, or beacons, marked the supposed line of the channel leading into the lagoon. The beacon nearest to the sea was 150 yards from the reef edge and marked the start of some shallower, but still quite deep, water. From it, we made good progress to the next post, several hundred yards ahead, which marked the narrowing of the channel at the start of a band of superb, but ominous, coral heads. Their presence had the effect of greatly restricting the average depth of the channel, thus speeding up the water emptying from the lagoon.

The outflow was impressively fast and Gerry had a hurried conversation, through our intepreter, with the helmsman, as it was still not too late to turn back. However, with a nonchalant smile, the helmsman assured us that we could make an entrance and then committed us to his decision. Unlike others who have passed the point of no return, like a ski jumper, or a canoeist shooting the rapids, acceleration into the unknown was not our problem. Our danger lay in going progressively slower, or even perhaps stopping, at which stage we would be at the mercy of the tide race.

For examples of really impressive coral heads, Aranuka could have won prizes. From the second marker post, we were confronted by a dense forest of them for the next quarter of a mile. They were ten or more feet in diameter and broke the surface at low tide: the bottom depth varied from about six to thirty feet, with the sand still easily visible through the gin clear, but rushing, water: the deeper the water, the more formidable were the coral heads. There was nothing to show that their cores were of hard white limestone, as the lichenlike algae which coated them gave their outer surfaces an astounding variety of colours: there were all shades of oranges and lemons, plenty of deep reds and purples and some dark greens.

"What a perfect place for underwater photography," I was thinking, but those thoughts soon turned to survival. Every one of those coral heads, whether just proud of, or just under, the surface, was capable of toppling us, as the emptying lagoon water, urgently and unpredictably, churned around, and cascaded over, them.

So far as our helmsman was concerned, those obstacles merely added spice to his life and gave him an opportunity to demonstrate his skills. He invariably made the correct decision on whether to go left or right of the next pillar in the maze that confronted him. It would have been easy to enter a dead end, in which case the launch would have spun across the current, with consequent disaster. The helmsman's problem was no longer to miss the great cauliflower-like clumps in front but to ensure that we were not washed sideways or backwards into others. The launch was said to be capable of five knots in still water, but with its engine on full throttle, as it had been for minute after minute, it possibly went a little faster. Now it could not roar any louder and the roar was not a happy one. In contrast, the helmsman remained his very happy self.

Our forward progress gradually decreased until we were sitting stationary in the swirling water. Unable to shout over the engine noise, I was gripping the gunwale, as the launch started to edge backwards, first by a few inches, then by a few feet, before making a few encouraging inches forward again. This irregular oscillation was like that of the handkerchief on a tug of war rope approaching the winning line but, exciting though that may be, our launch's efforts were merely frightening. We grew to know the half dozen coral heads nearest to us all too well and longed for the equivalent of a punt pole to fend off the heads directly behind us but, almost miraculously, the flow of water kept us clear.

I hope that I looked as calm as everyone else but we all admitted later that we had planned in which direction to swim, had the current allowed any choice. The nearest land was a mile and a half away and the nearest boat or vessel was *Nareau,* well down the coast, not looking out for us, and with us using her only launch.

Happily, the flow of water started to slacken and we made headway, passing more of the marker beacons nearby. As we passed the eighth post, we entered the still, and now relatively shallow, lagoon, with its water of the lightest emerald green gleaming in the sunlight. On our way across it we revived sufficiently to express our views on the official who had positioned posts numbers three to seven, with any relationship between them and an obstacle-free channel being purely coincidental, but Gerry said, "That gentleman left the colony years ago."

Half an hour later, we reached the government station on the lagoon shore, where we were met by what must have been a high proportion of the island's total population, all of them showing more than usual interest. After what we had just experienced in reaching them, Jack and I were not surprised to hear that Aranuka had very few visitors.

Yes, the entrance to the lagoon was indeed "hazardous" and Jack and I fully agreed with Gerry that improvements to the channel were essential. The thought of making the trip, even at slack water, with copra boats in tow, appalled us, yet that feat had been achieved by launch helmsmen as a matter of routine for many years. If a large number of the coral heads could be removed, a much safer route would be opened. How I wished our divers had still been with us to give advice! The Aranuka channel was just their kind of task, even though their work would be severely restricted by the tides. However, in their absence, we had to make our own assessment, so took some trouble to foresee the sort of questions divers later might ask.

Many of the headings on our questionnaire were not appropriate for a channel through the barrier reef at Aranuka, but that on *Hazards to Working Parties* certainly was. The primary hazard was the current while the lagoon emptied and filled, even though the local boys fished at the lagoon entrance at slack tides. "If they are swept away, all they have to do is swim to still water, and then wait until the current allows them to reach a dry part of the reef." Simple perhaps, but we were assured that the conditions we had experienced were truly unusual and probably the worst in the whole year. It had been doubly unfortunate that our traverse of the channel had coincided with both a spring tide and the mis-timing of slack water. Gerry did not blame the mis-timing on *Nareau's* late arrival but that must have contributed strongly to our problems.

We were shown the government rest house, bare but spacious, and we knew that a small working party would be happier living in it than in tents. We then sampled the local drinking water, definitely brackish; just who ever stayed in the rest house as a visitor, or sampled the drinking water, we never established. There were no tourists to the colony, let alone Aranuka, in the tripper sense, nor was there any point in trying to encourage visitors until travel between, and access to, the islands could be improved.

Now that we had seen the coral heads through which any channel would have to run, Jack and I considered the demolition tasks involved. Given sufficient explosive, positioned correctly, it should prove fairly easy to break them up, which we planned to confirm when we were back on Christmas Island, where plenty of explosives were available. However, the Aranuka coral heads were literally miles from anywhere, absolutely clear of people, pastors and panes of glass. Tons of high explosive could be detonated without bother to anyone, always assuming that those involved with the firing got well clear of the explosions.

We were perhaps excessively keen to catch the slack water at the lagoon entrance on our return to *Nareau,* so, after only an hour ashore, the launch took us back through the coral heads, most of which were now showing above the water. Gerry had asked us to plan for a channel at least forty feet wide, to allow some swinging room for a copra boat when on tow: with this in mind, I undertook to count the heads within twenty feet of one side of the launch, with Jack doing the same on the other side.

The tide was dead low and the water almost still, so we hoped to be able to traverse the channel really slowly, but the helmsman needed to take us along his favourite obstacle course faster than we would have wished. "Steerage way," Gerry said.

Our total count added up to seventy large coral heads that would need attention, a figure with which Gerry's personal estimate tallied. We could not be sure that the line the helmsman had taken would be the best for a permanent passage, but divers could check that later.

We had only a vague idea of the quantity of explosives required to clear each coral obstacle. With some of the coral heads twenty or more feet high, and with copra boats only needing three feet of water under them, it might be sufficient to knock the tops off some heads, rather than breaking them up completely. An added uncertainty was whether, and how quickly, the coral might grow towards the surface again after it was chopped down. My first guess was that five tons of explosive would be needed for the Aranuka channel and we thought that the task could be done with surplus munitions, were any available. With the Japanese and Korean Wars not so long before, they might have been, but we never traced any.

Following this visit I thought more seriously about coral and its growth, hoping to understand how channels could best be cut through coral in its various forms. I hope that my findings, at the end of this book, may provide a basis for discussion for those to whom the subject is new. It took no deep thought, though, to realise that coral polyps were living creatures, which explained why the sores on my shins were reluctant to heal. My stockings were not the answer for abrasions, and I never learned what I should have worn on my legs when clambering on the reefs.

* * *

We were now over half way through our reconnaissance and Jack and I were delighted still to have had no experience of stonefish. We knew that they were flat fish of greyish colouring and horrid ugliness, and did not doubt that the poison which exuded from the spikes on their backs would cause agonising death.

However, the subject of stonefish was not one to pursue and we just hoped that our tennis shoes would provide the necessary underfoot protection. I was thankful not to know until many years later how wrong we had been, when I heard that Beryl, the wife of Percy Roberts (the Christmas Island District Commissioner) had stepped on a stonefish on an Australian reef. I asked Percy to record the circumstances for me, which I will now quote:–

"I have never seen a stonefish, but Beryl tells me they are very like a sole, with about nine spikes on their backs, which they raise when disturbed. They camouflage well on coral sand.

"In September 1969 we had gone to Wonga Beach, seventy miles north of Cairns, particularly to catch a low spring tide, when the beach would extend out for a mile or more. Beryl was seeking shells about a couple of hundred yards from the shore when she trod on a stonefish. Two of its spikes penetrated the sole of her right foot, *despite the fact that she was wearing sandshoes with thick rubber soles.* (My italics – DR.)

"Fortunately some local residents saw her collapse, rushed out and took her ashore. They phoned for an ambulance, put her in their car and met the ambulance about half way from Mossman Hospital about ten miles from Wonga. When I heard what had happened, I immediately set off for the hospital and found Beryl virtually unconscious. The doctor was very consoling, saying his last stonefish patient had died. However, thanks to those local people, Beryl survived."

This incident confirmed what we had heard about stonefish, except for the important detail that rubber soles did not provide protection. To cut any suspense, I will say now that Jack and I never saw a stonefish, so never knew whether we had really been in danger from them. Clamshells were obvious, when the sun was out, because of the brilliant, lovely and almost luminous, blue of the meat between their rock hard jaws. Stonefish remained my greater worry throughout our reconnaissance but, if asked what part of it left the most vivid impression in my mind, my answer would be the tide race at Aranuka.

Chapter Ten

MYSTERY TOUR

Once we and the launch were safely aboard *Nareau* again, we headed south for Nanumea, the most northerly of the Ellice Islands; Bill estimated that we would arrive in two days. The sheer slowness of our progress was exasperating, but Gerry dared not press for greater speed, lest *Nareau's* engines disagreed and left us drifting a long way from anywhere.

At eighty-four tons, *Nareau* was hardly an ocean liner but Bill and his crew made sure that their few passengers followed a strict routine. We all slept with windows and port holes open, but at 6.30 a.m. these had to be closed while the decks above and alongside were washed down. Gerry or I shut our French windows over the stern but our cabin also had small windows either side that were closed by the crew.

This deck washing was one of the strictest rituals of the day's routine, but Bill recollected that, when he first carried the Bernacchis, he relaxed it with a view to giving them a longer, undisturbed, night. Doors and windows would be shut half an hour later, at seven o'clock, and scrubbing down was to be restricted to five minutes only. The split second timing proved all too much for the crew, who, knowing the importance of their passengers, were keen to achieve spotless results. Unfortunately, scrubbing down started just before the side windows were closed and His Honour the Resident Commissioner received a bucket of deck washings fairly and squarely over himself in bed. Sitting up to protest, H.H. knocked over a bottle of lemon squash, which happened to be open, and the relationship between captain and passengers remained tense for some days. However, I doubted if that incident alone could have induced Mr Bernacchi's intense dislike of *Nareau.*

We caught a small tuna on a trailing line over the stern just after we left Aranuka, therefore we had tuna for dinner. Gerry had told Jack and me earlier in the day what boring eating he always found tuna, so we enjoyed hearing the appreciative remarks he felt obliged to make to "Daddy", as Bill was known, while manfully swallowing his boiled fish. In anticipation of the privations we might experience in *Nareau,* we had taken the precaution of bringing plenty of beer aboard with us, two cans of which we each drank before lunch and dinner daily. The demand for whisky thus slackened, but a tot in everyone's coffee after dinner mellowed the memories of tuna.

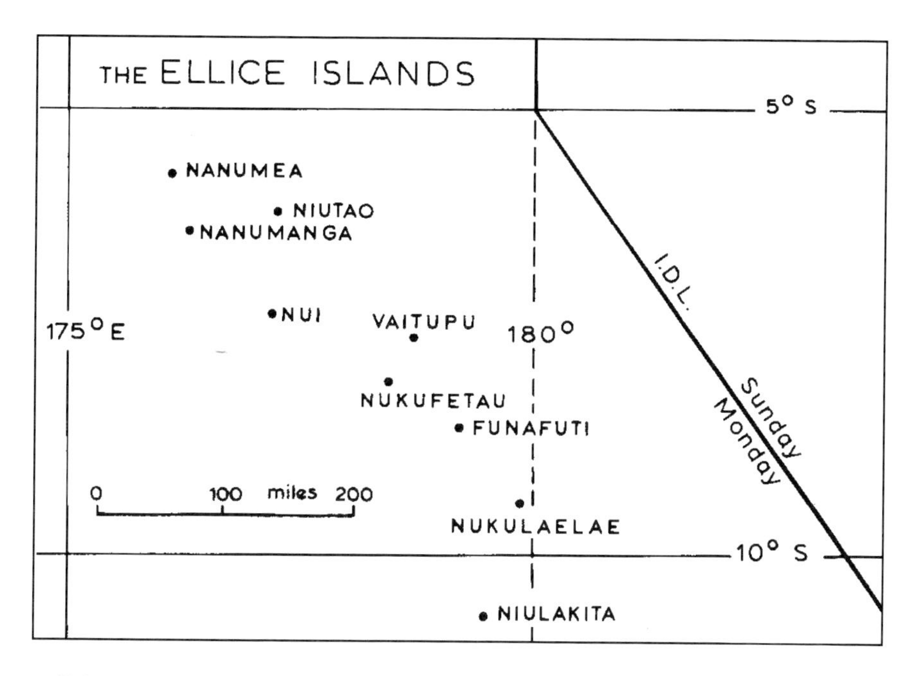

Friday the Twelfth of August 1960 found us just about as far from a grouse moor as was possible at a particularly unfrequented spot in the Pacific Ocean, some six degrees south of the equator and one hundred and seventy six degrees east of Greenwich. When the island wireless stations had opened up "on sked" for an hour the previous evening, Nanumea was warned to expect us at 6 a.m., just before dawn, but at 8 a.m. no land was in sight. Bill was a little sensitive at breakfast and explained how difficult the two knot east to west "set" could make navigation with a ship as slow as *Nareau,* particularly on a night with no stars. Gerry tactfully agreed, adding that the variations in the speed and direction of the set throughout the year could aggravate any difficulties.

Soon after breakfast *Nareau* crossed an unexpected stretch of shallow water. Just how shallow it was we had no means of telling, unless we cared nearly to stop and plumb it with a line, but the water looked milky. We were over those shallows for about fifteen minutes, or two land miles at *Nareau's* speed, and during that time we caught fish on the troll lines as quickly as they could be brought aboard. There were five in all, including a fifty pound tuna and three small barracuda. The latter, fried in steaks and with chips, made a welcome alternative to the perpetual tuna.

There was no sign of that shoal on the charts, even when later we knew our correct position, nor could I fit its existence into my theories about atoll formation, thus confirming how dangerous a little knowledge can be! Had the water depth turned out to be much shallower than the forty feet we estimated, the danger would have been real; even at *Nareau's* slow speed, none of us would have wished to run on to an uncharted reef. After a tactful delay, Gerry asked if he could borrow the sextant to make his own check of our position, but he would not tell us his findings.

Nareau pressed ahead as fast as her engines would allow and at 11 a.m. an island came into sight on our port bow. Quite why we should be six hours late on an unhampered thirty-six hour trip was not explained but, after another half hour, the appearance of a conspicuous white church made members of our crew say, "That's not Nanumea, that's Nanumanga." How right they were! Nanumanga lay seventy miles to the south and slightly to the east of our intended destination, Nanumea, which we must have missed in the dark. Just how we could have missed it, when it lay very nearly on the line we had been trying to take, again nobody explained. We must have passed very close indeed before dawn, but we had not hit it!

It did not matter to Jack and me at which island we arrived, providing that it was included on our list, and Nanumanga was. We could see that it was a small reef atoll, only two miles long from north to south, and a mile at its widest. Gerry told us that eight hundred Ellice islanders lived there so, hardly surprisingly with such a dense population, they ate most of the coconuts they grew and very little copra was exported. However, it would still be tactful to provide them with a reef channel if possible.

A message was passed round *Nareau* that the change of island had been intentional, as the state of the tide would have been unsatisfactory at Nanumea; I believed this, until the first two canoes from Nanumanga arrived beside us. The occupants shouted up, as Lotto our interpreter told us, "Delighted to see you, but the wireless said you were going to Nanumea today." A few minutes later another canoe arrived carrying the Chief of Kaubure, or Headman of the island. He apologised profusely for not having been the first to greet us but, unfortunately he had not been expecting us.

The Ellice race, who are Polynesians, are of a lighter skin colour than the Micronesian Gilbertese, and this Chief of Kaubure was a splendid looking man, probably in his late forties, whose authority few would have questioned. Sadly, though, his legs were grossly swollen with elephantiasis. That unpleasant disease had been prevalent in the Ellice Islands and could now be prevented but, unfortunately, not cured. The C of K had difficulty in coming aboard, poor man, and it dawned on me that I myself would be expected to go ashore in the same type of canoe.

* * *

Those canoes were dug-outs made from buka trees, hollowed out so as to leave the remaining shell very thin and certainly not strong enough to take the impact of a man's foot if he casually dropped in. My mind went back to Cambridge and the rowing eight in which, for a short while, I had been member of Peterhouse's "row for fun" boat. It, too, had been excessively flimsy and I had the greatest trouble entering and leaving it in the prescribed manner. There, I had been on the dead calm River Cam, with friends holding the boat steady. Here, we were out in the Pacific Ocean, with its swell and its set, on which the canoe danced unrestrained.

Across the gunwales of the canoe were a few lengths of squared two inch timber and it was on to one of these, and nowhere else, that we were permitted to put any weight; a paddler sat at each end, which left space between them for two passengers. Together with its outrigger, a lightweight log which extended along one side and over fully half the central length of the canoe, its overall width was about six feet; but, even with an outrigger, it was still easy to capsize a canoe if it were loaded off centre.

We needed two canoes to go ashore, one for Jack and me, complete with crowbar, recce gear and six foot measuring rod, and one for Gerry and Lotto, who was required to know English, otherwise he could not have been the ship's apprentice officer. They boarded their canoe first, to show us how to lower ourselves into ours.

As may be apparent, I was never the agile or athletic type, so was full of qualms. As instructed, "all I had to do" was to stand on the walk-the-plank-type length of wood that projected over *Nareau's* side, hold on to the rope provided, and wait. The canoe would rise and fall with the swell alongside the ship, perhaps four feet up and four feet down, and, at the top of the oscillation, the cross bar of the canoe, on to which I was expected to make my feather light descent, would be a mere three feet below the perilous plank. It sounded nothing but, with my head five feet, or so, above my feet, I would need to judge a distance of eight or nine feet very precisely; not quite so easy.

I asked what I was required to do after I was down and balanced on the cross bar. "Just let go of the rope and then crouch so that you can place a hand on each gunwale," had been the answer. If I did not let go of the rope at the right instant, and the temptation to hang on would be great, then down would go the canoe again, and I would be left dangling. "Once you are crouched," said Gerry, "you should take your full weight on your arms, so that you can extend your legs forward and lay your feet gently on the bottom of the canoe."

Jack and I lowered our impedimenta down to our paddlers and it became clear that they were not used to carrying sharp and heavy crowbars in their flimsy and valuable canoe. However, "T ker-o-ba", as both the Gilbertese and Ellice called it, was safely stowed. I then gave Jack the honour of leading the way and he boarded the canoe as if he had performed such a feat every day of his life. I followed, with considerably less grace, but found the process not quite as bad as I had expected.

The tide was dead low and there was a dip in the reef edge opposite the church, which led into a natural chute, or channel, just wide enough for the canoe to be paddled nearly as far as the shore. Our paddlers hopped on to the reef flat, then helped us out, and we had the satisfaction of knowing that we had successfully made our first trip in an outrigger canoe.

The Chief of Kaubure, who would normally have been our guide, was still aboard Nareau, so Lotto had to find another man who could speak with authority on the island's requirements for reef channels. His choice was not very fortunate and our suspicions rose as we tried to run through our visit questionnaire. We were receiving none of the normal answers, though those given, mainly either "Yes" or "No", could hardly have been more definite.

When it came to the *hazards to men working in the water?*, we expected to be told "None", just as on all the other islands, but back came a strong "Yes". This was doubly interesting, not only because of the implications for a working party, but also because it was pleasant, at last, to think that Grimble's accounts of the perils of the deep may have been more accurate than we had begun to believe. I asked Lotto to try to discover to what hazards our informant referred, but that proved too difficult and no reply was forthcoming.

The Church, Nanumanga.

When we were nearly at the end of our pro-forma, I asked Jack, who had been the scribe, to let me look through it. Sure enough, the answer to every question was opposite to that which our previous experience would have led us to expect. I expressed my doubts to Lotto who, intelligent young man that he was, took the point and said that he would try to clarify matters. After a long and seemingly complicated discussion with our guide, Lotto was able to turn to us to say, "You are quite right and there has been some misunderstanding. He wants you now to realise that when he answered "Yes" he meant "No", and that when he answered "No" he meant "Yes"!

All was now clear! We had had a little trouble on Gardner Island obtaining reliable answers to our questions but, for sheer ambiguity, it would have been hard to beat Nanumanga's representative. What with having been taken to the wrong island as well as having to substitute "No" for "Yes", we were not having the most straightforward of days, but at least the requirement for a reef passage was plain to see. All that was needed was to widen and deepen the existing natural channel and it was a pleasure to be able to say that it could easily be done with explosives; easy, that was, except for the usual snag.

The large and, in its way, beautiful, church lay directly in line with the channel and only seventy-five yards from the end of it. My report on the proposed work tried to explain the problem:

"The very fine London Missionary Society church is dead in line with the channel at present used. This church has twenty wood-framed glass windows and also a large north window with eighty panes of glass. The locals said that they could remove all the windows, but that this would require the blessing of the LMS pastor, whom we did not meet. The church roof is of corrugated aluminium, with (luckily) no glass in it. The locals expressed a strong preference for this line of channel, rather than for one more to the south of the church."

The channel was only ninety yards long but, to improve it, more than a ton of explosives would be needed which, even if fired in small charges, might damage not just the windows, but the structure of the church. Jack and I had little experience in limiting the effect of explosions (there is seldom this requirement with wartime demolitions), but just hoped that, if the charges could be fired with the tide over them, the water would blanket the blast. Fortunately, our experiments later proved this to be the case.

Before coming ashore, Gerry Douglas had decided with Bill that our next call should be at Nui Island, which would be as far south as time would allow us to go, and we would then make our postponed call at Nanumea on our way back to the Gilberts. With Nui only a few hours away, there was time for us to stay ashore until dusk, so we borrowed bicycles to have a quick look around Nanumanga. Without notice of our requirement, the bikes were inferior to those we had been lent on Marakei: mine had its handlebars round the wrong way and a buckled rear wheel which delighted everyone except me, and Jack's had a very high saddle. None of them, of course, had brakes as atolls are popularly thought to be flat but our circuit of only four miles included some steeply sloping humps. Luckily I could gain some control with my feet dragging the ground, but Jack could not, and became a real menace. It would have been simpler, and more peaceful, had we walked the whole way.

Nanumanga turned out to be a pretty little island, solidly covered with coconut palms and with only a tiny lagoon. However we saw frogs and large, dark blue butterflies, with purple patches on their wings. Naturalists, please note those frogs; we didn't know that frogs on atolls were rare, but now I understand that they are, very! My reconnaissance reports could have done with some lighter touches but, as we flitted from island to island, it was a constant struggle to keep them up to date and *Nareau's* pitching on the way from Aranuka had tested my sea-sickness pills beyond their limits.

Before going aboard again, we held a prize giving for those who had helped us on Nanumanga. We gave the island scribe, who had taken over from our first informant, some baccy, but I asked one of the village elders to hand out the sweets to the hordes of eager children. The task must have further aged and deafened him, but he was pleased with the twenty-five cigarettes he received for his efforts. Some of the children did not get any sweets but much their greatest disappointment was our failure to blast a big channel for them, then and there.

* * *

Nareau's master was really on his mettle to deliver us to Nui on time the next morning and it was not his fault that our reception arrangements were less than perfect. There was a motor vessel of about *Nareau's* size, the London Missionary Society's *John Williams VI,* lying off the island; for two ships to visit an island at once was unusual and likely to raise problems: her launch was towing an apparently capsized canoe to the shore. It was a foul, squally day and, if the visiting missionaries, with the Almighty on their side, had capsized, the prospects for us poor sinners could be none too promising.

The erratic and strong swell was throwing the canoe that would take Jack and me ashore up and down *Nareau's* side, so I had great difficulty judging when to drop off the ship, as the crossbar on the canoe never seemed to be directly below me. The paddlers, assisted by many members of the ship's

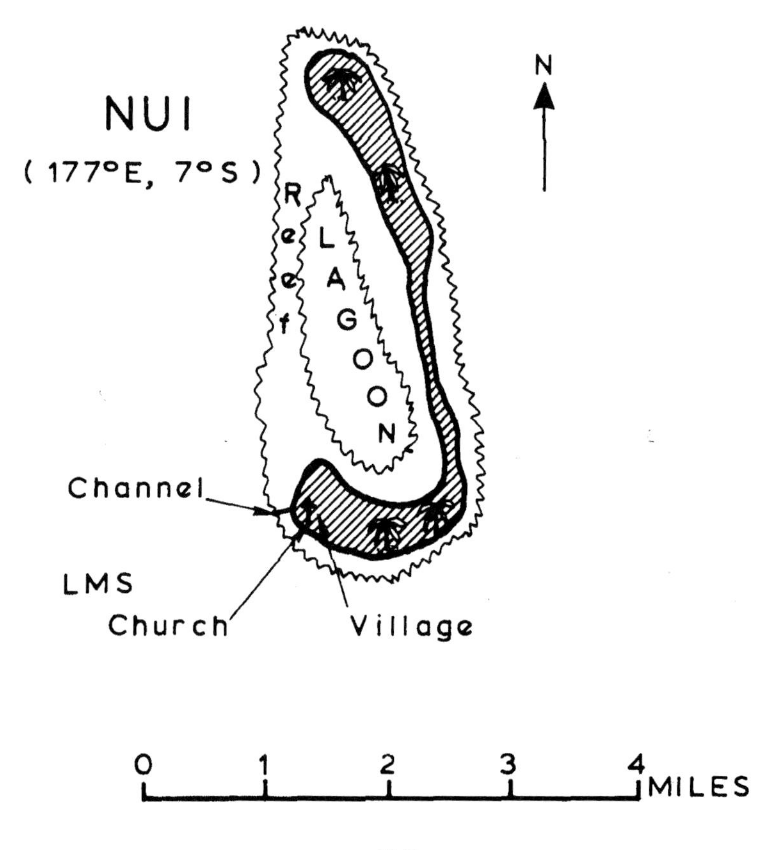

crew shouted something which I assumed meant "Now!", but twice I hesitated and missed my chance. The third time was lucky, but only just, as the soles of my tennis shoes were wet, and so was the crossbar.

Nareau was unable to anchor, so my inelegant transfer to the canoe took place a quarter of a mile outside the reef, just as a thunderstorm, of the type normally reserved for tropical films, broke overhead. Thunder, lightning, high winds and torrential rain, that could have been hail, were all competing, but my main concern was to hang on to the sides of the canoe. As usual, because I would be working in the water on the reef, I was not wearing a shirt, and Jack's was only a soggy encumbrance. Never had we expected the cold to be our problem at sea level near the equator.

Our two minders stopped the canoe's forward progress about ten yards short of the reef's frothing and churning edge, from which hard and jagged coral pinnacles protruded through the sucking undercurrent. They held the canoe in that position, waiting for the right wave on which to surf, before the man in the stern made the decision and, with a mighty yell, he and his companion paddled madly ahead. We grazed the edge as we crossed it, but the canoe remained sound. Jack and I, much relieved at our safe deliverance, tried to congratulate the canoeists on their skill and, from the way they grinned, we thought they understood.

There were unexpected advantages in having the important LMS visitors ashore ahead of us. There was no doubt that the Methodist missionaries had gained a strong footing in the Ellice Islands and, in the eyes of the locals, senior visitors from the Missionary Society were more important than Government folk from Tarawa. We were pestered by many fewer children than normal and were able to wade on the reef flat with an unusual lack of attention.

The storm cleared as quickly as it had started and the day, and our morale, improved greatly. We were further heartened when we found that, in the 1930s, a resourceful District Officer, Mr Kennedy, had blasted the beginnings of a boat channel in the Nui reef and here it still was, plain for all to see. Mr Kennedy's cut in the reef flat was over a hundred yards long, just over a foot deep and ten to fifteen feet wide. It seemed amazing that no one had told us of this work, but probably its significance as an example of a reef channel had been forgotten. It gave us the lead we so much needed, and Jack and I were enormously encouraged. If Mr Kennedy, with no outside help, had managed to make such a good start on a channel, then surely the Royal Engineers, with time to make plans, could achieve something better!

What was even more encouraging was that Mr Kennedy had left evidence of how he had done the job, for there, at one end of his incomplete channel, were three obvious boreholes down into the reef flat at four foot centres: each hole was two inches in diameter and two feet deep. We already knew that the right way to quarry rock, and this coral was as hard as marble, was to lift it out with explosives filled into boreholes. However, none of the conventional means for drilling boreholes were available in the colony, so we had discarded the hope of using them.

On Nui we were told that Mr Kennedy might still be alive in the Cook

Islands and later we heard more of his doings. Before Pearl Harbour he had been transferred to an outlying island in the Solomons, one, which, when the Japanese arrived later, they never garrisoned. However, they sent occasional small patrols to it, which, with the help of two policemen and their rifles, Mr Kennedy had ambushed, putting the captured weapons to good use. Tiring of this, the Japanese sent a punitive force, but Mr Kennedy and his friends had already disappeared to another island.

After the war Mr Kennedy was involved in resettlement work in Fiji. By repute he was a man with a healthy thirst, a real character, well worth meeting. However, the Cook Islands, which were administered by New Zealand, were thousands of miles away and, sadly, there was no hope of my reaching him.

Now that we had seen the old boreholes in the reef, we asked if anyone could be found who had worked for Mr Kennedy, whereupon a middle aged man called Papua was produced with commendable speed. In his time, Papua had probably been a very good labourer. He was not an easy man to interrogate, but we managed to discover from him the basics of what we wanted to know. Our primary question was, "How were the holes drilled in the coral?" Lotto interpreted the answer for us, "The holes in the reef were made by hitting iron bars with hammers."

Light was starting to dawn! Both Jack and I had seen "bars, jumping and boring" listed in old vocabularies of ordnance stores, but neither of us had known what they were. We now deduced that boring bars were sharp steel spikes that could be thumped with a sledge hammer, or otherwise jumped up and down, to drill holes in rock. If we were right, and we became convinced that we must be, the quality of work achieved at Nui would fully meet our needs.

When it came to asking Papua questions of detail, such as, "How long did it take to make a hole?" or "How did you clear the crumbled coral from the holes?", it was evident that they were quite beyond him. His job had been to thump the top of the iron bar with the hammer and to keep thumping it. Judging by his fine pair of shoulders, he must have thumped well.

With the islanders' magnificent physique, doubtless developed from countless generations of children coming into the world with paddles in their hands, I had been surprised to see no football or cricket grounds, nor even volley ball pitches, on our tour. I asked Gerry why such born athletes had not taken to sports ashore, to which his simple answer had been, "They can't afford the land." As almost always in the colony, it came back to coconuts: with the total land area of the nine inhabited Ellice atolls being so tiny, there was precious little land to spare for sports fields.

Talking to Papua made us realise that the most valuable engineering resource that the colony could offer was strong and willing labour. Another asset, with which Jack and I had seldom been accustomed on military tasks, was that time, and plenty of it, would be available for making any channels through the reefs that we might recommend.

Papua was becoming restive and obviously wished to return to his own affairs, but we walked up and down Mr Kennedy's channel with him twice more, to see if further questions came to mind. There was no need to ask what had been done with the coral after it had been blasted, as piles of coral slabs were lying some twenty yards from the side of the channel. It seemed amazing that they had not shifted after twenty years of surf in the westerly seasons, but that knowledge helped our planning, as did the fact that very little new coral had grown in the channel since it was cut.

The Nui reef flat was composed of the hardest coral we saw, and the crowbar bounced straight back off it. However, it was apparent that the coral lay in layered slabs, and we could hear water gurgling through a few natural holes as the tide changed. When Mr Kennedy's borehole charges had lifted the slabs, they had broken into sheets about six inches thick, which men must then have humped to form the piles at the side.

These were the kind of slabs from which Lance-Corporal White was building his church on Christmas Island, and we wondered how he was getting on. It was only a month since we had been there but that all seemed an age away. As no daily news sheet was on offer on *Nareau,* we were completely out of touch with world affairs and even more so with matters military.

Between the Nui reef edge and the end of Mr Kennedy's channel there was a gap of about a hundred yards, just where a channel was most needed. It struck us that he had probably not been able to extend his project due to the nature of the explosives then available to him, which may have been unsuitable for use in the wet: the nearer the edge, the wetter the reef became. If our proposals were put into practice, more modern explosives should not, fortunately, suffer from such limitations. We decided that, after lunch, this would be a good place to experiment with some of the explosive Gerry had obtained for us. Meanwhile, a rather apprehensive Papua was dismissed, with many thanks and a goodly supply of baccy.

With the weather calm, we returned to *Nareau* in the canoes, well satisfied with the information that the morning had yielded. After lunch, we pulled out the fifty pound box of what I shall call "Forcex" explosive from beside my bunk and removed the lid. The contents were divided into five parcels, each of which contained twenty half pound sausages of Forcex wrapped in greaseproof paper.

Gerry and I had grown used to the strong smell of almond icing in our cabin but now, with the lid off, the effect was almost overpowering. We decided that ten pounds of explosive should satisfy our immediate needs, so lifted out a parcel from the end of the box. Some oily brown liquid dripped from it into a small puddle on the bottom, which was sodden.

We boarded our canoes with the Forcex in one sandbag and some detonators and safety fuse in another, and were soon back on the Nui reef. The *John Williams VI,* with its important and religious passengers, had sailed, so now we became the island's main attraction for the afternoon. Lotto had to use all his authority to impress upon the village policeman that the hordes of children must be kept clear when the explosive charge went off. Initially, though, we let them swarm around like flies, of which there were also many.

The name Forcex was new to us, and we only knew that what Ocean Island had kindly sent us was a commercial blasting explosive. We decided to use our ten pounds of it in a single charge on the reef flat and chose a place near the ocean edge, as far as possible from the church and its windows. I unwrapped the sausages and moulded their explosive contents into the shape of a cone, which I pushed well down on to the coral.

Forcex reminded us of a service explosive that had been known as Nobel's 808, with which Jack and I had done our early training. Its basic ingredient was nitro-glycerine, the handling of which could be guaranteed to give me a headache if I did not wear rubber gloves. Too late, it struck me that the liquid oozing out of the Forcex must be nitro-glycerine and, needless to say, I was not wearing gloves. Forcex was reputed to explode satisfactorily when initiated by only a detonator, meaning a little open-ended tube of very sensitive high explosive into which a length of safety fuse could be inserted. This was the most simple method, but I was surprised that it was said to work, as most explosives cut better if a special booster charge is added to the detonator.

Gerry and Jack stayed near the church to ensure that the policeman kept the children under control while I went to insert the detonator and light the safety fuse on the charge. I had cut a length of fuse to burn for three minutes, plenty for me to walk back to the shore with the prescribed air of confidence in the precision of my planning and, after exactly three minutes, there was a powerful bang. The children were held back while I went to inspect the damage to the reef but, within seconds of the smoke clearing, they uttered a loud groan of disappointment. They had been expecting the end of the island to disappear but, from a distance, it looked just the same as before.

From nearby, also, I found the coral looking much the same as before and had some difficulty in discovering the exact spot where I had placed the charge. Then I found a small dish on the reef surface, less than a foot deep and with a little coral dust resting in it: the only fair description of my experiment had to be "wholly ineffective". The one point in that explosion's favour was that it had not broken any glass. Seldom can a group of spectators have been more disappointed and seldom had I been more embarrassed. Gerry Douglas, very understandably, showed his concern: if this were the best we could do, there was little hope of his reef channels ever being built.

Once we had had time to think, Jack and I decided that the ineffectiveness of the explosion must have been due to the manner in which the Forcex had been initiated. What I had been told, about a detonator alone being sufficient, might well be true if the explosive were used in boreholes, as it would have been for phosphate quarrying on Ocean Island. In that case, the relatively slow development of the explosive's power, with the charge fully contained in the phosphate, would be perfectly acceptable. However, a surface charge would never have a chance of cutting into the coral unless it delivered its energy as quickly as possible.

We were convinced that, another time, it would be better to add a booster charge, or primer, to the detonator. "It is such a pity we have no primers with us," was our excuse to Gerry. He, polite fellow, said that he was relieved to know there was an answer to our problem. Meanwhile, Jack and I remained ill at ease, as there would be no means of confirming our theories until after we returned to Christmas Island, and before then our firm proposals would be required.

We were very happy to abandon coral blasting for that day but did not want to leave Nui without buying some of the beautiful fans for which the island was renowned. Like most things locally, they originated from coconut trees, with the boiled and shredded leaves providing a form of stiff raffia, rather like chair cane, that could then be woven, usually into concentric circles of differently dyed colours. Six inches across was the normal diameter for a fan, but that was increased by weaving coloured feathers in around the edge. With a handle added, these fans made good fly whisks, but making contact with the flies was difficult in the constant breeze.

The Government Rest House, Nui.

Lotto knew we wanted fans and, after a while, a man arrived with two, saying that not many were made nowadays. In a place where money was seldom used, we found it difficult to put a price on what was on offer, but one Australian pound (78 new pence) for the two was happily agreed, and we were assured that those who had made them would be pleased.

Just as we were going to leave Nui, the Chief of Kaubure arrived, saying how very sorry he was not to have been able to give us his attention earlier. He brought with him three beautiful fans, one each as gifts for Gerry, Jack and me. This was as kind as it was unexpected, and we were hard pressed to keep our earlier purchases hidden, as we were wearing very few clothes in which to secrete them.

The Chief of Kaubure invited us to honour him and Nui by signing the island's visitors' book, which, with due ceremony, we were pleased to do.

Our signatures followed that of Sir John Gutch, High Commissioner of the Western Pacific, a personage of excellent repute, to whom H.H. Mr Bernacchi, the Resident Commissioner of the Colony, reported. We could not help noticing that the signatures of those highly influential London Missionary Society visitors, who had been ahead of us that morning, did not appear in the book. Perhaps, in the excitement, someone had forgotten to ask them to sign.

Chapter Eleven

A HEADACHE THAT LIFTED

By the time the canoes took us back to *Nareau,* I had a splitting headache. If you are sensitive to them, and I am, nitro-glycerine headaches have a very special power. That headache gave me positive confirmation that the Forcex we had just used was based on nitro-glycerine, so the liquid in the box beside my bed must also be nitro-glycerine.

As many burglars' widows knew, nitro-glycerine was not the kind of stuff to keep around the house. It was known in the trade as "burglar's soup", because, in its liquid form, it poured well into the keyholes of safes. In the same form, though, it was highly sensitive and, let alone needing a detonator, a good shake could prove sufficient to make it go off.

The forty pounds of Forcex that remained beside my bunk would easily have blown the stern off *Nareau* and, much as I wished to rest my aching head, I knew that I would not sleep soundly with it still in my cabin. Gerry gave me his instant permission to dump the rest of his hard won explosive; in no mood for charitable thoughts, we could now understand why those on Ocean Island had made us the gift of it.

Soon after we left Nui, Gerry cleared the aft end of the ship while Jack and I disposed of the Forcex. We opened the French windows of the cabin, put the box on the small patch of deck and then, as gently as was possible, dropped it into *Nareau's* foaming wake. There was no explosion and the box soon disappeared. I laid my sore head on my bunk and missed dinner; Gerry said later how wise I had been to miss the meal, stewed tuna in onion sauce.

We would have liked to go further down the Ellice Islands and Bill would have taken us, but there could be no question of keeping a Hastings aircraft waiting for us at Tarawa, so time simply would not allow. The more was the pity, as Vaitupu, that island of beautiful repute, was only another day away. Instead, we headed north, back to Nanumea, the island we had previously missed.

The next morning I still had my nitro-glycerine headache so, as Gerry expected the task at Nanumea to be very much the same as at Nui, I asked Jack if, with Gerry's help, he could make the reconnaissance without me. Feeling as I did that morning, I would happily have entrusted my responsibilities to others much less capable than them.

Nanumea Island sent out three canoes to greet us, each manned by four

Rover Scouts, Nanumea.

extremely smart Rover scouts. They all wore well pressed khaki shirts and shorts and their red and white neck triangles were secured with just the same kind of toggles that I remembered from my prep school scouting days. Two of the twelve, presumably the leaders, wore best quality broad-brimmed scouts' hats, of which Baden-Powell would have approved. The whole effect was most impressive and we wondered, with some embarrassment, whether a similar reception had awaited us two days before when we had gone to the wrong island.

Gerry and Jack went ashore in *Nareau's* launch, with which the scouts, in their outrigger canoes, easily kept station. Jack was, as usual in his working clothes, bathing trunks and favourite loose blue shirt but Gerry added a little tone with his khaki topi. Pith helmets had gone out of fashion in India well before I left in 1947 but Gerry still wore his with an air of authority. Even before the visitors and their escort reached the shore, my headache started to lift and I regretted not being with them, but welcomed the chance to catch up with my visit reports.

Jack and Gerry returned to *Nareau* in the afternoon, well satisfied with their day's work. However, Jack was obviously not his normal cheerful self, with something weighty on his mind. Although I was his officer commanding and he was my squadron sergeant-major, our relationship throughout the trip had been informal and relaxed. Now, out of the blue, he addressed me in an excessively military manner. "How, sir," and he stressed the "sir", "did you know not to come ashore with us this morning?"

"But sergeant-major," I replied, "You know that I would have liked to be with you, but I had that shocking headache." He gave me a real old soldier look of disbelief but soon repented and told me his story.

"You saw those canoe loads of scouts. Well, the moment we got ashore, they, plus some others, lined up in three ranks, ready for inspection. That would have been your job, sir, but Gerry wouldn't do it, so I had to take the salute and inspect every one of them, dressed in this shirt and these bathing trunks!"

I thought that all had been explained, but worse was to come and, with every fresh word, I thanked providence for preventing my attendance ashore. Knowing that the instructors on his guards' drill course would haunt him for ever, Jack had completed his inspection, whereupon the scouts sat down in a neat circle and asked that either Jack, or Gerry, should brief them on current affairs, such as the trouble in the Belgian Congo. Now, one of *Nareau's* pleasures was our complete lack of contact with the outside world, so we had no recent news of anything.

However, Lotto had proceeded to translate some thoroughly awkward questions, thus showing that his qualities as an interpreter were improving. After a sticky start, Jack and Gerry had handled them jointly, and claimed to have bluffed their way through the session better than they had expected.

Not for me, or anyone else, though, did they wish to repeat the experience.

Despite my questionable luck in remaining aboard, I really wished that I had met those enterprising young men of Nanumea. It was ironic that Jack and I each had a suit of Army uniform with us and, had he known what to expect, Jack could so easily have worn his that day.

Later, I was told about the reef channels. Mr Kennedy had started to blast one on Nanumea, just as he had on Nui but, again, had been unable to join it to the sea. Then, in the war, the Americans attempted to build a major passage into the lagoon, much as we saw on Canton Island. However, the tide race proved excessive and they had to drop the project.

Jack's recommendation, which I fully supported, was for Mr Kennedy's channel to be deepened and completed. He then gave me the copious notes that he had written, with his long lists of measurements and left me to write them up into another report. Never again would I desert my team in its hour of need! Later that evening, I found Gerry and Jack on the stern deck, both with beer and the latter with his pipe well alight, whiling away their well deserved rest. They were making a good start at eating a gigantic bunch of bananas that they had been given ashore.

On Tuesday, 16th August 1960, we were chugging from the Ellice Islands towards Arorae, the most southerly of the Gilbert Islands, when *Nareau's* wireless operator received a telegram for us from Tarawa. It told

Gerry Douglas and Jack Cheeseman on Nareau.

The reef flat, Arorae, with Nareau *in distance.*

us that an unexpected visit by a Royal New Zealand Air Force Sunderland flying boat had used up all the fuel on Tarawa that had been reserved for our return flight. Christmas Island had been informed and new plans had been made. Instead of making direct trips, a Hastings from Christmas Island would now divert through Canton both ways and refuel there, so that no fuel would be needed on Tarawa.

We wondered how many other uncertainties were still ahead of us, but realised how lucky we were to have good friends on Christmas Island acting on our behalf. However, the plane would arrive two days later than previously scheduled, so we need be in no hurry, after all. If only we had known earlier, we could have seen more of the Ellice Islands.

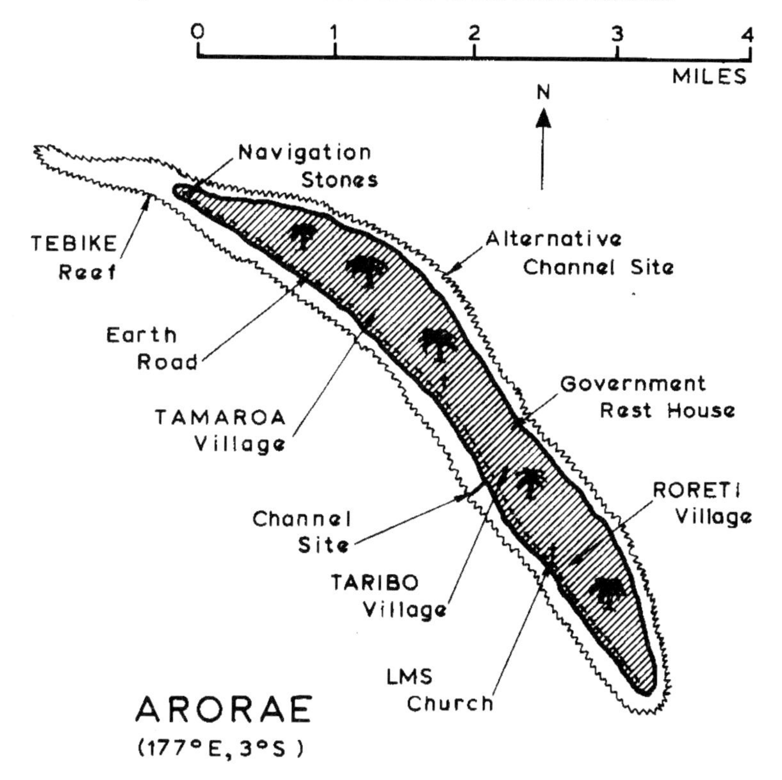

Instead, Gerry Douglas was delighted that we could now spend more time in the southern Gilberts and immediately added another couple of islands to the list of those we would visit. I did not fully share his enthusiasm, as every island meant at least one more formal report, of which the writing, now that we had perfected our methods ashore, took longer than the reconnaissance itself. Those reports reminded me of writing up many, many, practical afternoons in the engineering laboratories at Cambridge. One or two could be interesting, but too many became tedious.

I still had little faith in the explosive techniques I was recommending and needed some happy reassurance, which the Island of Arorae gave us. Percy

Roberts had told me that it was one of his favourites and I soon saw why. A reef island with no lagoon, Arorae was about five miles long and only half a mile wide, with some 1,700 Gilbertese living there. *Nareau* was able to anchor opposite the landing place on the west coast; it was a lovely sunny day, the sea was calm and I had eaten a good breakfast.

The invariable cheerfulness of the islanders added greatly to the pleasure of our visits. Both in the Gilberts and in the Ellice Islands, the local populations were obviously happy with their lots, to the extent that they kept telling us, without being prompted, that British rule suited them fine and that they couldn't understand all they heard of so many other places demanding independence. Apart from on the capital atoll of Tarawa, there were next to no white men in the colony so the islands were left to make their own way, which, they apparently did efficiently to their own satisfaction and, so far as it mattered, to that of the government. There was probably an advantage in being able to ask for help from Tarawa, if needed, but mainly the islands preferred to be self sufficient.

It was a great pleasure for Jack and me, who had seen things very different elsewhere, to find everyone well fed and generally fit. Nobody needed to be a beggar and everyone had time to behave with dignity and politeness. Even the children, about whom we had our reservations when they were at their most boisterous, knew that they were loved.

Both the Gilbertese and the Ellice were proud races and, as we had seen with the ships' crews, worked well together. The Ellice were lighter skinned, a more apricot brown than the darker Gilbertese, but they all had black hair which, on some of the Ellice, tended towards fuzziness. Not a great number of the grown ups with whom we dealt spoke English, so it was a pity that we had to converse through interpreters, thus never had a proper chance to make friends.

* * *

Before we arrived, I had had some forebodings about the islanders of Arorae, as I had read in Grimble's *Return to the Islands* how he had been sent there, more than thirty years before our visit, to investigate what had nearly become a mutiny against British rule. The trouble had been caused by an ignorant and officious colonial officer on temporary duty. He had been quickly removed, so far as anything could happen quickly in the colony with communications as they were, after which peace and the British had happily reigned again. That unfortunate affair was never mentioned during our visit and, the longer we were on Arorae, the more we were impressed with all we saw and the less we could believe there had ever been trouble there.

Arorae was strongly Protestant, with the London Missionary Society having a firm hold, so we expected to find a church at the end of the channel we would be asked to plan. In fact, the nearest church was seven hundred yards away, so, in that respect also, Arorae gained our approval. At that distance, to break windows with reef blasting would be quite an achievement.

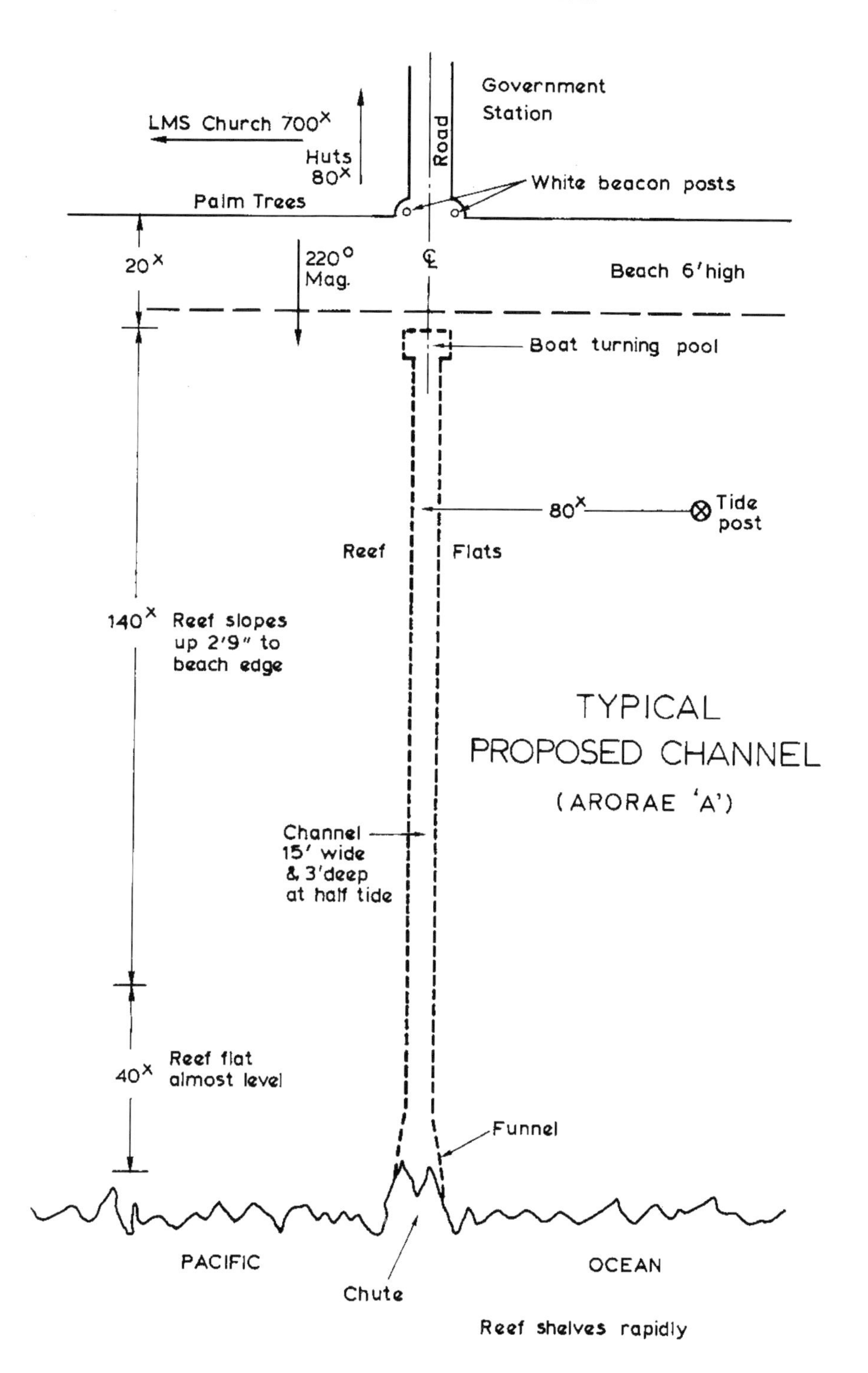
Government
Station
LMS Church 700^x
Huts
80^x
Road
White beacon posts
Palm Trees
20^x
220°
Mag.
℄
Beach 6' high
Boat turning pool
80^x
Tide
post
Reef
Flats
140^x
Reef slopes
up 2'9" to
beach edge
TYPICAL
PROPOSED CHANNEL
(ARORAE 'A')
Channel
15' wide
& 3' deep
at half tide
40^x
Reef flat
almost level
Funnel
PACIFIC
OCEAN
Chute
Reef shelves rapidly

The Chief of Kaubure, named Tavia, was obviously an outstandingly strong character. He made all the village children sit in rows and kept them there while Jack and I took measurements in the water lying over the reef flat. I nearly lost control of my own legs near the reef edge, where the current was much stronger than I expected and, for a moment, I thought I was going to be washed over it. Even on a lovely day, the idea of swimming out to sea and waiting to be rescued did not attract me; at least that taught me not to become over-confident.

When we emerged from the water, Jack and I went to the telegraph office to send telegrams home, an excitement for the telegraphist and an experience for us. Jack's younger son's first birthday was the next day, and it took him an age to cut down all he wanted to say to the small number of words necessary to qualify for the cheap rates.

My message home to Judy was more easily drafted and fitted into the prescribed form, so, while Jack was again rewording his, I reminded Lotto, who found his duties as the ship's interpreter more varied than his apprentice officer routine, that he had failed to buy me a grass skirt to send home from the Ellice Islands. "Please, can we try again here in Arorae?" I asked. No sooner had I said this, than a wizened old lady wearing a grass skirt pedalled past on her bicycle. Without hesitation, Lotto called her back imperiously and must have said something like, "The English Major wants your grass skirt".

The poor old girl looked horrified and embarrassed but, both on the grounds of modesty and of hygiene, I felt worse. I quickly uttered a desperate "No, No !", to the extent that Lotto took my point, but he was obviously highly disappointed that his fine effort had been in vain. Blushingly, I then managed to explain, at least to Lotto, that: (a) I did not mean *that* grass skirt, (b) My requirements were not immediate, and (c) I only had one Australian pound with me that I could spare.

The lady then adjusted her skirt around the saddle again, with much rustling, and bicycled off with evident relief. I imagined that some good stories might develop in the maneaba (meeting house) that evening: I also began to realise how easily trouble could be initiated, not only by inexperienced colonial officers.

As we made our way around Arorae, Jack's demeanour became more and more sergeant-majory, with his chest puffed out and his voice booming ever deeper: it was the whitewash that had most impressed him. It was said in the Army, "If it moves, salute it and if it doesn't move, whitewash it!" Arorae had kept the latter rule to the letter. Every possible building, wall or stone, had been recently whitewashed and the whole island was spotlessly clean, as if ready for an annual inspection, though we had arrived almost without warning. Arorae was like that every day, as whitewash was available in abundance. Just bake some coral on a fire of coconut husks, and you end up with the same kind of lime that comes from the baking of chalk in other parts of the world.

We walked across to the other side of the island to look at the very good government rest house. The main furniture consisted of a couple of four-poster double beds with string springs: the posts were, presumably, for the hanging of mosquito nets. There were also good outhouses, for the kitchen and for clothes washing, and the water from the well tasted drinkable.

As on most of the other islands, a party of up to eight people could have made themselves fairly comfortable in the rest house and, for various reasons, this was the number I envisaged might be sent from England to blast the channels. I had in mind a group of two officers and six experienced non-commissioned officers, so that work could be done on two nearby islands at the same time. As it happened, that was the size of the party which, in 1962, put many of our proposals into effect.

On our way back to our landing point by a fresh route, we passed some remarkably deep and well engineered babai pits, luxuriant with their root-like vegetables that could have been the envy of many timber merchants. We praised one particular pit of superb quality and the Chief of Kaubure was able to declare proudly that it was his. Neither he, nor we, could do wrong in each other's eyes that day!

There was said to be another potential channel site further up the island and, as Gerry was keen to study some old navigation stones on the northern tip, we borrowed bicycles. They were of a remarkably high standard, showing that money came into the island: evidently, local men were recruited for the relatively well paid phosphate excavation work on Ocean Island.

High standard those bikes might be but, as usual, they had no brakes. Our guide was a policeman, whose only word of English was "cowboys". Its relevance soon became clear, because the bicycle path lay along a three feet wide ridge, with babai pits up to fifteen feet deep on either side. The frequent corners in the path were often masked by pandanus palms and we found that short trip excessively exciting.

I performed my wading-on-the-reef act at the alternative channel site, of which we didn't think much, so carried on round to Gerry's stones. They could well be ancient, but looked like a set of dull and dirty rocks, which didn't catch my imagination. But, to Gerry, the Superintendent of Marine, navigation was an important subject and one which he did not wish lightly to drop. Even our guide lacked Gerry's enthusiasm for Arorae's most noteworthy antiquities but eventually was prevailed upon to try to find an old man who might be able to answer questions.

With lunch in mind, we cycled back to our starting point down a wide coral road that ran from end to end of the island. With coconut palms down both sides, it made an impressive boulevard, all the more impressive because there were no vehicles, not even a decent handcart, on Arorae. That road was a considerable status symbol and yet another sign of the island's pride. I estimated that its surface occupied over twenty acres of fertile land, also that each acre could have produced more than two thousand coconuts a year. When we asked how many coconuts everyone ate, the cautious answer was four to ten a day each for the Gilbertese with, for reasons unexplained, up to double that number for the Ellice Islanders. Small wonder that not many coconuts were spare for producing copra!

While we waited for the canoes to take us out to *Nareau,* we all agreed that the girls on Arorae were as pretty as any we had seen in the colony, and our judgement was influenced not just by time at sea. Their grass skirts were undyed, so could have appeared dull, but when hung from the hips over a longer and brightly coloured cloth skirt, with a bra of the same material, the overall effect was very attractive. Sadly, though, the girls all seemed to acquire babies while still very young, then quickly lost their beautiful figures.

* * *

After lunch our policeman was still away looking for the old man who knew about the navigation stones, so we walked to inspect a second fine church, also sponsored by the London Missionary Society and also, fortunately, nowhere near where explosives might be used. The LMS was akin to the Methodist Church at home, whose chapels were often ugly, but these colony churches were in happy contrast.

While we were still walking, a young mother approached us carrying a brand new grass skirt. She told Lotto that she had only finished making it that morning, but would be happy to sell it to me. The young lady was wearing a rather dowdy cloth around her middle so, not wishing to cause further misunderstanding, I was keen to establish that she possessed another grass skirt for her own use. Lotto assured me that she did and my price of one Australian pound was readily agreed. Later, Lotto told me that I had got good value for money as, in his view, the true beauty of a grass skirt lay in its seductive rustle, and the one I had bought rustled just right.

The mass of children now attending us kept mimicking our every movement. They were convinced that the nearly naked Englishman had bought the skirt to wear himself, and their anticipation of my discovery that it was much too small was proving hard to contain. I had to ask Lotto to impress upon the children that I would be sending the skirt to my wife in England, also that I was sure she would wish to thank the lady who made it. Dare I say it but, when it eventually arrived home, Judy herself found it a little tight, also rather tickly around the tummy. Lotto had done his best for me, but the children continued to giggle and smirk until the Chief of Kaubure took personal control.

For those who have not seen a Gilbertese grass skirt of the then latest (1960) fashion, it may be worth giving some details of what was in vogue. As I have mentioned, they were not made from grass, but from the backs of coconut leaves that had been torn into thin strips and dried in the sun. These were boiled and again dried, to produce strands of vegetation that looked like light brown hay, thus "grass". One half of the hay-like strands were left in their brown form, to be worn next to the body, but the outside layer was bleached in more sun, to a greyish white colour. The waistband, also a misnomer, as the skirts were designed to be slung around the hips, was formed from a double length of coconut string on which, inside, were knotted the brown strands and, outside, the bleached material. Eight knots to the inch was about the norm and, when complete, the skirt was carefully combed and then trimmed to a length of sixteen inches. The skirt I purchased had a "hip" of thirty inches and weighed one and a half pounds.

Our policeman friend at last brought in Arorae's oldest inhabitant on the handlebars of his bicycle, from three miles away. The old boy looked exceedingly ancient, but only claimed to be seventy-two; he was certainly game, even if he was as deaf as he was old. After much shouting through interpreters, I managed to get him to smile for a photograph. A shocking toothless grin was the result, but the dear old man seemed to be enjoying all the attention.

We returned to the navigation stones, where Gerry and the old man sat facing out to sea, but with Lotto and the old man's own interpreter sitting between them. Lotto translated Gerry's questions into Gilbertese and then the No. 2 interpreter shouted the questions to the island's oldest inhabitant. In the same way, the relay of messages brought the answers, except that Lotto told the No. 2 interpreter that there was no need to shout. After a little while, Lotto realised that he could shout the questions himself, but No. 2 interpreter was slightly hurt to be left out of the fun. Unfortunately, the old man remembered very little about the stones, which was hardly surprising, as he lived at the far end of the island, and seldom came to the north.

The very idea of navigation stones made us marvel how anyone managed

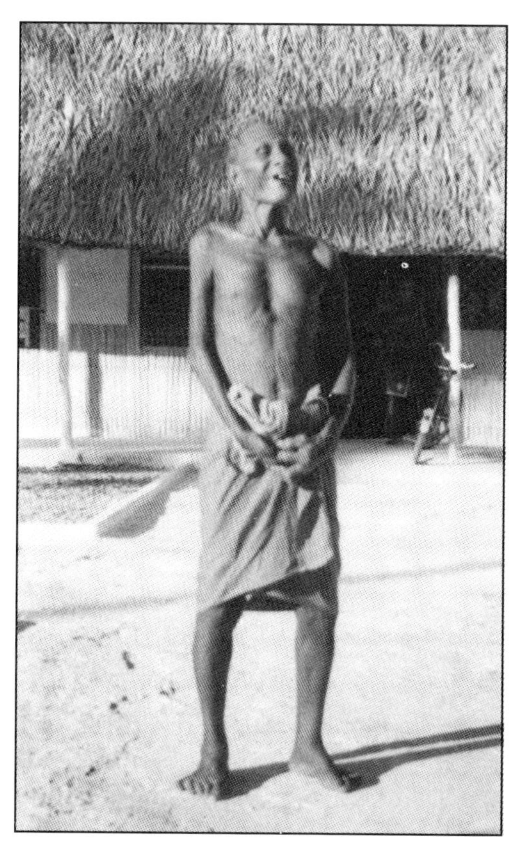

Arorae's oldest inhabitant.

to find their way between the islands, very few of which were in sight of each other. Quite apart from direction, there was always the "set" cross current, as we had ourselves learnt. If *Nareau,* complete with compass, chronometer and sextant, still had difficulties, navigation in the central Pacific could never have been easy.

On our way back to the landing place, an islander offered us two Gilbertese swords, for each of which we managed to find another pound. They were beautifully made and, even if models, were certainly not toys. The straight handle and blade were of pandanus palm wood, on to which sharks' teeth and the pincers of "pen-knife" fish had been sewn, all resulting in weapons of decorative but awesome appearance.

As we had seen with the Nui fans and now the grass skirt and swords, the islanders were capable of producing lovely craft work from materials that cost them nothing, and yet there were not many of such items on offer. It cannot have been a case of "So sorry, but we are too busy to make them," as filling the days must have been a problem for many of the inhabitants. We supposed that, with no trippers to buy them, there was little point in making them. Our impression was that most of the islanders, and the government of the colony, were glad not to have tourists.

We were very sorry to leave Arorae, of whose inhabitants the Chief of Kaubure was such a splendid example. We gave him baccy for himself, the policeman and the oldest inhabitant, and sweets for the children, who, for the first time that day, became utterly out of control.

We helped carry our canoes the couple of hundred yards across the dry reef flat, to be launched in a small natural chute on the reef's edge. They were heavy and we wished that the channel we had planned had already been built.

Chapter Twelve

"ONE MORE ISLAND"

We had been warned to expect cockroaches on *Nareau* but had not met any. Ants were a different matter and the ship's speciality was very small ones, which quickly discovered the sweets reserved for the islanders and stowed in the desk drawer of Gerry's and my cabin. As I wrote up my report about Arorae, the ants were all over the paper but, as they did not bite and were messy if squashed, co-existence became the rule.

I was recommending just one channel for Arorae, the one where we had landed and was feeling a little more confident about the amount of explosive required to do the job. Gerry was talking of work on ten or twelve islands so, if Arorae were typical, we would be thinking of a total of thirty or forty tons of explosive.

The procurement of explosives in adequate quantities now became the greatest unknown factor in my planning. In wartime conditions, we just asked for the explosives we needed and someone else provided them, probably with some to spare. Things would be different in the middle of the Pacific Ocean in peacetime.

Gerry had very little previous experience with explosives but, the more he learnt about them, the more he realised that, in his position of authority, he must stick to the safety rules. I asked for details of them, but Gerry said he would have to check his manuals back in Tarawa. Basically, any ship carrying explosives needed to have a designated magazine with a sparkfree lining, meaning wooden, not metal, walls. The magazine would also have to be well clear of fire hazards, such as people smoking or cooking. As far as he could see, the only legal answer would be to reserve a ship's hold specially as a magazine, then have it lined in wood and sealed against fire. That would be easier said than done, because all the colony vessels had only one hold each.

Even if the problems of transporting and storing explosives could be overcome, that of their cost still remained. In England I had been given a figure of £700 a ton for plastic high explosive with which to plan, so forty tons would knock an appreciable hole in my total budget of £70,000. We talked again of wartime surplus explosives but, even if offered free, they would probably prove more trouble than they were worth.

Despite his official reservations, Gerry was increasingly enthusiastic about the whole scheme succeeding and now wanted to visit as many islands as possible before returning to Tarawa in just under a week's time. By then, *Nareau* would be short of fuel, and a lack of variety in the menu was already evident!

The next morning at 7 a.m., before dawn broke, we were ashore on Tamana, our next island. It was a reef atoll, very similar to Arorae but sixty miles to its west and, at only three miles long, even smaller. We got very wet in the canoe going ashore and then very cold, all a mistake before breakfast.

When we discovered there was a superb LMS church, with all its windows of stained glass, just at the end of the channel that was requested, I said, "No!" so firmly that Tamana's Chief of Kaubure then admitted that it would matter very little if the channel were cut three hundred yards further along the reef. We then planned a task very similar to that at Arorae. We were only ashore for an hour, an adequate minimum for a now standard requirement. The children were still at home, which helped enormously but, with finishing so quickly, we had the nagging thought that we must have forgotten something vital.

Gerry had planned to do another island the same day, so we immediately sailed for Onotoa, a lagoon island fifty miles to the north-west. Our short visit to Tamana had produced me three hours of report writing and I had run out of seasickness pills. Each coral atoll had its own reef characteristics and I knew how easily I could muddle things up, right proposal, wrong island, if I did not write them up immediately.

At 4 p.m. we arrived off Onotoa, which turned out to be quite a big island, with a population of nearly 2,000. The location of a leper colony was marked on its elderly chart but had nothing to do with the islanders' reputation for remarkable average stupidity, of which they were rather proud.

Proven or not, that reputation had been perpetuated since pre-war, when a District Officer lived there. He had had a white obelisk built and, when asked what it was for, replied, "To commemorate the stupidity of the people of this island!" There had been no resident DO for many years, but the obelisk remained for all to see and had recently been whitewashed. Stupid or not, we found the requirements for boat channels, as requested by the local populace, completely incomprehensible. Those who tried to explain them to us were out to be helpful but confused us further.

Onotoa's lagoon was full of coral heads and we had an unpleasant trip dodging them in *Nareau's* launch. Bill had come with us, as he wanted to buy some chickens and, on enquiry, was offered four at £5 each. He looked horrified, and said that he had bought birds just as good for ten shillings each in the Ellice Islands only a week before, which we knew to be true. "Well, fancy," uttered the chickens' owner, "if that should be the price, of course you can have them for ten shillings each." If Bill had asked for the chickens as a gift, he might well have been given them. This little encounter only confirmed that money meant very little; apart from the items on sale in the Wholesale Society stores, there were no means of comparing prices from island to island.

While trying to discover Onotoa's requirements for reef channels, we were shown a well constructed, quite modern, stone mole. It jutted out a couple of hundred yards into the lagoon but the water at the end of it remained shallow. It must have taken years to build and we all tried to look appreciative, before Gerry dared to ask what it was for. "We are sorry, but no one can remember," came the answer.

* * *

What with trips from India as a child and many journeys in troopships, I had spent nearly a year of my life at sea, so had often heard of the "green flash" at sunset, but had never met anyone who had seen it. It was said that, at the instant the sun went down over the ocean, occasionally a green flash would be seen on the horizon. If a young man had his girl beside him at such a time, the omens for marriage were good; here, on *Nareau,* though, there were no girls to enter competition with our wives at home.

However, after Onotoa, Bill and I were watching a lovely sunset, when we both said together, "That was the green flash!" It was vivid and of the shade emitted by a barium salt placed in the flame of a bunsen burner. That was a bit of school knowledge I never thought I would use, but I wished someone had also explained the reason for the green flash!

Gerry told us the next island at which we would call, Beru, was worth study, as more copra could be produced there than could easily be shipped out. He had said the same before we visited Maiana, where we had failed to make any useful proposals, but he promised Beru would be different. Its chart had been issued by the Admiralty Hydrographer but was headed "From the Japanese Government chart of 1943". So far as we discovered, it was accurate, so something good had stemmed from the wartime occupation of the Gilbert Islands!

Gerry was out to use every opportunity to extend the scope of our reconnaissance and it was at dawn again that we headed for the shore. We soon understood the first of Beru's two requests for reef channels as, even in a light sea, the canoe in which Jack and I were passengers bashed the reef edge, throwing one of our paddlers into the water. His friend followed him over the side, after beckoning to us to stay where we were. I, for one, had no intention of doing otherwise, and continued to grip the gunwales.

With the canoe lighter without their own weight, our two paddlers managed to swim it and us back seawards, a few yards out from the churning suction of the reef edge. They then held the canoe with its nose towards the reef and waited for a suitable wave on which to surf us over it. That they achieved, and we did not know whether to feel proud or embarrassed while they almost carried us, in the canoe, well up the reef flat. Both of them were completely unscathed and thought the episode a huge joke.

Had Jack and I gone overboard in the same circumstances, we would almost certainly have been severely grazed on the reef edge; that thought reminded me that the coral sores on my legs were no better. With the need for me to be in the water so frequently, they were having no chance to heal. "They'll get better when we are back in Tarawa," said Gerry soothingly.

Our plans for Beru could have met with complications, as the island was the local headquarters of the London Missionary Society, but we were delighted to find both the suggested channel sites were well clear of churches. What was more, we believed both the channels could be blasted. However, each of them was three hundred yards long (above average length), and could use up to ten tons of explosives each. With no habitation near either of the channel sites, a riotous nightlife could be excluded from our *hazards to working parties* answer.

At every place we went, Lotto continued to ask whether a visiting British party would be in danger when working in the water. He obviously thought that this was unnecessary and became shy when we pressed him to enquire. The answer, "None", which we regularly received, was the opposite to what we expected before we started our trip; reassuring perhaps, but we dared not be absolutely certain. Grimble might have been right.

The most memorable things we saw in the water were many lovely lumps of lichen coated coral and an amazing variety of small, multi-coloured fish. Unfortunately, the colours of both species faded quickly when they were out of the water. A small item but, to me an important one, was that on none of the islands we had visited, sixteen so far, had stonefish been reported.

* * *

I knew that, once we were back on Tarawa, I would be expected to present my preliminary recommendations to the Resident Commissioner and his Colony Secretariat. My outline plan was in constant flux, because there was always new information but, as expected, all questions boiled down to time and cost. Gerry gave me guidance on shipping costs, which fortunately were less than I had expected. *Nareau* was charged at only £50 a day (though few would have chartered her for fun), and *Moana Raoi*, the largest colony vessel, would only be about double that.

Considering those figures included the wages of the ships' crews, I concluded that it was not only Army pay that was poor. My pay, as a major, was just under £5 a day, which included twenty-two shillings of marriage allowance, all before tax.

The cost of a Hastings four-engined transport aircraft was still quoted at £1 for every three miles, so a return trip from Christmas Island to Tarawa, via Canton Island, was going to cost around £1,300. Overall, therefore, our six weeks reconnaissance would be charged at £4,000, which would have to be subtracted from the total of about £70,000 that was probably available for the whole project.

Whoever had estimated the project budget had set a tight target, particularly when the cost of transport of a small working party from England, with their pay and food for, say, nine months, would have to be included. However, it looked as if a full half of our proposals could be undertaken for the money. I very much hoped that that would prove to be the case!

I still imagined that enterprising individuals from somewhere in the

Pacific would offer to take over the reef channels project where our reconnaissance left off. To a reputable engineer, let alone a sea tramp, over £60,000 could sound like a fortune but, fortunately, no competitors had become apparent. Gerry was reassuring, saying there could be great problems in supervising an "unofficial" programme from Tarawa, also in inspecting such work before payment was made. He stressed that H.H. had his background in the Royal Navy and would, he was sure, like the job done by the services, so that he would know with whom he was dealing.

On 18th August, after supper and following another beautiful sunset (but no green flash!), we were sitting on deck and all noticed an unusually bright star scooting across the heavens.

Gerry said that it must be a satellite, and sightings of satellites, which were still novelties, were to be reported without delay. As Superintendent of Marine, he was keen to set a good example and took great trouble in measuring the bearing and positions of the assumed satellite against exact times. He transmitted his "satellite sighting message" in the prescribed form and returned to us and his coffee in the satisfaction of a job well done.

Soon, though, a further aspect to his report came to his mind. Before it was forwarded from Tarawa, the reliability of its source would have to be graded, from 1, meaning "wholly reliable" to 5, meaning "highly suspect". Gerry said that he would take it as an insult if his report were not awarded Grade 1 and would check back in Tarawa. He later found that his report had been rated only at Grade 4, meaning, at best, a poor source. Hardly surprisingly, this low grading hurt him, particularly as his own staff had made the assessment. Jack and I thought Gerry's low place in the grading table was exceedingly funny, as was its explanation, "No message initiated by a colony official after dinner should ever be awarded higher than Grade 4."

If I have not already made it clear, may I stress that Gerry Douglas was one of the most level headed men I ever met. Perhaps I should add that I never saw justification for the automatic downgrading of the reliability of colony officials after dinner! It turned out that the satellite we had seen was the American *Discovery XIV,* an enormous aluminium foil balloon that had been inflated in space to form a mirror that could be seen from the earth. Months later, after I had returned to Christmas Island, satellites adopted an important and unexpected place in our lives. Because of the vast expanse of ocean around there, with so little land for thousands of miles, both the Americans and the Russians had chosen that area as a harmless place to land the earliest of their space projectiles. It became anybody's game to see who could first find the nose capsule of whose rocket floating in the sea!

* * *

Tabiteuea, pronounced Tab-it-u-ear, was the next island we planned to visit and the manner in which Gerry talked about it sounded ominous. Its population of over 4,000 Gilbertese was, among the islands of the colony, second only to that of the capital, Tarawa. Nearly a thousand tons of copra a year were produced there and more would be possible, if it could be shipped out more easily than at present.

"Just like Maiana, again," Jack and I said to Gerry. He agreed but then was charitable enough to add, "and Beru, and you had some useful ideas there!" Tabiteuea would be a challenge for us and, as before, we could only promise to do our very best. We should never have made that promise, as many hours of thoroughly unpleasant wading on Tabiteuea's barrier reef yielded absolutely no prospect of success. My report told the disappointing story:

"We examined the barrier reef west of Utiroa with a view to clearing a ship passage eighty feet wide and fifteen feet deep but concluded that nothing could be gained by blasting at this stage. The reef is wide and indefinite in structure and the chart of Peacock Anchorage is dangerously in error. It is possible that, after a proper nautical survey, selected coral heads could be blasted to give a passage ten feet deep. However, this would still be of little avail, as the lagoon "beach" in front of the copra loading point turns into three-quarters of a mile of mainly mud at low tide. The shore at the alternative site, Terikiai, is wholly mud.

With no positive suggestions for a route from the lea shore through the lagoon, I examined the weather on the east shore of the island. Its fringing reef flat is fully four hundred yards wide, so any channel through it would be a major undertaking of doubtful value."

During our day at Tabiteuea, Lotto thought I might like to know that, on Beru, various people had commented on how brown my skin was. Evidently the few other Europeans they had seen, including the missionaries, were white, and it had caused great interest to see an Englishman who was so brown.

I had, in fact, noticed that I had received more than my share of attention on Beru and was now relieved to discover the reason. I just hoped that being considered brown, by brown people, could be taken as a compliment. "Did they not say the same about the sergeant-major and Mr Douglas?" I asked.

"Not really," said Lotto, "because they wear shirts." I explained that I had arrived quite brown from Christmas Island, where we worked wearing only our shorts, boots and socks, and had got browner working on the reefs around the colony. Lotto appeared satisfied and hoped that I had not minded him asking; I hadn't but had never previously viewed myself, in the circus sense, as a curiosity.

To visit the weather side of Tabiteuea we borrowed bicycles at the government station, with the kind assistance of the island's assistant medical officer, or AMO. Despite his title, he was the only medical officer on the large atoll, so his responsibility for 4,000 people, with no normal medical chain behind him, was considerable. He hastened to explain to us, in perfect English which he can seldom have practised, that he was not a fully qualified doctor, but was happy to tackle any problems that came his way. Like all the colony's AMOs, he had done his four years medical training in Fiji.

He showed us round his hospital with great pride, much as had the matron of the Colony Hospital on Tarawa and, as we saw there, if one member of a family were admitted to hospital, so were an adequate number of relatives to nurse the patient. As on Tarawa, it was often difficult to tell which was the ill member of the family. The hospital had twenty huts, with a family, including a patient, in each: apart from a couple of medical dressers and the AMO himself, there was no permanent staff, a fine example of economic management.

We were greatly impressed by that young AMO of Tabiteuea, who was a great credit to the education system of the colony. Primary schooling was still in the hands of the missions but government higher education had made great strides since the war, so that most of the younger people on the islands were literate and keen to learn more.

Like Maiana, Tabiteuea needed some constructive ideas from us regarding reef channels and we felt sorry, almost guilty, for having none. We tried to explain this to the AMO as we congratulated him on his achievements and thanked him for helping us. As it was, it was he who thanked us profusely for our visit and interest, so perhaps all had not been in vain.

Jack and I expected Tabiteuea to be the last island we visited before our return to Tarawa but Gerry proposed that we add just one more, Kuria, to end our programme. From the channels point of view, Tabiteuea had proved something of an anti-climax, so we hoped that Kuria might revive our spirits and arranged to call there the next morning.

The small island of Kuria lay west of our old friend Aranuka and only a hundred miles south of Tarawa. We crossed the equator from south to north overnight and arrived on 20th August. That was the day, we learnt later, that the Soviets launched their *Sputnik V* satellite. It had two dogs, (Strelka and Belka), two rats and forty mice on board, and was successfully retrieved after eighteen revolutions of the earth. I don't know what happened to the animals but would like to think that they lived happily ever after.

Meanwhile, life in the Gilbert Islands carried on as normal and Kuria felt a very long way from the modern world. We thought it one of the most lovely islands we had visited, the only snag being that the inhabitants wanted a passage blasted in what we were sure was the wrong place. By now we had visited over thirty suggested channel sites, so had a fair idea of which were, and which were not, likely to prove successful.

Kuria consisted of two small reef islands, linked together by a sandbar only a hundred yards across, which dried out at low tide. Most of the copra came from the southern island, so it had perhaps been logical to build the copra store there. Logical, except that the shore there could only be reached by copra boats on the highest of spring tides; otherwise it was inaccessible across half a mile of mud.

We pointed out that, if we blasted a channel through the mud, it would fill in again in no time. Only with great reluctance was this accepted, but we were then taken along a good track towards an alternative site on the other islet. At half tide, we were just able to wade across the sandbar from south to north; the most direct route would have taken us out of our depth, so we were glad to have a guide who knew which way to go. Personally, I was pleased to be carrying the wooden measuring rod, which floated, rather than Jack's crowbar, which did not.

Once we were out of the water we saw a natural channel in the coral lying between a ledge and a spit of sand; it looked attractively sheltered and would be easily approachable with a copra boat at most tides. In addition, a new copra store could be built there without difficulty. "Then what's wrong with this place?" Jack, Gerry and I all asked almost together. The answer was, "We couldn't get the copra here, because of the ferry."

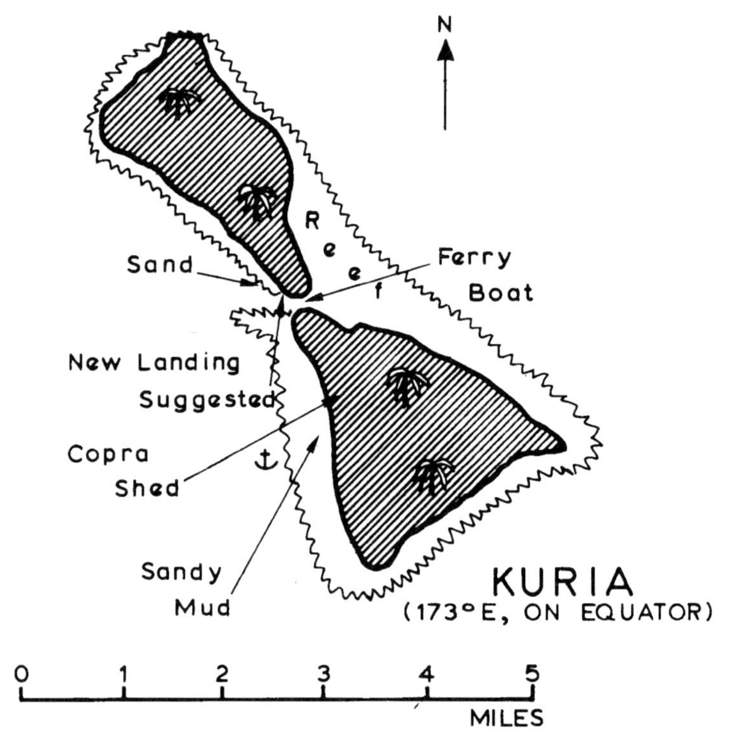

The flat bottomed boat lying on the beach by the sandbar turned out to be the ferry. It was privately owned, and a toll of three old pence a head was extracted from every passenger who wished to be paddled or poled across the gap between the islets. It could carry three quarters of a ton of copra, but its owner, who happened to be away, had (unusually for an islander) a good eye for business!

Our recommendation for a new channel on Kuria was to use the northerly site, with the Wholesale Society buying out the ferry owner and his rights, then providing a more suitable boat for ferrying the copra across from the south islet. Gerry thought this sounded too simple and was sure there must be a snag, but the plan was worth trying. We heard later that the new system worked; how we wished all our recommendations could have been as effective!

During the first three weeks of our trip, when we had been for much of the time with the Resident Commissioner and his wife, Mr Bernacchi had made it clear that if any ideas, however unorthodox, came to mind for improving the economy of the colony, he would be very glad to hear of them. H.H. had stressed that Jack and I would be making an unusually extensive, and in its way unique, tour of the colony, and hoped we would not restrict our interests entirely to advising on reef channels. This may have been why he had given us some background to the financial affairs of the colony; with the phosphate deposits nearly worked out, and with the increasing population eating more coconuts, he had admitted that the long term prospects looked anything but rosy.

Jack and I were not, of course, the first to think of tourism as an alternative, but we soon saw its snags. The three main ones were the lack of communications, the danger from the sun and the scarcity of good bathing beaches.

We had noted the possibility of sea bathing at Marakei but, here on Kuria, we found an attractive bathing spot. It was a beach of silver sand, close to the natural channel on the north islet and we all agreed that it would be a lovely place for children. That said, it wasn't a very big beach and mothers just might have worried about sharks and other dwellers of the deep. Swimming pools ashore were coming into vogue elsewhere, but we thought that Pacific atolls should be able to do better than that.

We were probably over sensitive about the capacity of the reflected sun to burn and almost blind newcomers, but the necessary precautions could well prove irksome. When it came to communications, we hoped that our proposed channels would make access to many islands easier but the problem of reaching Tarawa to start a holiday remained. The colony needed proper airfields, but these would be unlikely to materialise unless a flow of tourists was assured. The more we saw, the more we considered that the exploitation of tourism in the colony would not be easy.

That very few visitors would be likely to follow us in the foreseeable future made us all the more aware of the opportunities we had been given. We would have much liked to come forward with some money-spinning suggestions, but we did not, and the more was the pity, as we had formed a great respect and liking for those fine and charming islanders. We just hoped that some of our coral channel proposals would one day come to profit.

Chapter Thirteen

TAKING STOCK

From Kuria to Tarawa was another overnight trip and there was no point in pretending that I would not be glad to be leaving the Motor Vessel *Nareau* very soon. I had no stomach for the way she wallowed, nor for her culinary speciality, tuna in onion sauce. Gerry Douglas had the advantage over Jack and me, as he could say that he was looking forward to being back with his family. However, we hoped that we thanked Bill and his crew appropriately, of whom the indomitable helmsman of the ship's launch and our long suffering interpreter, Lotto, were the most memorable. It was not their fault that their ship had been built the way she was.

The Bernacchis were still away at the magistrates' conference when we arrived back on Bairiki. With them away, Jack and I obviously could not stay at the Residency, as we had on our two previous visits to Tarawa, and we were put up at the local club. It, like some of the government rest houses on the smaller islands, was available for visitors but, because there were so few of them, was seldom used. If the Residency equated to Buckingham Palace, unfortunately the Bairiki Club did not equate to Claridges. It took us a couple of days to settle in as the only occupants of the club and soon realised how very spoilt we had been at the Residency. However, many kind social invitations were waiting for us and we had no hope of fitting them all in.

I had arrived back with a nasty headache, one which, this time, I could not blame on nitro-glycerine. As my leg was throbbing as well as my head, I sought help from the local Gilbertese assistant medical officer. He diagnosed some blood poisoning, started by the coral sores on my shins and that accounted for my temperature of 103°F.

The AMO wanted to send me to the Colony Hospital, the one that we had visited with Elaine Bernacchi as our guide, but I would have to wait until the tide had dropped sufficiently for a vehicle to make the trip. In the meanwhile, he gave me a goodly dose of penicillin, which acted so quickly that, by the time the tide was down, so was my temperature. With a booster dose, I was as good as better the next morning but the AMO told me firmly to keep my legs dry, so as to kill off the coral in the sores.

Mr Roy Davies, the Secretary to the Government, called at the club to confirm that H.H. the Resident Commissioner hoped that, soon after his return, I would brief him on my preliminary recommendations. The

Bernacchis would only be back for a short stay before setting off for Ocean Island to celebrate the Diamond Jubilee of phosphate discovery there, so we agreed a time on Wednesday 23rd August. That gave me two days to bring my reports up to date and to clear my thoughts; as I had foreseen, it was a puzzle to remember what had happened on which atoll. Hull and Gardner, the first islands we had considered for reef channels, seemed a very long way away both in time and space, though it was only a month since we had been there.

Those were two very busy days for me, when, despite Jack's offers of help, I was best left alone. He put up his fishing rod but found that the prospects off the shore of Bairiki compared unfavourably with our own fishing spots on Christmas Island. His thoughts turned to what would await us back there, at work, and he became increasingly convinced that everything would not have been kept in a manner to his, the sergeant-major's, liking. I hoped that he was being pessimistic, but knew that he would enjoy sorting things out if needed. I, too, would have plenty of loose ends to pick up on Christmas Island, and was all the keener to press on with my coral channel work as much as possible while we were still on Tarawa.

When the Bernacchis returned from the conference, Elaine came to see us to say how sorry they were not to be putting us up but, apart from going away again, they had a visiting missionary staying for a couple of nights.

I made my presentation to H.H. in his office that Wednesday morning. Jack was with me, and Roy Davies, Gerry Douglas and a couple of other colony officials were also there. I had qualms about what I had to offer but received a better reception than I ever dared to hope. I foresaw that useful work could probably be done under Royal Engineers supervision on at least ten of the islands we had visited, but just how much could be undertaken depended on the cost limit of £70,000. I emphasised that my estimates, particularly for quantities of explosives, were highly approximate, as we still had not tried out most of the techniques we were proposing.

H.H. understood the uncertainties and made various encouraging comments; indeed, his personal enthusiasm for the project had been a tremendous boost to us throughout our trip. He and Gerry Douglas had originated the idea of the reef channels and it was clear that they would be as sad as us if they did not materialise.

On points of detail, I did not need to explain the complete lack of engineer resources around the colony, but did mention the great asset of a strong and willing labour force being available. I envisaged about thirty men being recruited for a few weeks on every island and had been told to plan their pay at seven shillings a day each. The greatest difficulty anyone foresaw with labour was that there would be an overwhelming number of volunteers.

Some work on most of the islands would involve divers and I could only hope that we had gauged their requirement sensibly. As shallow water diving was a Sapper skill, I recommended that as many as possible of my suggested party of two officers and six NCOs from England should be trained as divers. H.H. nodded and then took his pipe from his mouth to say, "Please remember how very sorry we are that Lieutenant Commander Mitford and his companion were unable to be with you, but we are delighted to hear that Bill is recovering so well."

I then came to the timing of the work, running through a list of inevitable delays before it could start. It would take say, six months, to collect and select a suitable party of Royal Engineers and to give them special training and, before that, the Colonial Office would need to agree the project formally with the Ministry of Defence.

Meanwhile, I would have to edit my large and detailed reconnaissance report and have it reproduced and distributed; in spite of the lack of clerical assistance on Christmas Island, I hoped that it would be posted off within a month. It would then take a further month for a copy of it to come round the world and back to the office in which we were sitting in Tarawa.

So far as I could see, it would take a full year before a properly trained and equipped party could reach Tarawa from England, which suggested a start date of September 1961. However, the annual westerly winds would come to blow about then and all the required channels would be westward facing. Some of the work would be dangerous, even under good conditions, so the westerly season needed to be avoided. That would, unfortunately, put the start from Tarawa back to March 1962.

H.H. had become increasingly sombre as I ran through the dates and delays and now looked disappointed. He sat in silence for a while, puffing his pipe ever harder, before he said, "March '62 is nearly a year later than I had contemplated. However, I can understand all your reasons and can see no alternative." Nor, sadly, could anyone else.

I had arranged that Gerry Douglas would explain the problems of transporting explosives to and around the colony, which he then did. A ship with a wood lined hold would be essential but, even supposing a ship could be spared, it would be expensive to send one of his existing vessels many thousands of miles to Hong Kong and back to have the necessary modifications carried out.

Gerry suggested that the provision of *Nareau's* replacement should be hastened, with her construction to include a wood lined hold. If she were built in Hong Kong, then Army explosives could be obtained there, and two birds would be killed with one stone. H.H. said that the money for the new ship had not even been approved, but he took Gerry's point and would see what he could do.

One of the others present suggested extending *Nareau's* life to become the explosives ship, but the hollow laughter that followed was soon quelled by H.H. saying, not for the first time, "Please, no! *Nareau* must go and the sooner the better!" He added that the building date of *Nareau's* replacement might just fit in with the schedule I had suggested and again promised to do his best to hasten the necessary approvals.

H.H. did not encourage questions at the end of my presentation but said that he would be happy to offer the job to the Royal Engineers, providing the necessary funding could be arranged. Turning to Roy Davies, he continued, "I can see no harm in us telling England by telegram of my decision." The Resident Commissioner then thanked Jack and me profusely for our efforts, and also thanked Captain Douglas; however, only Jack and I could properly appreciate how great had been Gerry's contribution to our reconnaisance.

Nobody actually clapped, but Jack and I felt well pleased. I had been told to "get the job for the Corps", and now it was to be offered to our Corps, the Royal Engineers.

* * *

Our Hastings aircraft was due in two days time, the same day that the Bernacchis would have to leave earlier for the Ocean Island celebrations. H.H. explained that their programme was tight but we were bidden for tea with him and Elaine on Thursday.

Tanaka was, as usual, raking the gravel outside the front door and greeted us in his normal cheery manner when we arrived at the Residency. Elaine had been busy with her staff in the kitchen all day, preparing for a large cocktail party which, "she and her husband might care to give" immediately after their arrival on Ocean Island.

Mr Craig, the London Missionary Society senior missionary, was there, and, together, we were allowed to sample the cocktail eats for tea. We told him of the strong possibility that the proposed blasting would break some of the church windows, news which he took very well. His attitude was much less touchy, and more broad-minded, than that of the Roman Catholic pastor on Marakei, but the latter not only lived with his flock, but also next to his church.

While H.H. was seeing Mr Craig on his way, Elaine said she wanted a good gossip. She was intensely interested to hear what we had been doing, what we had thought of the islands, how many sweets had we given to the children, had we been given anything ourselves, and what did we think of the ships? Most of all, she was interested in the people we had met.

We told her what we could but kept off the little matter of being taken to the wrong island. We were sure that all our views would get back to H.H., and knew that he would relish any hint of wrong doing by his pet hate ship *Nareau*. We later heard that he already had personal experience of *Nareau* losing her way.

Elaine had two main items of news for us. The first was, "Have you heard of the affair at the prison?" No, we had not, and were delighted to listen to her account of it. While we had been on *Nareau* we had received literally no news of the outside world, but plenty of news and rumours about the upheavals in the Belgian Congo (now Zaire) had been reaching Tarawa. This proved altogether too much for the imagination of the Gilbertese policeman on duty at the colony prison, the one we had visited just close to the Residency, who decided to lead the prisoners to revolt. He had knocked out the prison warder and unlocked the prisoners, telling them to help him collect the Resident Commissioner and the other colony officials on Bairiki, then lock them up instead of themselves.

The policeman had not realised just how much the prisoners enjoyed being in jail, well away from their family responsibilities and with food provided free. "Dear Tanaka", as Elaine called their pig keeper and gardener, had not been prepared even to get out of bed. Only three of the prisoners left the jail, but soon asked of their own accord to come back in. "And now the silly policeman is a prisoner." We never asked whether the female jail had also been unlocked but Elaine would not have missed anything worth relating.

The second item of local news was that one of the British wives on Betio, next to Bairiki, had been assaulted by a Gilbertese. She had recently arrived in the colony and was a good looker with good legs. "Have you met her?" asked Elaine and continued, "What a pity, but I am sure you would agree with me." The good looker had been wont to wear shorts that were too short, not the kind of thing that ladies did in the colony and her manner of dress had proved all too inviting. Luckily the assault had been of such a minor nature that there was no need to give us details.

The Gilbertese man concerned had been apprehended and now understood that he had overstepped the mark. Meanwhile, the lady, and more particularly her husband who should have told her the form, had incurred displeasure, and were considered the more to blame. Little had we realised what exciting times we had been missing while at sea!

When Mr Bernacchi returned, he and Elaine took Jack and me for a final stroll around Bairiki, during which H.H. mentioned that he would be fifty next year and then expected to be retired, as he had little hope of being made a governor or a high commissioner. Fifty seemed to us to be a very early age for him to retire, especially as we had seen so much that he and his wife had achieved in the colony. Their probable departure from Tarawa in a year's time explained why he had been so disappointed when I had said that I couldn't see the reef channels project starting for nearly two years. He would have liked, personally, to see the job done.

While we had a final drink back in the house, we asked if we might say goodbye to the servants, and they were all called into the drawing room. When I had enquired earlier, Elaine suggested we gave them tobacco and ships' biscuits, both of which we had purchased, even though plenty of biscuits had been on offer and uneaten in *Nareau*. The way that those little presents were accepted made us all the more glad to have given them.

I had also bought a few tennis balls for the staff, as they used the Residency court with tremendous enthusiasm. When we left, though, that beautifully smooth surface featured some large Gilbertese children pulling chains of smaller children round and round on their tummies, to the noisy delight of all.

* * *

Our immediate interest in the arrival of the Hastings was in the mail from home that it should bring us but we were surprised to discover how many others on Bairiki were also associated with the arrival of that plane.

Roy Davies, the Secretary to the Government, had asked if Percy Roberts, our District Commissioner on Christmas Island, could make the round trip, so as to meet the current colony staff; apart from the

Bernacchis, there was hardly anyone left on Tarawa who knew him. Percy, himself a one-time Secretary to the Government and now its longest serving ex-patriate, was delighted to hitch a lift. Those in Tarawa who had not met Percy seemed to regard him with awe and had been surprised when Jack and I dispelled their impression. As can so easily happen, Percy's true character had been misjudged from the terse, but correct, phrasing of his telegrams and from the wording of his official letters, always received many weeks after writing.

The RAF padre on Christmas Island was, despite the missionaries of other denominations, the only Church of England priest in the colony. The Davieses wanted their daughter christened, so had asked for the padre to visit, thus the Reverend Douglas Jones, who wore the badges of rank of a squadron leader, was also on the plane. It was due at Tarawa at four o'clock, which meant the tide on the way to the Bonriki airstrip would be sufficiently low for us to make the journey over land.

Jack and I still had our unworn sets of uniform, so chose the occasion of the plane's arrival at last to wear them. Roy Davies, as the senior official on Tarawa (with the Resident Commissioner on his way to Ocean Island) wore his regulation white shirt, shorts and stockings. His wife, Laurel, in her coloured shirt and blue slacks, was the most suitably dressed of the four of us, as we trundled the fifteen dusty miles from islet to islet along the south coast of Tarawa in a couple of old lorries.

With great relief we sighted the plane precisely on time; had it been late, we would all have been stranded on the airstrip for the night because of the tide. The pilot brought his Hastings low and slow over the runway, before circling over the ocean again to make his approach. The plane looked enormous or, more precisely, the airstrip looked extremely narrow. In messages back to Christmas Island, I had not mentioned the new rows of coconut palms that had been planted since the last plane landed on Bonriki; true, they were still small trees and mainly near the ends of the strip, but my conscience was not entirely clear.

To our great relief, the pilot made a perfect landing. He seemed a little tense as I thanked him for coming to collect us and said that he never wished to land on a strip an inch narrower. He added that if the cross wind had been a knot stronger, he would have turned back to Canton. Just what would then have happened to Jack and me was not our immediate worry, because we were opening the mass of mail from home that had been brought for us.

That no fuel was available at Bonriki, meant that no time need be spent refuelling, which was just as well. However, a couple of ground crew who had come with the plane made some routine checks, but they were kept to a minimum once everyone appreciated the urgent need to be ahead of the rising tide as we motored back to Bairiki. Meanwhile, the Hastings was left overnight at Bonriki.

Douglas Jones christened Susan Davies in a charming little service held that evening in her parents' house on Bairiki; real French champagne was served, to the delight and amazement of us all, and goodwill abounded. As predicted, Percy Roberts was found to be much more approachable than had been imagined and he later admitted that he had much enjoyed putting faces to the names of the colony staff. Not to be outdone by Ocean Island, Tarawa staged its own Phosphate Ball that evening and, with the well timed influx of visitors off the Hastings, the Bairiki Club became unusually alive.

* * *

News from Christmas Island was mainly good. Bill Mitford had recovered wonderfully from his hospital treatment in Honolulu and was on his way home. Lance-Corporal White had made remarkable progress with the building of his church, so much so that Douglas Jones had arranged for the Bishop of Honolulu to come and consecrate it in two weeks time. However, the young man in charge of Christmas Island's Military Post Office had gone off his head and had thrown his entire stock, stamps, savings certificates, the lot, into the lagoon. He was now under arrest and I knew that, unfortunately, I would become involved in the enquiry. As expected, it sounded as if I would be busy "back home" and that it would never be easy to find time for experiments to confirm our recommended techniques with explosives.

Because of the high tide early the next morning, all of us for the Hastings had to pile into a launch to make the three hour trip along the lagoon edge before dawn. This involved wading to the launch with all our kit and then ashore again at the far end; we had never found our lost crowbar so, after returning the bar which H.H. had borrowed for us, were glad not to be lumbered with one. However, I was finding that to comply with the doctor's well meant instructions to keep my legs dry was proving impossible.

We refuelled on Canton Island on our flight back to Christmas Island. I would have liked to call on the Bristows who had looked after us when we had been there on *Moana Raoi* seemingly years before, but there was no time.

We took off from Tarawa on Saturday, 27th August 1960, crossed the International Date Line from east to west, the equator from north to south to Canton and then from south to north again, and arrived back on Christmas Island on Friday 26th, the day before we left! Jack and I had checked carefully that we would not lose a day's pay thereby and could not believe that we had only been away for forty days.

* * *

That might have been the end of my story, but experiments with the blasting of coral en masse were essential and, when I eventually was able to undertake them, I had to think again.

Chapter Fourteen

TRY, TRY AGAIN

After living cheek by jowl with my good companion Sergeant-Major Jack Cheeseman for what seemed an age, our ways had now, domestically, to separate again, as we went off to our respective messes, I to the officers', and he to the warrant officers' and sergeants'. Next morning we were both on parade at eight o'clock, when he handed my squadron over to me, "Ready for your inspection, sir," as if we had never been away.

The Base Commander, Wing Commander Richardson, told me that, as I had expected, my second-in-command, Captain Dick Sullivan, had carried my Army responsibilities without the slightest difficulty. However, the affair of the postal lance-corporal throwing the stamps into the lagoon had been tiresome; it was now apparent that, when the garrison had been reshaped, the postal job was severely undergraded.

Dicky Richardson had been a constant supporter of my reconnaissance and I tried to thank him for the splendid assistance we had received from behind the scenes. He brushed my thanks aside but said, "When we heard that the fuel at Tarawa, reserved for the Hastings that was coming for you, had been used by that seaplane, it was nearly the last straw. Things were going very well here without you and your sergeant-major, so I was strongly tempted to stop bothering and leave you both there." When, evening after evening, I worked on my detailed reconnaissance report, which included endless little maps and diagrams, I began to wish the plane had never arrived to pick us up. However, a questionable advantage of an unaccompanied overseas tour was the lack of other pressing calls on my spare time in the evenings.

Lance-Corporal White's church was almost finished, there for all to see, and was larger than I expected when I saw its foundations less than two months before. With its white coral walls and glistening silver roof of corrugated aluminium, it made an impressive building; a porch was being added to break up its rather gaunt rectangular shape.

White had trained two of Percy Roberts' Gilbertese labourers to help him break up and lay the natural coral slabs, which they had collected near the reef flat. Then, with the help of a crane they had positioned the large roof trusses, made by the squadron carpenters; here on Christmas Island, there were still cranes, bulldozers and almost anything one might need. The contrast with the rest of the colony, where there was next to nothing, was

St George's Church, Christmas Island.

Consecration of St George's Church: Wing Commander Dicky Richardson, Rt Revd Harry S. Kennedy (Bishop of Honolulu), Revd Douglas Jones and the author.

sobering; those two thousand miles of Pacific Ocean meant that never could east and west meet !

In anticipation of the Bishop of Honolulu's visit, the padre appointed the Base Commander and me as churchwardens and asked us each to read a lesson at the consecration of St George's Church, Christmas Island on Sunday, 11th September 1960.

"Harry Honolulu", as he signed himself, was Bishop of Hawaii and the Pacific in the Episcopalian Church and it was fascinating to hear of his travels around his See. He was with us three days and we found him a most impressive and likable man. He was the proud father of three sons, one of them a US Marine Corps officer and the other two both US Air Force jet pilots, so he was well acquainted with life in the services. Never before, though, had he met a junior serviceman who had built a substantial church on his own initiative. The Bishop was wholly delighted and heaped sincere praise on Lance-Corporal White, who, a shy fellow, neither expected, nor really wanted, it.

A few days later, I finished writing my reconnaissance report and, with no dramatic afterthoughts since briefing the Resident Commissioner in Tarawa, I left my main recommendations unchanged. I laboured the point that, unless the colony could provide a suitable ship for transporting explosives around the islands, the scheme could never start. I intended that the Colonial Office should pick this up, in order to free funds for the building of the new ship. Luckily, those funds were approved, probably because the Resident Commissioner had already made his own convincing case.

I did my best to prune the report but it still ran to book length and I was embarrassed to hand it over to our busy clerks for urgent typing and the re-drawing of my diagrams on to skinlike stencils, all highly tedious. I particularly felt guilty as the clerks knew that the Base Commander and I were off to Honolulu but they promised to have everything ready within the week for our return.

There were many good reasons for that Honolulu trip: Dicky Richardson would be meeting his successor, who would take over as Base Commander; I wanted to meet my US Navy reef blasting friends to discuss our own reef blasting proposals; the Bishop of Honolulu had issued a pressing invitation for us to visit him and, by good chance, the visit would include my own thirty-fifth birthday.

* * *

Honolulu was, in 1960, already one of the world's most expensive places and even modest sightseeing would have been beyond my means, but my US Navy friends, Lieutenants Al Kennedy and Frank Shissler organised a full programme for me. Al used his car and Frank arranged a special launch to take us round Pearl Harbour, beautiful but awesome, with a bevy of nuclear powered submarines contrasting with the wrecks from the fateful attack. Only later did I realise just how lucky I had been to have such privileged and generous guides; I needed embarrassingly little money but more than normal stamina.

Lieutenants Al Kennedy and Frank Shissler, US Navy, with launch coxswain at Pearl Harbour.

Al and Frank well remembered, and asked after, Jack Cheeseman from their visit to us on Christmas Island and were intensely interested to hear of our trip around the colony. As divers, the idea of tackling the coral heads at Aranuka, with or without the tide race, greatly took their fancy. It was reassuring that they thought my estimates for sizes of explosive charges under water were of the right order; if anyone knew, it was they, and I certainly needed guidance. They were particularly keen to have details of the sharks and other marine hazards we must have encountered and were downright disappointed to hear that our experiences had been so tame.

Bishop Kennedy, as good as his promise when he had visited us, asked Wing Commander Richardson and me to meet him at his house. It lay on the most exclusive bit of the Hawaiian coast and would have been well worth the visit on its own account, but he and his wife then took us out to dinner at an equally exclusive restaurant on Diamond Head overlooking Waikiki Beach and the lights of Honolulu City. During the evening, the Bishop mentioned that he often conducted baptisms on his travels and was in need of a portable font. "When you next come up here, Dan," he said, "please bring me half a small clamshell."

The Bishop must have been thinking of one of the sea-scoured, sun-bleached, shells which made such good door stops, but I forgot his request until the day before I next visited Honolulu, two months later. Without further delay, I took a Gilbertese worker with a crowbar and we found a suitable clam on the Christmas Island reef. In no time he had cleaned out the flesh, and I put half the shell in a sandbag and took it with me on the plane to Honolulu the next day.

The Bishop was out when I called at the cathedral, so I left my present there. Soon I received his thanks for his font; "just the right size" but he added some highly secular remarks about the stench of fish with which the cathedral continued to be pervaded.

My overriding memory of several short trips to Honolulu was of the magnificent hospitality with which we "from an atoll" were greeted by our American hosts. They set an example hard to surpass.

The bulky folders containing my reconnaissance report were despatched from Christmas Island before the end of September. I should have felt relieved, but I had become increasingly uncertain as to whether the methods recommended would be feasible. I wanted to complete some practical trials with explosives before Jack Cheeseman was due to go home in a month's time but, with the arrival of the new Base Commander, Wing Commander Charney, our workload would be reviewed.

Surface charges. Jack Cheeseman near the reef's edge at the Bay of Wrecks, Christmas Island.

I managed to make a start on my explosive trials just before Jack left. When we were seeing reef flats around the colony, we had assumed it would be simple to find similar stretches of coral for experiments back on Christmas Island. Now, nothing looked quite the same and Jack and I spent two days which we could ill afford just looking for suitable sites. Eventually we settled for two well separated reefs and hoped to find some representative coral heads in our main lagoon, but that would have to be after Jack had left for home.

We remembered that our only previous experiment in coral blasting, on Nui in the Ellice Islands, had been a pathetic failure, but we had convinced ourselves that the trouble lay in the explosives. Now, we had plenty of good explosives and expected immediate success. Our optimism was soon dashed when we fired a series of charges of increasing weight on some concrete-hard tongues near a reef edge with, just as at Nui, negligible effect on the coral rock. Our last charge was 40 lbs of the best plastic explosive, (equivalent to the filling of an eight inch shell), but its effect was limited to a deafening bang, accompanied by considerable blast, bad for church windows.

We then thought our best hope with charges on the surface lay in trying to blow a small pocket in the coral skin with a first blast, then filling the pockets with more explosive, and blasting a second time. This proved a little better, but was still very noisy and only loosened the coral to a depth of a few inches while we needed channels three feet deep.

Our next hope lay in firing explosive charges on the reef surface after they had been covered by the tide, on the assumption that the weight of water on top would make the explosive bite better into the coral underneath. Nearly two months passed before I could test that method and no, it did not work! In the meanwhile, Jack Cheeseman had been replaced by Sergeant-Major Hindley, whose main lines of expertise lay, unlike Jack's, in fields other than the use of explosives. Luckily, though, my new second-in-command, Captain John May, was a civil engineer with a healthy interest in demolitions; another new arrival, Corporal Jago, was also well qualified in explosive skills.

By the end of October I heard that my report had been read with interest in London and the Resident Commissioner in Tarawa had been contacted regarding its proposals. My recommendations were to be accepted almost in their entirety, news which should have made me proud and delighted, except that since writing the report I had learned that many of my proposed methods would not work.

I also heard that initial planning for a team of Royal Engineers to undertake the tasks was already in hand, even though they would not leave England for over a year. At that rate, there would be plenty of time for me to meet the team leader after I arrived home, which could prove awkward if I had little confidence in my own proposals. The only way round my dilemma was to find methods of blasting coral that worked, and I tried to plan accordingly.

After coming to meet me in Tarawa, Percy Roberts, our District Commissioner, had taken increased interest in my reef channel proposals and offered to help find suitable trial sites for blasting. One Sunday afternoon, he took me, with three of his Gilbertese staff, to the far end of the island in his Land Rover. The tide was low but none of the places we visited quite fitted my needs, though all of them were of great interest to the Gilbertese, because of their crayfishing potential.

At one point there was a small boulder sticking out of the reef flat, with a pool under it on the seaward side. The three Gilbertese showed great interest in it; then Bayonne, the senior of the party, lay down and plunged his arm into the water under the rock. He then wrenched himself backwards and we saw his arm fully entwined by an octopus, which still seemed to have plenty of spare legs for flailing around most dangerously. Without wasting time, Bayonne brought the head of the repulsive beast up to his own mouth and bit the octopus firmly between the eyes. It died immediately. I took a photo of Bayonne and his friends and their trophy, which, with its tentacles extended, spanned three feet six inches. "Only a small one!" Percy assured me.

Had this incident occurred soon after I first read Sir Arthur Grimble's *A Pattern of Islands*, I would never have questioned his frightening tales. However, since then, Jack and I had visited, albeit very briefly, most of Grimble's islands, and more besides, and despite precise questioning, we

A small octopus. Percy Roberts, Bayonne and two other Gilbertese.

had never received confirmation of his stories. With great impertinence, I had come to think that Sir Arthur had adorned his tales with incidents that were not entirely factual, but here I was having just seen an octopus killed by a bite to its forehead, much as Grimble had recorded.

I asked Bayonne, who spoke English, if he made a habit of killing octopi, but he became diffident and I only received a smile in reply. One thing was certain, that was not the first octopus Bayonne had killed. I concluded that it would be wise to take the dangers of the deep more seriously than I had suggested in my reports to England.

The section of reef I eventually chose for more trials lay, inconveniently, at the furthest point on the island from which we were living so, if we needed additional stores, they took several hours to collect, by which time the tide would have changed. The surface of the reef flat was, however, very like what I remembered at many of the channel sites in the colony, as hard as marble and almost as bare. My plan was to lay the explosive charges on the reef when the tide was out, wait three hours for a couple of feet of water to cover them and then fire.

To avoid the waves and surf of the incoming tide dislodging the charges, we tied them on to wire netting, which would be pinned to the reef. However, even this simple idea proved to have snags. Good six inch nails bent on the coral and so did the eight inch steel spikes which were then produced. Meanwhile, the tide came in and we had to retreat to the shore, dragging our explosive laden wire netting behind us.

Overnight we made a special tube to prevent the spikes distorting when they were hammered, but then their points buckled. Eventually we positioned the wire netting, with explosives all in place, weighted it down with sandbags full of coral rubble and left it overnight again to be subjected to the rise and fall of two spring tides. The next day, everything was still in place, so we waited another three hours until the charges were well covered with water before firing them. The way that the blanket of water deadened the blast of nearly 100 lbs of explosive led me to hope that we had been over-cautious regarding the breaking of church windows.

The only effect of the explosion that was immediately visible was a splendid wall of water and spray but we had to wait a further five hours for the tide to drop again before we could examine the effect of the explosives on the coral. For my companions, those were five pleasant and restful hours on a beautiful Christmas Island day. For me, they were worrying, because my trials were eating up so much time. Small though my work force was, it could, and should, have been doing other useful things in support of the base. Much as I and my superiors in the Royal Engineers wished to develop techniques for coral blasting, the island's small garrison had been established for other purposes.

When the tide had dropped nearly sufficiently to allow us to examine the effect of the charges, I hoped, like Archimedes, soon to shout "Eureka!" but, as we waded out to inspect the damage, I immediately realised that here was another case of "Wrong Again Dan!". Scraps of shredded wire netting remained, but so did almost all the coral. The pockets blasted into the reef surface were even smaller than before, when no water had covered the charges; it wasn't until ages later that I realised I should have given thought to Archimedes and his principle much earlier. Instead of pressing the explosive charges down into the reef flat, the covering of water was doing just what I least wanted, giving them some buoyancy!

My morale plumbed new depths, and the unbelieving looks that our Gilbertese helpers gave me were the hardest part to bear. British soldiers understood that their officers' plans might not always work, but the Gilbertese had been brought up to believe that the British were infallible.

Back in the Port, I apologised to the new Base Commander for wasting effort that could well have been used otherwise but he understood the need for me to continue with my trials. Our failures continued, but slowly we learnt that better effects could be achieved if the explosives were pressed very carefully into natural, or man made, depressions on the reef surface.

At last we were able to try boring holes into the reef flat, then filling the lower ends with explosive. This was the method upon which my main hopes had rested and, thankfully, they worked. However, a series of little practical problems had first to be overcome. We had no "bars, jumping and boring" for drilling holes by hand, as would, we hoped, be provided for work in the colony. However, here on Christmas Island, we had an air compressor, so cheated, and used it. A borehole was a borehole, however it might be drilled!

Charges fired under water on a reef flat.

Clearing coral rubble from an experimental channel.

Royal Engineers coral clearance party. Sapper Eke, Corporal Truckle, Sapper Caffrey, Lance-Corporals Davies and Cook, Sapper Cousens and Lieutenant Stephen Sheen.

The hardness of the coral under the surface varied enormously, even for boreholes only three feet apart and, the softer the coral, the more likely the drill was to jam in the hole.

The delays in staging these trials had allowed me to keep my legs dry; I was thankful that my coral sores had healed, which was just as well, as I was now constantly in the water again. The reef flats were only dry for an hour or so around low tide, so most of our drilling had to be done under water. This proved possible, providing that the top of the compressor tool could be kept dry; not easy once the small waves rolled in. As soon as the drill was removed from the two inch diameter hole, silt off the reef started to fill it remarkably quickly. The answer was to kneel down and plug the hole under water with a piece of rag.

Inserting explosive into a vertical borehole full of water proved easy. Wait for the tide to drop and for the reef to dry out, then bounce a broomstick up and down in the hole: the water jumps upwards, straight in your face, but the squelch is very satisfactory. Then, using the same stick, gently push the explosive, with its detonating fuse attached, down the hole.

We tried various depths of boreholes at various spacings, and ended up with three feet deep holes, four feet apart. By this means the coral could be loosened to the necessary three feet depth over any required area. The more we carried on by trial and error, the more we thought that others must surely have done all this before, but we never heard of them!

Our problems with boreholes seemed to be nearly over, but not quite. We needed a channel in which a laden copra boat could float, not a channel that was full of coral rubble. Clearing the fragmented coral from the channel was an even more tedious and tiring job than drilling the holes. The reef flats turned out to be in layers, three to nine inches thick, in the form of the slabs, naturally broken by the waves, from which White had built his church. I later surmised that varying sea levels, perhaps during the ice ages, might have accounted for the layering.

The art of making a channel with boreholes was to break up the coral into the smallest number of large, slab-like, lumps. These were much easier to move than millions of coral chippings that needed to be cleared by wheelbarrow and shovel, again not easy under water. The secret was to use just enough explosive to break the reef into layers; too much pulverised the debris. Even so, channel digging by these unsophisticated methods was a slow business and, as I soon discovered, hard and painful work.

The clearance of rubble from a channel that was usually full of water had to be done by hand, and those with long arms had the distinct advantage of keeping their heads above water as they sat or knelt in the channel. My arms are short, thus not good for finding the soap in a foamy bath, nor coral fragments under milky sea water.

I needed to write yet another report to supplement my earlier one, which required many amendments, and on coral debris clearance, I wrote :

> "The edges of the coral, whether in large slabs or smaller stones, were very sharp. All the British had cut their hands within an hour of the start of manual clearance. The four Gilbertese with us suffered only sore hands after eight hours, but they did not enjoy the work! Leather gloves, tried by the British, proved

> useless, quickly falling to pieces in the sea water after becoming cut. Metal reinforced gloves, as used for barbed wire fencing, might prove effective, but we had none, and the consumption rate would be heavy. The Gilbertese said that they were happy with bare feet but we noticed that on the second day some of them wore shoes."

I could only hope that, with coral rubble clearance, where there was a will, there would be a way. For planning purposes I managed to convince myself that once a visiting Sapper party had done the necessary blasting on an island, they could move elsewhere to start blasting again, while the locals on the first island finished off the rubble clearance in their own time.

My report continued:–

> "Even with surface charges, a covering of a foot or more of water reduces blast enormously. Similarly, the blast from borehole charges is small. The danger of breaking church windows would, therefore, be less than I thought when my original report was written. However, initial caution would still be advisable."

It was a great relief to know that the revised methods, even though they lacked elegance, could be made to work and that it was not too late to take account of them. The problems of blasting coral heads and coral on the reef edge still needed to be tackled and, as both needed divers, I turned again for help to the Royal Navy.

Chapter Fifteen

BUT FOR A CROCODILE

An incident from my more irresponsible past came back to me during my continued blasting experiments on Christmas Island in 1960 and was soon to prove more relevant than I ever dreamt.

Early in 1945, I was an officer cadet in the Royal Engineers, starting a month at a jungle camp in India's Mysore State; my companions and I were being trained for the Japanese War in South East Asia. We lived high up on the bank of a deep, but not very wide, river, in which we bathed and washed our clothes. Most of our training was on the far side, so we needed to cross the river many times a day in all manner of small boats. The setting was truly beautiful but the overall attraction of the place decreased dramatically when we found that we were sharing the amenities with a large crocodile.

Sapper officers were expected to be specially skilled in the use of explosives and, as appropriate to wartime training, we were encouraged to undertake unusual tasks. Many of us knew that poachers stunned salmon by dropping explosive charges into their pools, so we planned to deter our crocodile by similar means. Our instructor, a young and clever captain, willingly approved our outline proposals and left us to carry on with the task. We decided that 25 lbs of high explosive should make a crocodile feel unpopular, so stuffed most of that quantity into a sandbag.

I was proud to be selected to prepare the initiation set for our small depth charge; it consisted of a length of safety fuse inserted into a small detonator of highly sensitive explosive. In the prescribed manner I tested a separate length of the fuse to see that it burnt at the correct rate of two feet a minute and also checked that it continued to burn under water.

We decided on a delay time of two minutes, so I cut off four feet of the fuse and carefully inserted one end into the open mouth of the detonator, which I sealed with watertight tape. Carefully, I wrapped up the detonator in the last sausage of explosive and tied it in, leaving the free end of the fuse poking out through the sandbag's neck.

With keen anticipation, my friends and I discussed the probable effect of our highly lethal bomb, which was large enough to knock down a good house. We paddled our boat to the middle of the river where the crocodile had last been sighted, the fuse was lit with a match and the sandbag of explosives was lowered overboard; it sank immediately. Before the two minutes of fuse burning time elapsed, we had reached the bank and taken cover.

After two minutes, nothing had happened. After two minutes and fifteen seconds, we thought something had gone wrong and, when three minutes had passed, we knew that we had had a misfire. At just the place we would be churning up the river most frequently we now had, certainly, a large and sensitive explosive charge and, probably, a large and sensitive crocodile. Sheepishly, we told Captain Peter Garnell, our officer, what had happened, and he replied, as we might have expected, "You put the charge there. You get rid of it!"

Too late, we remembered his own teaching, "Never position a detonator where it is not accessible." Our detonator, embedded in its bomb, was now lost on the bottom of a murky river perhaps twelve feet deep. The most likely reason for the failure of our croc buster was water entering the joint, which I had made, between the fuse and detonator. I, therefore, was unanimously elected to dive and retrieve the explosives.

My proficiency as a swimmer had always been poor but I hoped that my determination showed as I entered the water. I also hoped that my lack of real intention to reach the bottom of that river was in no way evident. I could not help thinking that the crocodile might prefer me, as a snack, to the evil smelling parcel that must recently have arrived at the bottom of his pool.

My efforts were quickly seen to be hopeless, so two of my friends, stronger swimmers and much braver than I, started to dive, and kept diving. At increasingly frequent intervals they came to the surface, saying that they could touch the bottom, but only felt mud. We were all just about to admit defeat when, to our great relief, one more dive was rewarded with success. As the sandbag and its puffing retriever surfaced, the former was eagerly grabbed and hoisted into the boat. Captain Garnell arrived at the critical moment and said, "Next time, put the detonator on a float!" As we cautiously opened up our misfired bomb, we wished that we had taken the point earlier.

We now brought into use an additional explosive accessory, known as detonating cord, which looked like other fuses but, although it was itself very insensitive, could transfer a detonation wave instantaneously from one explosive charge to another. I cut off a length of the detonating cord rather longer than the depth of the river and inserted a knotted end of it into the main 25 lb charge in the sandbag. We prepared another, highly watertight, initiating set of safety fuse and detonator and secured it to the other end of the detonating cord and thence on to a small log to be used as a float.

The sandbag was lowered, with its detonating cord attached, to the river bottom. The time fuse was lit and fizzed merrily, floating on its log, all still connected by the detonating cord to the charge on the river bottom. When we were safely ashore, after two minutes exactly from lighting the fuse, a gigantic plume of water sprang directly upwards. When it subsided, there was no sign of the crocodile, and he never bothered us again.

* * *

Here on Christmas Island, two Royal Navy divers had arrived to replace Bill Mitford and AB Williams but one of them then broke his leg, so there was further delay before I could stage demolition trials on underwater coral obstacles.

We were asked to remove a coral boulder from a shallow pool used for bathing, and this small task provided a useful introduction for the divers, as neither of them had previously worked with explosives. They found that they could drive pins into the rock under water and then secure small charges on either side, which I was able to inspect by flopping around on the surface wearing my face mask and gas mask specs. We fired those charges in the manner that had eventually proved effective for crocodile scaring, with the detonator and safety fuse on a float. The obstruction in the swimming pool disappeared, no windows were broken and everyone was pleased.

That boulder did not compare in size with the enormous coral heads elsewhere in the colony which would require attention later, so I borrowed the RN motor cutter, its coxswain and the divers, and we spent a pleasant afternoon on Christmas Island lagoon searching for heads similar to those I remembered. There was any number to choose from but none was as large as those we had seen at Aranuka and Marakei, where the water had been deeper.

Royal Navy divers with "Ginger".

The representative coral head which I chose lay about two miles out from the lagoon shore and looked like an enormous cauliflower covered in greeny-grey lichen; it just broke the surface with the tide out, when the water depth was eleven feet. We marked it with a small buoy and the divers wrapped a length of line round it, to tell me the circumference five feet from its top. It had a convenient depression in its crown, just the place to pack in some explosive to give it a good thump at the same time that other charges were fired around the sides.

My demolitions assistant, Corporal Jago, and I spent the next morning making up the charges that the divers would position around the coral head. There was to be a 20 lb charge of plastic explosive on the crown and four 10 lb charges in the form of a necklace around the head five feet down. Corporal Jago was quite surprised by the trouble I took preparing those charges and their connections. All the lengths of detonating cord were duplicated and strengthened with cod line, so that it, not the explosive cord, would take any unintended tension. I am labouring these points because, when you are about to be hoist by your own petard, details matter! Only the detonator and its associated safety fuse were not duplicated, as they would remain floating on the surface.

How long to make the time delay between lighting the fuse and the charge exploding was an important but difficult question. We needed plenty of time to motor the cutter to a safe distance and I tended on the side of caution, yet we did not want the nerve-wracking waiting to be too long. I decided on a five minute delay, a choice that proved to be more important than I could have imagined.

Five minutes delay meant using a ten feet length of fuse and, rather than have this vital link flapping about in the lagoon waves, I coiled the black coloured fuse around the wooden plank that would be the float, driving in a few nails to ensure everything stayed in place. Our preparations were taking longer than planned and Corporal Jago asked why we were adding complication by putting the initiating set on a float. His highly understandable, and tempting, theme was, "Surely it would be much simpler to put the detonator into one of the charges?" I told him of my hard-earned experience with the crocodile and, tiresome as it was, I was determined to use the float.

After lunch, Corporal Jago and I took our completed necklace of explosives to the motor cutter, which was much like a ship's lifeboat. Its coxswain and the two divers were there to meet us, plus four others who wished to be spectators; they included one of the RAF doctors (Flight Lieutenant Malcolm Sleight) and Squadron Sergeant-Major Hindley, who had taken over from Jack Cheeseman. Hindley believed that a sergeant-major should set an example in his bearing and dress at all times, all very commendable, but his formal turn out of smart bush jacket and shorts, with boots, dark blue stockings and puttees looked highly incongruous in the cutter on the lagoon.

The divers and I would be going into the water, so wore our bathing trunks and I had on my tennis shoes; they put on their flippers and air bottles before they went overboard. The leading seaman coxswain and the doctor were in their shorts and flip-flop sandals; Corporal Jago wore shorts and his favourite pair of boots, thus confirming that he had no intention of going in the water; just as well, as I understood he could not swim. I made sure to wear my tinted spectacles under my officers' service dress hat, both of them to reduce the tremendous reflected glare off the light green lagoon.

True to form, the easterly winds that had blown across the Pacific until September had changed to westerlies and the breeze was pronounced as we approached my chosen coral head. The buoy was bobbing up and down erratically in the choppy water and I wondered if the divers would have trouble in swimming our heavy necklaces of explosives over the great lump of rock. In fact, they handled the explosives as if they had been trained to do so all their lives and accomplished everything necessary without difficulty.

The cutter on Christmas Island Lagoon. AB Burke, Sergeant-Major Hindley and Flight Lieutenant (Medical Officer) Malcolm Sleight.

While the divers were working, the cutter went up wind about fifty yards and dropped an anchor. We paid out its cable until we could hold our position back near the coral head. When the divers said they had finished, I changed my specs for the gas mask variety, put on my face mask, and lowered myself over the cutter's side to swim around in an effort to inspect the positioning of the charges.

So far as I could see, all was fine, but I realised how much better I could have made my inspection had I been a diver myself. I was then heaved back into the cutter, to be reminded again of its high and hard gunwales. The gas mask specs were uncomfortable and I again changed to my favourite pair.

Before the divers came aboard, they passed up to me the free ends of the duplicated detonating cords that led to the 60 lbs of explosive under water on the coral head. Very carefully I incorporated them into a junction with the initiating set mounted on the plank float. The coxswain had kept the cutter's engine ticking over and all was now ready for me to light the safety fuse and for us to make our get-away to a safe distance.

* * *

The cutter was still swinging gently on its long length of anchor cable, with a goodly length of spare cable still aboard in the bows. Rather than waste time, after lighting the fuse, by taking in the cable and lifting the anchor, we decided to cast the whole cable into the water and to pick it and the anchor up later. We realised that some of the cable might be damaged by the explosion, but there was plenty available ashore. The divers kept their gear on, as they would soon be retrieving the anchor for us.

With my audience watching with an air of eager anticipation, I ordered the anchor cable to be dumped overboard and, when that had been done and with the coxswain still managing to hold the cutter in position, I lit the safety fuse. I carefully noted the time on my watch, at the start of what turned into five very sporting minutes.

Next, I gently lowered the plank with the ten feet of safety fuse coiled around it, into the water. As soon as I released it, it floated very slowly down wind behind us, until its connections to the main charges became taut. We could see and hear the burning fuse fizzing and spluttering on its float, just as prescribed. All was going as planned.

The coxswain was highly professional and quick in the uptake, so it was with an air of confidence that I said to him, "OK, take her away!" Not until a few seconds later did I realise the error of my phrasing. I should have added the word ". . . gently". Meanwhile, the coxswain had opened up the cutter's throttle, so that his craft, which I had always considered to be a wallowing old tub, leapt forward like a speed boat.

We were most impressed, that was until we had gone forty yards or so up wind from the charge and its burning fuse, when the boat's engine cut out. The coxswain tried to restart it, but nothing happened. It was then that someone noticed we were trailing the anchor cable astern, and the awful truth dawned: the cable had somehow been churned off the bottom of the lagoon and into the single screw of the cutter. My arrangements, so carefully planned, had resulted in the cutter, with eight others and me in it, being anchored just up wind of a large charge of high explosive that was shortly due to detonate.

* * *

The forward movement of the cutter had been checked by the drag of the anchor cable and now we were drifting with the breeze very, very, slowly back towards the coral head. At a distance of nearly fifty yards we could intermittently see the floating plank bobbing about in the small waves. Before I had time to think, though later they assured me that I had given my permission, both divers went overboard with their knives unsheathed, saying that they would cut us free. They disappeared from view as my watch showed that fifty seconds had elapsed since I had lit the fuse.

For what seemed an age, the remaining seven of us just sat in the cutter, listening to the divers tapping and scraping near the propeller under our stern. We knew they were under us, from the occasional surge of bubbles from their air bottles popping through the lagoon's surface under the gunwales.

Probably Corporal Jago and I were the only people aboard that cutter who can have fully understood what might be in store for us all, but I was amazed how little concern anyone showed. The fault for anything going wrong could only be mine, so I expected to sense a lack of popular approval for my efforts to date. Not so! My companions gave the impression of continued enjoyment, in fact, they were revelling in the excitement which had been added to the day's programme.

The fuse had now been alight for one minute and thirty seconds and my only thought was to get the divers back into the boat. Without doubt they would be killed by the explosion if they were still in the water but I judged some of us might just have a chance if we were aboard the cutter. None of us knew how to communicate with free swimming divers under water but still we could hear them working near the propellor. We tried hammering on the bottom of the boat and they, maddeningly, just hammered back! To my great relief, just after my watch showed that two minutes had gone by, one of the divers surfaced, to tell us that they had cut the anchor cable, but could not free the screw.

I decided that our only remaining hope lay in cutting the safety fuse at a place that the burning had not reached. However, I was all too aware that nearly half of the length of fuse would already have burnt, so the choice of places to cut was rapidly diminishing. The only person, apart from me, who might know what to do was Corporal Jago and he couldn't swim. There was no need to waste further time. Overboard Dan must go!

The diver who had surfaced had his knife in his hand, so I grabbed it and told him to fetch the other diver back into the boat. Out of curiosity, I had handled divers' knives before but the one now in my hand turned out to be much heavier than I expected. My main worry was not to drop it as I plunged into the lagoon with my pathetic imitation of a racing dive. The result was a prize belly flop, very painful on my tummy. Someone had removed my parade hat from my head but no one, least of all me, had remembered my most prized of accoutrements, my green tinted spectacles: they were knocked off when I hit the water, never to be seen again.

Without my specs I could no longer see the float and had difficulty in making progress with my cumbersome side stroke; the knife weighed down my forward hand and my tennis shoes weighed down my feet. Mainly by good chance, I judged the correct direction towards the float, helped by the spluttering of the fuse and by some well meant, but mainly inaudible, advice from the boat. I reached the float, with its fuse still fizzing viciously, at about three minutes and fifteen seconds. The plank was still down wind of, and well away from, the coral head, so there was no question of my standing on the crown of the head; as it was, I was well and truly out of my depth. Keeping afloat was a problem in itself but cutting the fuse in the right place was worse.

Safety fuse of the type in use in 1960 was black in colour and, after it had burnt, it remained black, so, even in a good light, it was difficult to tell how far the burning had progressed along a given length. With no specs and with salt water splashing in my eyes, there was no point in my trying to see where the burning had reached. I knew that I must cut the fuse as close to the detonator as possible, but all my careful preparations with waterproof tape had not made that any easier.

Because of the way the fuse was coiled round the plank, I found that I could not, in fact, attempt to sever it any nearer than six inches from the detonator. However preoccupied I was, I was still well able to equate fuse length with burning time, and calculated that I had rather less than a minute left in which to achieve the cut.

Safety fuse was normally fairly easy stuff to cut; just lay it on a hard surface and part it with a sharp knife. However, I was trying to perform the task in a popply sea, while treading water, wearing shoes and with both hands occupied. The left was trying to hold the plank steady, while the right clung on to the divers' knife and tried to cut the fuse. The plank had negligible buoyancy to help me and, as soon as I started my sawing motion with the knife, down went my head under water. On resurfacing, my own spluttering competed with that of the fuse and its accompaniment of urgent hissing. I had given up trying to look at the watch on my wrist, but after what must have been another fifteen seconds, I had managed to cut the fuse.

My urgent wish then was to get back into the cutter, not that its protection would have been of much avail had I cut the fuse in the wrong place. By four minutes and thirty seconds I was back aboard and able to reassure everyone that all was well, a pronouncement in which I had greater faith when, a few seconds later, the noises from the fuse suddenly went blissfully silent.

My companions were still as calm as before, perhaps more than ever interested in my antics, but certainly not frightened. Minute five from lighting the fuse passed uneventfully, just as we drifted over the coral head, still draped in its necklace of high explosives, all peacefully undisturbed.

The cutter continued to drift slowly downwind and it was a great relief, for me at least, not to be in a hurry to do anything; I only hoped that I looked as calm as the others in the boat but certainly didn't feel it. The divers went over the side again to cut the propeller free. That took a few minutes, then the coxswain started the engine and brought us back up to the coral head.

I leant over the side, lifted the float from the water, and cut it free from the main charge, then gently removed the detonator, with the short length of unburnt fuse attached to it, and all was again safe.

I thought that we must all have had enough of explosives for the day, so we left the main charge, completely safe without its initiating set, in position on our coral head. We marked it with the buoy and then the coxswain took us back to the Port for tea.

When we were ashore again, I went in search of the Base Commander and reported that I had nearly caused a nasty accident. I knew that all aircrew members of the Royal Air Force were on their honour to report dangerous "incidents" concerned with their flying, however they were caused. Wing Commander Charney said that he viewed my episode in the same light as he would an RAF incident and thanked me very much for letting him know what had happened. We went over to the mess together. It might be tea time but whisky proved much more appropriate for the occasion.

My incident occurred on 8th December 1960, since when I have been thankful that, before it happened, I had remembered what a crocodile had once taught me.

* * *

Preparations for Christmas on Christmas Island were already under way but when, the next morning, I announced, "We really will blow up that

Blasting a coral head in Christmas Island Lagoon, second attempt!

coral head today," all sorts of people found that they had no pressing duties and asked to accompany us as spectators. We had to limit the numbers. Blessed with hindsight, we changed our method of approaching the coral head. We anchored the cutter on a short cable, so that I could make the connection from the initiation set on the float, with a new five minute fuse, to the main charges that were still in position. Next, we chugged ahead to pick up the anchor and its cable before dropping back to light the fuse. The coxswain then took us gently astern and down wind, so that, had the engine cut out, we would have continued to drift in a safe direction.

Five minutes after I lit the fuse, we were nearly a quarter of a mile from the charge. We felt a sharp smack on the cutter's side, as a beautiful column of water and coral rocks leapt a hundred or more feet into the air. The subsequent cascade continued for many seconds and, had the cutter been near the explosion, it would certainly have been destroyed.

When we went back to inspect the damage, we could find no trace of the coral head, just a white scar on the bottom of the lagoon. Unfortunately, many vividly coloured small fish had been killed by the explosion and we picked some of them up. Sharks could well have been attracted to the spot but, even if our fascinated spectators were disappointed, I was glad that none turned up.

When all was over, we had established that 60 lbs of high explosive would fully destroy a good sized coral head. I had also learned that some of my estimates for the quantities of explosives required for the tasks in the colony might be on the generous side and I sent off yet another supplement to my report to London.

* * *

Though I was only a junior major, I was the senior British Army officer in most of the Pacific Ocean and there was plenty to keep me occupied for the remainder of my year out there. Senior visitors, who included Earl Mountbatten, various rocket capsules, both Russian and American, landing nearby in the ocean, and many lesser diversions, ensured that the time passed quickly, so I undertook no more coral blasting.

When my year away from my family was over, I realised more and more just how lucky I had been to be sent to the Gilbert and Ellice Islands Colony when the reef channels were being considered. As no great enthusiast for the sea, I would not have been the man to select for a coral blasting reconnaissance, but I was now glad to have been Hobson's choice.

I realised that I had been fortunate in many other ways too, not least in having Jack Cheeseman as my companion when we visited so many of those remote islands in the colony. One of our mottoes in the Royal Engineers is "Ubique" and, even if Jack and I had not been "Everywhere", we liked to think that we had trod some ground new even to our Corps.

Chapter Sixteen

THE OUTCOME

After being exactly a year away, I was back in England in June 1961 and Judy and I spent most of my disembarkation leave staying with her parents near Malpas, Cheshire. Bill, our elder son, was now aged three and a half and Henry was nearly two; they had changed enormously in that year, but all was obviously very well and my family had certainly not suffered in my absence!

When Tony Younger, a distinguished Royal Engineers officer, came to lunch with us, I discovered that the planning based on my reconnaissance around the colony was more advanced than I realised. The Ministry of Defence had eagerly accepted the Colonial Office's invitation to undertake the work and a unit under Brigadier Younger's command was forming a team to do it. A couple of captains, Terry Hardy and Mike Addison, both of high repute, had been selected, and the problem now was to choose from the great number of non-commissioned officers who had volunteered, to keep the team total down to eight.

By the vagaries of post-war training, Tony Younger and I had once been on the same pre-Cambridge course and knew each other fairly well. He had appreciated the remoteness of the islands and the need for the team to operate completely independently; his questions were more about the personal qualities each individual would require, rather than about the intricacies of the necessary engineering.

It sounded as if the rigorous selection procedures that were in hand would result in the right men being chosen, but I stressed that I still lacked faith in some of the explosive methods that I had proposed. The brigadier said that he was sure that good men would find ways that worked and, thankfully, they did. Captain Hardy's team, consisting of two captains, four sergeants and two corporals, all of them Royal Engineers and all of them divers, spent nearly ten months working in the colony in 1962 and, according to the many appreciative reports that were received, accomplished all that was asked of them.

The time between my departure and their arrival had fortunately allowed for the new colony vessel, the MV *Nivanga,* a close relation to the MV *Ninikoria,* to be designed and built in Hong Kong with a properly authorised explosives magazine. *Nivanga* was able to dump explosives appropriately around the islands as the project started; over thirty tons were used and over a mile in total length of boat channels were blown in the fringing reefs of eleven islands. In addition, the channel through the towering coral heads at the entrance to the lagoon at Aranuka had, as anticipated, provided a task of very special interest. Three and a half tons of explosives were used there in a single blast, to produce "a great white strip along the lagoon bed, over half a mile long." (Lest environmentalists worry, countless thousands of coral heads remained untouched on either side!)

In accordance with my suggestions, the team had started work on Nui atoll in the Ellice Islands (now Tuvalu), where evidence of Mr Kennedy's earlier work was still on view. Once techniques had been established, it split into two parties of four for most of the rest of the project. During their work in the water, there were plenty of encounters with potentially dangerous fish, particularly barracuda, but no mishaps occurred.

Both parties reported that they were nearly killed by the kindness of the charming and hospitable islanders but, as time went by, many months of living in such complete isolation from the outside world proved just as testing as had been expected. Both officers thought that the success of the scheme had been more due to the correct selection of the team than to any other factors.

Although Terry Hardy and I met occasionally over the years, neither of us heard to what extent the channels were proving useful. In late 1989, I wrote to Mr Charles Thompson in Tarawa, who was the British High Commissioner for Kiribati, asking for news. I received his reply within a fortnight, which showed that communications had improved since I was in the islands, and his letter included just what I had wanted to hear. After saying that he could only answer for Kiribati, which now includes the old Gilbert, Phoenix and Line Islands, Mr Thompson continued:–

> "Reef passages, presumably the ones made by Captain Hardy's parties, are still in use on all the islands in the Gilberts you mentioned. Further blasting is occasionally undertaken (usually by New Zealand Army personnel) to keep them up to scratch."

So, if the channels work in the Gilbert Islands, hopefully, they work in the other islands where they were provided. Just how much has been gained by their existence, I am in no position to judge, but they must, at least, make the crossing of the reef's edge easier and less hazardous than it was before the coral was blasted.

Annexe

THOUGHTS ON ATOLLS

Before I went to the Central Pacific, I assumed I could find out all I needed to know about coral and coral atolls once I arrived there, but no one seemed able to help me. When I realised how closely I was to be associated with coral, I hoped that if I could understand how it grew, I might learn how coral atolls were formed. In turn, I might then be in a better position to advise on blasting channels through coral reefs.

When I set off on my reconnaissance around the Gilbert and Ellice Islands Colony, I did not even know that Charles Darwin had published his theories on the formation of coral atolls over a hundred years before. And so, rushing in where others feared to tread, I started from scratch with ideas of my own but, the longer I continued, the more I realised that I would only be raising more questions. However, I dared to include a section on atoll formation in my September 1960 Reconnaissance Report but, even after that, no one drew my attention to Darwin's work.

In the thirty years since my trip round the islands, I have skimmed encyclopedias and asked questions, probably too superficially, but many doubts still remain in my mind. My impression is that the topic of coral atoll formation is full of misunderstandings and anomalies and that Darwin may not have told us all we need to know.

I hope to record some of my thoughts on atolls here, but please bear in mind that I am completely untrained in this field. If these notes are read, it should be more with a view to exposing fallacies, than to accepting my ideas.

Before starting, may I explain that the Pacific corals with which I was dealing were, beneath their outer surface, white and rocklike, much like limestone or chalk. They had little in common, other than in name, with the attractive, pink and jewel-like corals of the Mediterranean and elsewhere.

CORAL GROWTH

I understand that coral growth depends, to varying degrees, upon the following seven conditions:

1. *Life.* The tiny polyps that secrete the chalky substance known as coral

are living creatures. So long as their life can be sustained, polyps love living and multiply like mad, the result being more and more coral. If only I had studied polyps, rather than hydra and earthworms, in my brief encounter with biology at school, I might now be better placed to write on the subject!

2. *Sunlight.* Corals need sunlight for growth. Even in the clearest water, sunlight does not penetrate beyond a depth of about one hundred feet and, at that depth, the rate of coral growth is tiny. Near the surface there is plenty of sunlight and the polyps thrive.

3. *Temperature.* Reef corals only flourish at temperatures averaging over 75° Fahrenheit (24° Centigrade), so most reefs are restricted to tropical waters

4. *Salinity.* Polyps only live in salt water, in fact simply detest fresh water, so coral is not found at the mouths of rivers and streams of tropical islands. Atolls, however, are so porous under their flat surfaces that no streams flow from them.

5. *Food.* Polyps are prevented from moving by the coral they form. They are, therefore, dependent upon microscopic morsels of food being brought to them by the movement of the surrounding water. A polyp's diet sheet would tell it that nowhere does water provide more prolific food than in the race at a lagoon entrance, or in the breakers on the reef's edge.

6. *Submersion.* Reef corals die if they are exposed to air for more than a few hours, so their upward growth is normally limited to the level of mean low water.

7. *Freedom from Sediment.* Mud, sand and rubble kill live corals by cutting off the light and food supply.

⋆ ⋆ ⋆

I ticked off a check list of these points at various locations, and the entrance to Aranuka's lagoon (Chapter 9) provided an excellent example to fit my conditions for superb coral growth. Its water was constantly warm, sunlight beamed down the full depth of the coral heads and there were endless supplies of fast flowing food from all sides. Those coral heads and boulders were well spread out, so there was little chance of the debris from one, if it were to break asunder, smothering another. Everything there was set fair for the coral to grow fast.

How fast was an important question. Rates of up to an inch a year were suggested, though we knew that the flimsiest of branch corals could grow even faster for a short while, but then tended to break up. I now realise that very much slower rates of growth for coral rocks are more probable, with times being measured not in terms of tens, but of millions, of years.

ATOLLS AND MOUNTAINS

The more I thought that I understood the requirements for coral to grow, the more I realised how little I knew about the formation of coral atolls. I imagined, initially, that they were based on extinct volcanoes that had slowly emerged from the sea, with lagoons lying over their craters and reefs forming around their rims. However, this theory had obvious flaws, the main argument against it being that all atolls are of similar height, just proud of ocean level.

I would have expected some, or most, emerging volcanoes to continue to rise after they had broken through the ocean's surface, to result in a series of islands of different heights all thinly coated from their tops in coral. As far as I knew, no such islands existed and the mountainous islands of the Pacific, like those in Hawaii, had coral only around their shores but with none at their river mouths.

It was not until late in our reconnaissance that I came round to thinking that atolls must be based on mountains that had slowly sunk, not emerged, through the ocean surface. *Sunk* was the important word and I was not surprised to find later that Darwin had appreciated it much quicker than had Raschen.

I started to apply those conditions for coral growth to the formation of an atoll and found that the shapes of most I had seen, whether or not they had lagoons, might then be explained. Some apparent misconceptions fell into place when I realised that an atoll with a lagoon could have been formed from any sinking mountain, not just one that had been a volcano with a crater.

The sheer depth of the Pacific Ocean added further questions to an already complex subject. I knew that most of the islands we had visited in the colony were surrounded by ocean 2,000 fathoms (12,000 feet) or more deep, and very few shallower spots were marked on the charts covering vast areas. With the help of the staff of the Hydrographer of the Navy, I refreshed my memory when, in 1990, I pored over the updated charts of the old Gilbert and Ellice Islands Colony. I found that the recorded soundings indeed averaged 2,000 fathoms, with 3,000 or more being quite common.

This meant that some of the atolls had a height above the floor of the ocean of around 18,000 feet, much greater than that of Mont Blanc's height (over 15,000 feet) above sea level. Perhaps geologists could explain the phenomena, but the idea of mountains sinking more than the height of Mont Blanc was well out of my parish! The peaks of the Alps, say, vary in height by many thousands of feet. So, if a mountain range had sunk through the surface of the Pacific, I would have expected at least a few of the tallest mountains never to have submerged, thus never to have become atolls.

However, every island, nearly fifty of them, in the Gilbert and Ellice Islands Colony, lying in an area of two million square miles of ocean, was an atoll, with none of them higher than a few feet above sea level. No mountain or volcano top islands protrude above the level of that vast expanse of ocean, and I have still not met anyone who can explain their absence!

To complicate the arguments further, I considered three more factors, or possibly red herrings:

1. *The Ice Ages.* Over hundreds of thousands, if not millions, of years, the

levels of the oceans are known to have varied due to ice forming and melting. Those variations, I understood, were of less than fifty feet, so would not preclude coral growth, though some hiccups in the layering of the rock might occur. The ice ages should not, therefore, have greatly affected the way atolls formed.

2. *Depth of Coral.* Someone, towards the end of the Japanese War, was said to have drilled for water on Funafuti, the most important of the Ellice Islands and, after 1,000 feet, had met nothing but coral. To me, that meant that a mountain top had sunk at least 1,000 feet. I have since heard that, in connection with nuclear testing or oil prospecting, atolls have been drilled to reveal coral at even greater depths. They must have sunk very gradually over an awesomely long time!

3. *Coral at great depth.* Rock corals are said to have been found at depths of thousands of fathoms. By my rules, they can't have grown there, so how did they get there?

ATOLL FORMATION

Confusing though the subject was, I listed the stages in which I thought coral atolls came into being. The series of sketch diagrams which follow may help explain the evolution, which I thought would have been as follows:

1. A mountainous island, which may, or may not, have been a volcano, would find itself sinking slowly into the ocean; its shore, under the right conditions, would become fringed with coral (Figure 1). As the sinking continued, the fringing coral would grow deeper and the protruding peak would become smaller; so would any rivers on the island.

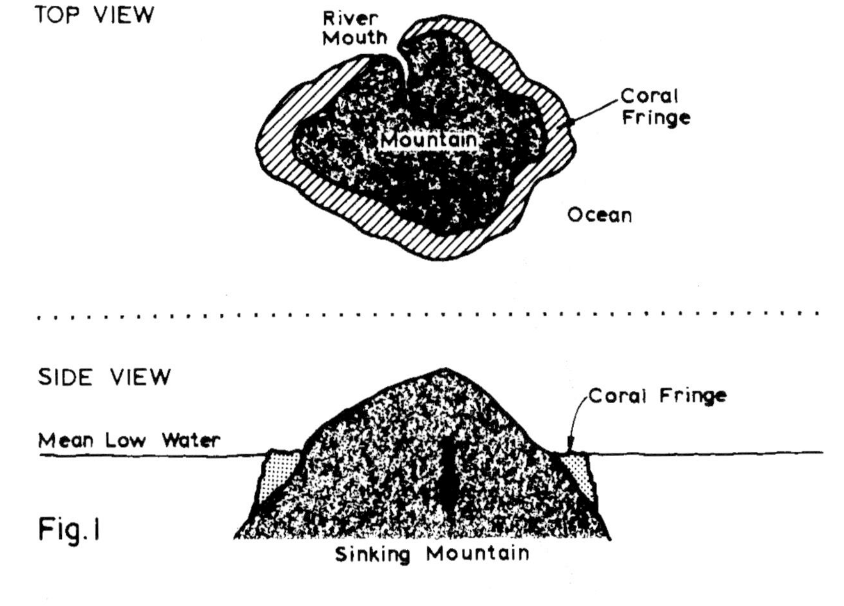

2. The peak of the mountain would be last to submerge, and the fringing coral reef would join over its top. In the absence of storms, the side view of the island would be of a flat plateau topped with coral, just breaking the surface of the ocean on low tides (Figure 2). Strong prevailing winds would, however, tend to break up some of the newly formed coral on the weather sides of the island and to throw it inland. The coral rubble would be spread over a wide area initially but, later, with the changing winds, would tend to pile up into walls, or dunes, not far inside the reef flat on the weather shores.

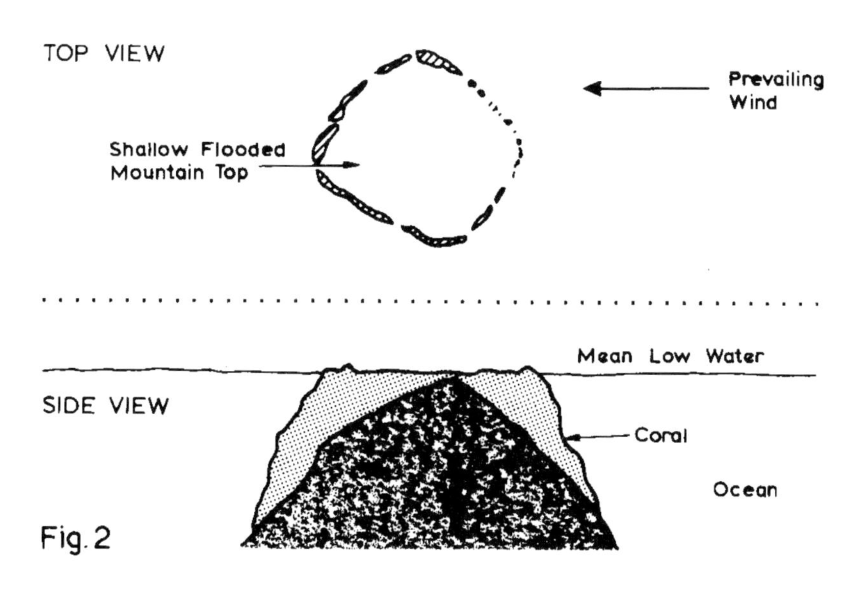

Fig. 2

3. The island would now have become an atoll. The growth of any living coral near the middle of its top would be smothered by the rubble washed inland and here a lagoon could start to form. Meanwhile, the coral around the outside edge, with the first choice of food from the surrounding ocean, would continue to grow (Figure 3). As the atoll continued to sink on the top of its parent mountain, coral would continue to form wherever the growing conditions were suitable. The scouring action of the surf would erode some of the new coral growing on the reef's edge and that could account for the very steep, but seldom vertical, slope of the edge downwards to the ocean depths.

4. Some of the broken rubble would roll down the outside edge but some would be washed inland, again to smother any secondary coral growing in the lagoon, which is why lagoons are never very deep. Had the parent mountain had an extinct crater in its top, it would long since have become filled with alternate layers of coral silt and living corals, all bonded together into coral rock (Figure 4). Because of the variations in the winds, rubble walls build up evenly around some atolls, so that their lagoons become completely enclosed. On others, part of the wall never builds up sufficiently to stop the flow of the tides and, here, one side of the lagoon is bounded by a barrier reef.

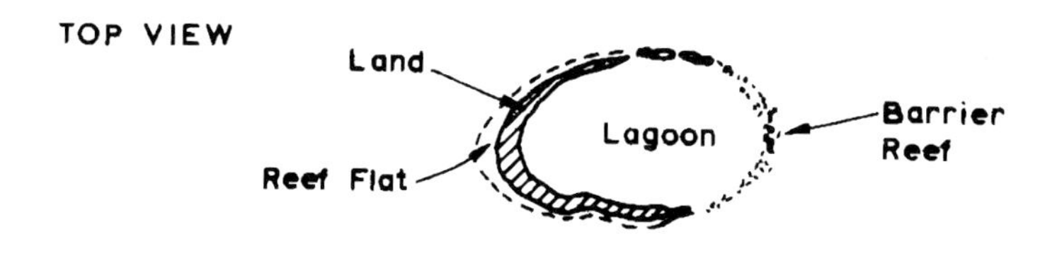

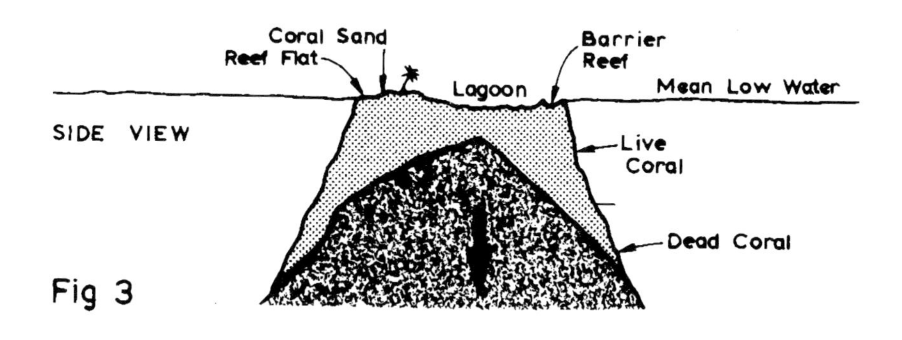

Fig 3

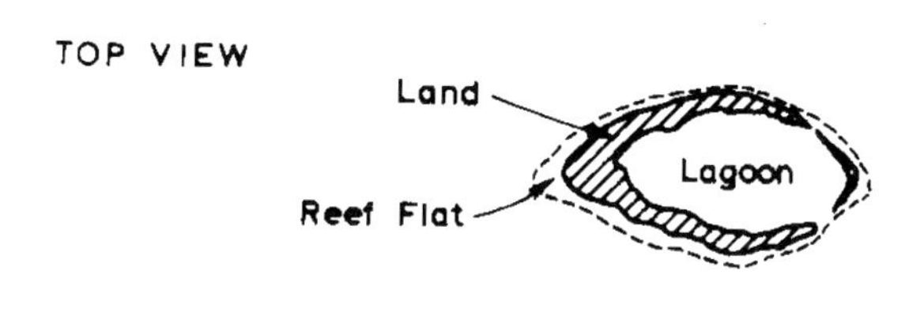

Reef Flat

Central Lagoon

Mean Low Water

SIDE VIEW

Live Coral

Dead Coral

Fig. 4

Some of the smaller atolls have neither lagoons nor prominent rubble dunes around their edges. These "reef" islands consist of just an elongated strip of almost flat coral sand or rubble, lying very little above the level of the highest tides. I guessed that these islands might have been formed from mountains that had not been far proud of sea level when they first started to subside.

* * *

"And where, Dan," you might well ask, "did all this rambling reasoning lead you?" My straight answer would have to be, "Sadly, nowhere!"

However, I hope that this Annexe may prove useful as an "Aunt Sally" at which to shoot. At least, in writing it, I have convinced myself that explanations of coral atoll formation are unlikely to prove easy. I should, of course, have known that before I started, because I had already found the planning of simple channels through the top few feet of "my" atolls difficult enough!

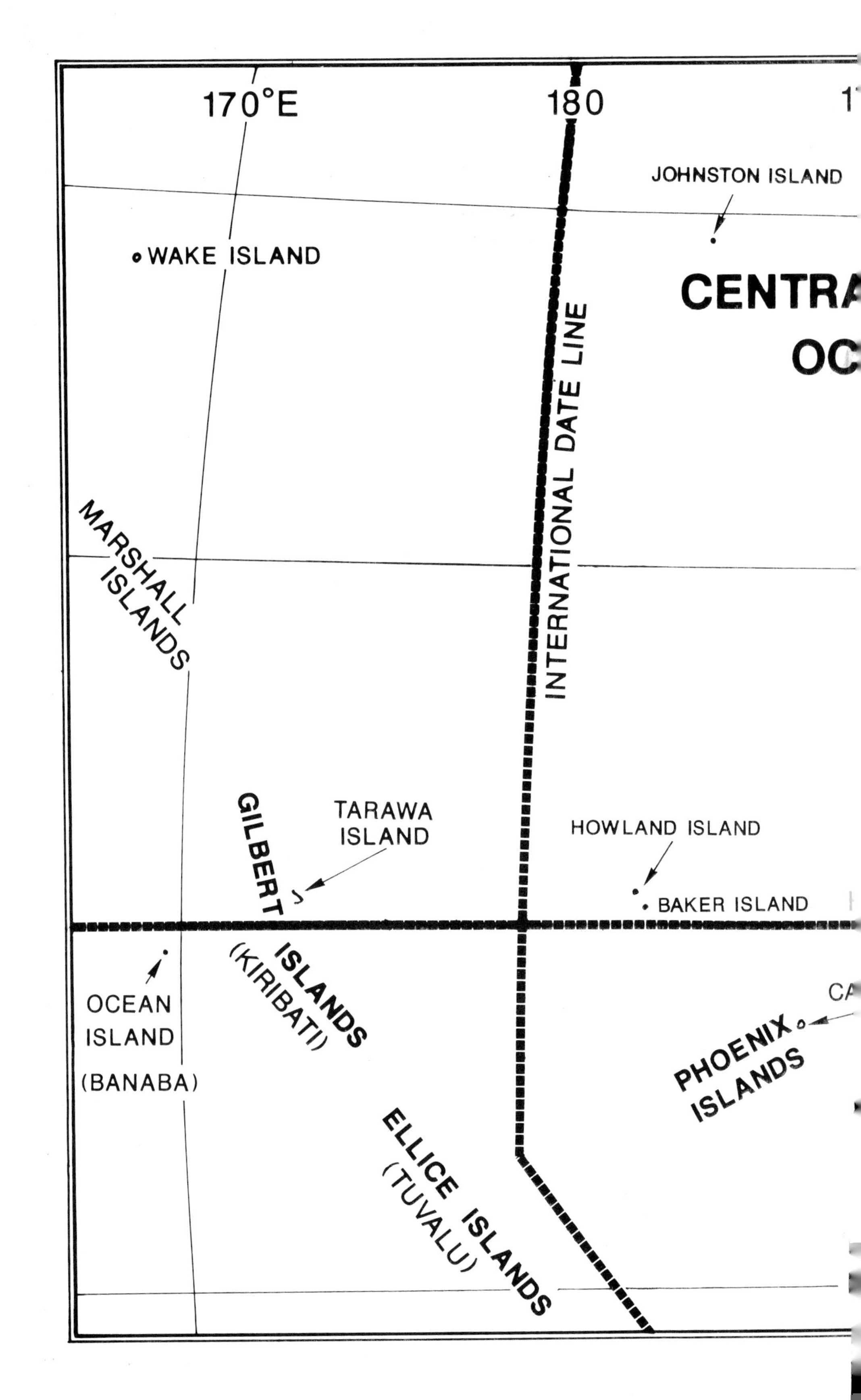

170°E
180
JOHNSTON ISLAND
WAKE ISLAND
CENTRA
OC
INTERNATIONAL DATE LINE
MARSHALL ISLANDS
TARAWA ISLAND
GILBERT ISLANDS (KIRIBATI)
HOWLAND ISLAND
BAKER ISLAND
OCEAN ISLAND (BANABA)
PHOENIX ISLANDS
ELLICE ISLANDS (TUVALU)